Sticks, Stones & Beans

The story of a rescue dog

To Bob
With Best Wishes,

Mart.

MARTIN JOHNSON

Not the least hard thing to bear when they go away from us, these quiet friends, is that they carry away with them so many years of our own lives.

John Galsworthy

For Jan.

CONTENTS

PREFACE

Beans

For most of her sixteen years of life Beans was our constant companion on our country walks and her enjoyment of these trips was equal to ours. The mere appearance of a rucksack or a pair of boots was enough to send her into a flurry of excitement that only abated once she was settled in the car. It was with very heavy hearts when we finally had to retire her from long walks when old age and arthritis got the better of her.

Shortly before she died I'd written and published an illustrated article on Beans' hiking adventures in *Dogs Monthly* magazine, in which I described how we coped with retiring her from the longer walks whilst at the same time ensuring that she still enjoyed shorter walks in her favourite places. I have always enjoyed photography and Beans had featured in many of my photographs, some of which I was lucky enough to get published. As well as being a treasured reminder of her life, it was this article that set me on the long road to a book.

In the days following her death I sat down and trawled through the hundreds of slides and photographs I'd taken of her over the years, reflecting on the wonderful life she'd had and all those adventures and funny scrapes she'd got into, many of which were immortalised on film. Although it was an emotional and at times almost unbearable process, the book idea grew larger in my mind. With help from my wife Jan, I started to jot down rough notes about every stage of Beans' life. Before long I had page after page of probably every funny, silly or naughty thing she had done. This actually helped the grieving process, as it was impossible not to smile when thinking of some of the tricks she'd got up to. As all these memories flooded back, the pile of rough notes grew larger; my notebooks quickly filled up and slowly, oh so slowly, a book began to emerge from these scattered jottings. My problem then was how I should present the book. People lose their pets every day, so why should mine warrant a book?

The answer to that question (and my own self-doubts) was answered as I recalled all those memories: she had made people laugh, so why not share that with those who had never met her?

As the book began to take shape, I decided that since all Beans' antics slotted (for the most part) into the stages of her life, then that was how I should construct the book. To present them in book form would be a wonderful tribute to her life and hopefully strike a chord with others who had loved and lost a treasured pet. It would truly be a labour of love; Beans deserved nothing less.

Pet owners will know about the joy an animal brings to their lives, but I hope that even non-pet owners will enjoy this book and perhaps gain a greater understanding of the close relationship that exists between people and their dogs. When people lose a dog there is still a bizarre and at times cruel attitude from others that it was 'only a dog,' as if losing an animal that had given a lifetime of pleasure and devotion was something not worth grieving over.

Despite the unfair bad press that dogs get, I'm pleased to say that in all her sixteen years, Beans never attacked anyone, child or adult, and those many children who met her on her travels ended up being enchanted by a very gentle and loving animal. I often wonder how many of those children went away begging their parents to get them a dog. Perhaps there are many more happy dog-owners out there because of their encounter with Beans. It would be nice to think so.

Some months after we lost her I sat on the side of the bed one morning looking at a photograph of her, which I always have on my bedside cabinet. It was one of the shots we'd taken of her on her sixteenth birthday. Looking at her that day on the Roaches, surrounded by the Peak District landscape she loved, I promised her there and then that I would finish my book and share her life with others. It is my sincere hope that I have succeeded in producing a celebration of Beans' life and hopefully raised more than just a few laughs along the way.

As a dog lover, what saddens me is that there are so many unwanted dogs in homes and sanctuaries that could give - and receive - so much love – if only they got the chance. The lucky ones find people who will give them a good life (as we did with Beans), but heartbreakingly, there are many for whom that chance will never come. It's a tragic example of the treatment meted out to animals by mankind. The only human kindness these dogs will know is the care they receive in the rescue homes.

My heart gladdens when I see the appealing faces of so many wonderful breeds of dog. It breaks when I read of dreadful cruelty inflicted on them, or the appalling statistics of how many have been needlessly put down. Dogs end up in re-homing centres for all manner of reasons, but shockingly, Christmas and its aftermath is the worst time of the year. Despite annual pleas from animal charities, people give puppies as gifts. However well-meaning this might be, inevitably, a couple of weeks later the novelty of a new puppy wears off, once the concept of what owning a dog entails sinks in. Another helpless animal is then dumped. Puppy love replaced by PlayStation love. The Dogs Trust, the UK's foremost dog charity, has even used Christmas as the basis for its slogan: *A dog is for life, not just for Christmas.* How true that statement is.

I cannot make any special claims for Beans. She wasn't the world's worst behaved, funniest, messiest, unluckiest or cleverest dog; she was like most other ordinary dogs who live with ordinary people, but whose lives become extraordinary when they take in a dog. When you own a dog you laugh every day, because at some point during the day the dog will do something to make you laugh. A horrible, stressful day at work is instantly forgotten the moment a dog greets you. In the darkest and saddest moments of life, a dog is there for you. No strings attached; no hidden agenda, just unconditional love. All a dog asks for is food, lots of walks and a good home.

Perhaps this story of how one little rescued dog changed our lives will compel others to give one of these unfortunate dogs a home. I really hope it does. Beans was special to us and after reading her story I hope she will become special to you.

CHAPTER ONE

Cooking Oil and Quiche

Beans Arrives

Thunder reverberated around the metal kennels. Lighting flashed, briefly illuminating the terrified eyes of the occupants. The panicked dogs began barking; first one, then another, until every dog had joined in, as if offering each other some mutual comfort from the frightening noise. A cloudburst followed, rain hammering on the roofs, the noise adding to the pandemonium.

We walked past the pacing dogs, coming to a kennel at the end of a row that appeared empty apart from a solitary drinking bowl. Before the storm arrived it had been a fine sunny day and we were totally unprepared for this sudden downpour. Hurrying to find shelter from the rain we'd almost walked past, but, as our eyes adjusted to the gloom, we realised that the kennel wasn't unoccupied. Tucked into a corner at the back, almost lost in the shadows, sat a tiny, beige-coloured puppy with floppy ears, quivering in terror. There was no barking from the little animal, just the odd whimper, nor was she pacing up and down like the other dogs. Hers was the *sit here and look pathetic* approach; a technique in finding an owner that was about to have the desired effect.

5

'Was she brought in on her own?' I asked the kennel assistant.

'No, there were six in the litter altogether. This one's the last,' she replied.

'How old is she?'

'About nine weeks,' she said, opening the cage door before we had even asked to see the puppy. I think she knew we were about to be smitten. With her siblings re-homed and now alone in the world, how could we possibly leave her behind?

Even when the cage was opened, the puppy didn't move. Gently picking her up, the assistant placed the trembling bundle of fur in Jan's arms. At that point I think we both knew that this helpless animal was coming home with us. The comical bent-over ears, fox-like face and cross of white fur on her chest were all it took. People have told me since that a dog chooses you and as far as this puppy was concerned we were the chosen ones.

Trying to pick a dog from a rescue home is heart-breaking; there are so many dogs and the evidence of man's cruelty to his fellow creatures is all too evident. So many sad stories gaze back at you from the eyes of these unfortunate animals, that there is often no need to read the disturbing notes pinned to the kennels: *ill-treated by previous owner; traumatised; will need time to settle in; found wandering the streets.* If they could talk, how much more distressing would the task be?

On that September day back in 1987, my girlfriend Jan and I were in need of an animal companion. Jan had recently lost her beloved cat, Crockett, and replacing him with another cat just didn't seem right. He had been her soul mate; there when she needed comforting and whose passing left a void that she felt another cat couldn't fill.

My parents had also rescued a delightful little cross breed named Benji from the same rescue centre near

Macclesfield a few years previously, and it was here that we'd begun our search for a dog. Neither of us had been to a rescue centre before and we soon met with that all-too-familiar problem that all dog rescuers face: which dog to choose? Puppy or older dog, small dog or large dog? You end up wanting to take them all home with you, thus starting a rescue kennels of your own!

I will never forget the pleading eyes of one German Shepherd gazing at me from his kennel, imploring me to take him home. At that moment I wondered whether it would be better to come away empty handed rather than taking one and not the others. I have been to other rescue centres since that day many years ago – it doesn't get any easier.

In the end, the decision was made for us, despite our reluctance to walk away from all those other dogs. That vulnerable little creature had already found a place in our hearts. There was no way we could put her back in the kennel.

With the puppy still nestling in Jan's arms, I dealt with the paperwork, left a donation for the animal sanctuary and we took our quivering bundle of fluff home.

Beans had entered our lives.

Cats

The thunderstorm ended as quickly as it had arrived and as we drove away from the kennels the sun came out again. Jan was stroking and cradling the puppy, who seemed to have calmed down now that the thunder had stopped, although every now and again her little body trembled from head to toe, despite calming words from Jan.

We made a detour via my parents to show off our new arrival, who by this time had perked up considerably and was starting to take an interest in her surroundings. The more I looked at the puppy, with her folded ears and cute little face – and that distinctive cross of white fur on her chest – I knew we had made the right choice. There was character in that face; in fact, there was character in her whole demeanour, even at this early stage in her life – or was it mischief?

'Do you want to come in?' mum said, as she came to the car to greet our latest addition.

'Might not be a very good idea,' I replied, imagining the chaos that would quickly ensue as soon as Benji spotted the puppy.

Benji was a loveable and loyal little dog, but not very tolerant towards other dogs, a trait that had got him into more than a few scrapes. Like our new puppy, he too was a mongrel, although, unlike the puppy, it wasn't difficult to see which dogs had got together to produce him. Benji was part Corgi, part German Shepherd. His body was Corgi-sized, but his tail, ears and face were undoubtedly German Shepherd, with a smattering of Corgi thrown in. The legs were Corgi-like, but without the length of the German Shepherd's. This blend of two very different breeds of dog gave him a slightly odd, though comical appearance.

Mum contented herself with stroking the puppy through the side window of the car, her hands receiving a good licking from the now happier animal, who, although still trembling, seemed to be positively lapping up all this attention from another stranger, all thoughts of thunder and lightning now forgotten. Perhaps the trembling was now more from nervous excitement than fear.

We said our goodbyes, promising to return with the puppy once she had settled in, although Benji, much to his annoyance, would probably have to be banished to the back garden.

Crockett had a younger companion, Zuki; short for Suzuki, whose loud purring was likened to the motorbike of the same name. Now that Zuki was on her own, the question was: would she accept a dog in her home? Driving the short distance to Jan's house, we wondered how the two animals would get on. That question was answered within seconds of opening the door. In that typically un-coordinated, floppy, bouncy manner that all puppies have, she trotted up to her new feline companion and was promptly and violently greeted by a well-aimed lash from Zuki's claws across the tip of her ear.

With a heart-rending yelp and blood pouring from the gashed ear she bolted away from Zuki. The cat calmly remained where she was with an I'll show you who's boss look on her face. Naturally we all panicked, because at first we didn't know how serious the injury was. What if her eyes had been caught in the onslaught?

The magic of bringing a new puppy home vanished in an instant. As Jan's parents – Bob and Rita – looked at the terrified puppy, together with the blood on the carpet, they wondered if we should take her to the vet. Once she had calmed down however, we discovered that the wound was only minor, so with some TLC and plenty of cotton wool the blood soon stopped flowing. It wasn't the nicest welcome our new puppy could have had. What with thunderstorms and now fierce cats, she'd had a traumatic day.

From that point on, puppy and cat kept a respectful distance from each other and, apart from the odd warning raised paw from Zuki, there were no more scraps; each treating the other with mutual respect and, for all we knew, some affection. The puppy had learned an early lesson the hard (and painful) way and as long as she resisted the temptation for a cat chase, Zuki was happy to have her around.

We soon learned that where cats were concerned, Beans only wanted to be friends with them, apart from when they had to be chased off her territory, a mission she carried out with zeal. If she met a cat when we took her out for a walk, her only intention was to say hello; there was no malice intended. Unfortunately for Beans, the cats never saw it that way and she would be left in no doubt that any closer inspection would be met by something distinctly more violent than an arched back and a hiss. She never grasped the fact that no cat was ever going to tolerate having a cold wet nose shoved up its bottom. That may be the way dogs greet each other, but not in the cat world. If Beans attempted this form of greeting, no warning was given and the encounter would be swiftly ended with one lightning-fast swipe of a paw.

Teething Troubles

We needed a name for our new companion. Various suggestions came to mind but were quickly discarded. Basil, after the famous television puppet, *Basil Brush,* was one idea, given her fox-like appearance, but that was thrown out for the obvious reason that she was the wrong sex. Trouble was we didn't want a common name for her; it had to be a name that somehow fitted her character.

After spending the afternoon with Jan and the puppy, I headed home for tea, with various names running through my head. Benji must have been wondering who this interloper was as he sniffed the strange new scent on my clothes. I think he took exception to the fact there was another dog in my life because he never accepted her on his territory. We tried several introductions both on territory and off, but the two dogs never got on. Benji was ignominiously sent out into the garden or another room every time Beans visited. He must have wondered why he was suddenly being shoved outside, but it was either that or a very nasty dogfight. I made sure my affections were shared equally between them both, especially when a rather disgruntled Benji was allowed back inside his home. If only they'd both got on.

'I've thought of a name,' Jan said excitedly, when I returned for my stopover later on.

'Go on,' I replied, half expecting she'd picked some typical doggy name.

'Beans!' was the enthusiastic response.

'Beans?' I replied.

But as soon as I'd repeated the name, I realised it was exactly the right choice. I had never heard of any dog called Beans before, but so what, it was perfect. The timid puppy we'd spotted in that gloomy corner of the kennel was beginning to show that she was indeed 'full of beans,' bounding around the house, cautiously taunting Zuki and investigating every nook and cranny, all thoughts of thunder and kennels seemingly banished, so what better name could there be for her? Jan's reasoning was spot-on – Beans it was.

With her name chosen, Beans gradually settled into her new home, although, as any puppy-owner knows, there followed many months of house-training, exciting new experiences and an aborted early attempt to introduce her to some formal training. Every now and again she taunted Zuki, approaching her as closely as she dared, perhaps hoping that the cat would put all differences aside, but Zuki had installed her very own personal exclusion zone around herself, which Beans learned never to cross. She wouldn't forget that first day in her new home in a hurry.

Naturally, with a new puppy around Jan's house, destructive behaviour of the very worst kind soon ensued. Whatever could be chewed, mangled or ripped was given due attention by the young Beans, although where personal possessions were concerned, Jan got off lightly. Angelina Brown however, an antique teddy bear given to Rita as a child, didn't escape Beans' rampage. The poor bear, who'd come through fifty years unscathed, suffered damaged feet and the loss of a considerable amount of her straw stuffing under the onslaught from Beans' teeth. The badly mauled and traumatised bear needed urgent surgery involving the use of foam and deft needlework from Jan, but Angelina Brown was soon restored to her former self. After that, she was kept well away from Beans, just in case she fancied another attack on the unfortunate teddy.

House-training happily didn't take long and Beans quickly learnt where she could – and couldn't – do her business. Inevitably though, there were accidents. Not long after Beans moved in, I received an unpleasant, but salutary lesson in watching where to put your feet when there is a new puppy around the house.

Jan was upstairs in her bedroom playing with Beans, when I walked in with my rucksack, which I dumped on Jan's bed. Beans was sitting at the end of the room, looking like she had already spent her first two months of life there, rather than in a rescue home. Talk about settling in.

'Would you mind shutting the curtains?' Jan asked, as she carried on petting Beans.

'Sure,' I said, clambering lazily over the bed to reach the curtains. It was a bad move.

Losing my balance a little, I trod on the rucksack as I turned around. As I was about to step back onto the floor, I noticed an ominous object on the carpet. I hoped against hope that it wasn't what I thought it was, but there was no mistaking; it was a turd. It had also been trodden in. No prize for guessing who'd trodden in it and no prize either for guessing who it belonged to.

The air was filled with expletives as my predicament revealed itself in all its glory. There was crap on the bed, crap on my bag and, if Jan had stepped in it as well, crap in heaven knows what other parts of the room.

Jan, seemingly unconcerned that her bedroom was probably plastered with excrement, started laughing. She checked her slippers. They were crap-free.

'Didn't you see it there?' I exclaimed as I stepped off the bed, ingraining even more crap into the carpet. The carelessness was undoubtedly mine, but it's funny how you always try to put the blame onto someone else, knowing full well the fault is yours.

'No I didn't,' she said, 'If I had, I'd have cleared it up.'

'Oh for crying out loud, how long have you been in here with her?'

'An hour or so,' Jan replied, 'but I did nip downstairs for a few minutes to make a cup of tea.'

Which, no doubt, was about the time when she decided to put down a small deposit on the carpet.

Strangely, there was little odour from the mess, perhaps because of the puppy food Beans was on, but I carried on with my irrational ranting.

'Didn't you notice anything – like a smell perhaps? I said sarcastically as I inspected the soles of my shoes.

'No, did you?'

The reply I should really have expected made me even angrier.

'Crap!' I exclaimed again.

'Exactly,' Jan said.

And then we both started laughing.

Although Jan and I had known each other for five years, it would be another three before we tied the knot. We both still lived at home in Wilmslow so much of my time was spent at Jan's, where I took an active part in Beans' development. Regular Saturday night stopovers were the norm, but if I thought I was going to get a nice Sunday morning lie-in I was sadly mistaken. Puppies are like babies – they cry a lot. As soon as Beans awoke, the incessant crying and yapping started in the kitchen. There was no let up from the noise. After a while, when we could stand it no longer, we'd have to go down to the kitchen and release her from the hell she thought she was in. I felt sorry for Jan and her parents; they would have this every morning – I only had to put up with it at the weekend. Although Beans was really Jan's dog, sooner or later, she'd be living with both of us, so I wanted to help as much as I could with her upbringing. It was only fair.

Until she could be trusted not to destroy everything in sight, or relieve herself in the other rooms, the kitchen was the only place we could keep her overnight. Unfortunately, this meant that it bore the brunt of her frustration. Cupboard corners were mangled, paintwork scratched and plastic pipes almost pierced as Beans' puppy teeth began to push through. Anything with the word Tupperware on it was butchered beyond all recognition. Not even her feeding bowl was left unscathed, when I discovered its chewed remains one Sunday morning.

Try and chew that up, I thought to myself, when I put a new metal bowl in front of her. But Beans was on the rampage and it was only a matter of time before disaster struck. She wasn't going to let the fact that she couldn't mangle her feeding bowl stop her.

Thankfully, due only to the toughness of the plastic, we escaped a major flood in the kitchen when she decided that the water pipe to the washing machine was well worth destroying. The teeth marks up and down the pipe bore testament to the ferocious assault she had made on it. We were lucky; the disaster we felt was imminent had been avoided – for now.

Confining the chaos and destruction to one room was, we thought, more manageable than having the same war zone spread throughout the house, but little did we know that Beans had other ideas - she learned how to open doors.

Despite the destruction of the kitchen, as the months wore on it soon became apparent that a clever and intelligent dog was beginning to emerge. As Beans grew taller, so did her ability to reach the door handle. Whether by chance, or by watching how we opened doors, she figured out how to do it. In her case all that was required was to jump up, place both paws on the handle and press down. Imagine her delight when she realised she could now spread her illicit behaviour to other parts of the house. It must have been like winning the lottery to her.

The problem of how to stop Beans escaping and leaving a trail of devastation in her wake was solved by some equally clever thinking on Bob's part. He turned the door handle around. To escape the confines of the kitchen Beans would now have to somehow press the handle up with her nose to open the door - a process she evidently found to be too much trouble. Round one to us!

Thinking a puppy will behave itself when taken out on a lead for the first time is like expecting a child to behave on its first visit to a sweet shop. Once all the initial vaccinations had been administered and it was safe to unleash Beans on the great outdoors, she was like a coiled spring that had suddenly been released. The big wide world was so exciting, not unlike the sweet shop, only the sugary goodies were replaced by a myriad of strange smells, dogs of all shapes and sizes to check out and lots of nice, friendly people to jump up at with fresh muddy paws.

A puppy wants to be friends with everyone, although some people, I suspect, won't be too delighted with a fresh set of muddy puppy prints adorning their clothes. Puppies are naturally endearing, but a bit of early training is vital. Most people have a reasonable level of tolerance when a puppy jumps up at them, but when it grows into a Great Dane, there are going to be some serious issues. Being knocked to the ground and plastered in mud by Scooby Doo is not going to win you any friends.

Inevitably, Beans did her fair share of puppy-greeting but the most unpleasant surprises came when she attempted to treat every dog she met as a long lost friend. Unfortunately, some dogs don't take too kindly to a bouncing bundle of fun who only wants to play, but the puppy soon learns that not all dogs are friendly. Learning dog language and reading the signs are all part of that learning curve.

Cooking Oil

When she was six months old we made the decision to have Beans spayed. This was the obvious and most responsible decision we thought we could make. What would be the point of taking in a rescue dog only to end up with a whole litter of our own puppies who would then need to be re-homed? Jan contacted the vet and the operation was booked.

Subjecting a dog to an operation, however small, is a worry, so we were relieved when the vet rang to say that everything had gone fine, Beans was recovering well and could be picked up whenever we were ready. Since Jan might be struggling on her own with a groggy Beans, I left work early and we headed for the vets together. Beans was awake, but it was obvious she wouldn't be able to walk properly until the effects of the anaesthetic had worn off. She stood there, swaying, her legs barely able to support her drowsy frame, a patch of shaved fur and a small dressing on her abdomen. Around her neck she wore one of those plastic funnels to prevent her from getting at the wound. Her tail wagged as she recognised us.

'Come on Beans, let's get you home,' I said. Her tail wagged again.

I carefully scooped her up in my arms and carried her to the car. Her head flopped uncontrollably to one side. All she wanted now was home and sleep.

Animals seem to recover from operations very quickly, taking everything in their stride. Despite the fact that she would have been in pain from the wound to her abdomen, she soon got back in to her routine.

The Sunday after the operation I watched her as she headed out into the back garden to do the necessary. After the preliminaries of sniffing and circling to find exactly the right spot, she got down to business. I don't normally make a habit of watching dogs relieve themselves, but on this occasion, perhaps out of concern for those stitches in her wound, I kept my eye on her. Things took a little longer than usual for obvious reasons, but I needn't have worried. As she finished, she slowly turned around to inspect the scar. Satisfied that everything was intact and the wound hadn't opened, she trotted back inside.

With the trauma of the operation over, it was time to start work on some basic obedience training. Beans was winding down as far as total destruction was concerned, but she still had her moments. Anything plastic that could be wrecked was duly set upon with relish – sometimes with dire consequences. It was time to instil some discipline, so Beans was enrolled on an evening dog training class at the local Scout HQ.

How long it was going to take to get her reasonably trained up was anybody's guess, but neither did we know that on the matter of training, Beans had other ideas. As if trying to lull Jan into a false sense of security, Beans allowed two classes to pass by uneventfully. Jan was even making some progress. Sadly, it was all too good to be true. Beans' taste for all things strange, plastic or exotic would prove to be her undoing.

The day the third training class was due, Rita went into the kitchen that morning to discover a disembowelled plastic bottle of cooking oil with the remainder of its contents spread liberally over the floor. Beans had obviously decided it was well worth a taste during the night. She seemed none the worse for wear following this culinary experiment, although the effect on her bowels was fairly instant and indeed, spectacular. I feel sure she had plenty of time to reflect on the results of swallowing what was, to all intents and purposes, an extremely effective laxative. Colonic irrigation could not have done a better job. Beans' rear end exploded over the back lawn, spraying Bob's neatly cut grass with sunflower oil. It was a miracle she'd managed to hold it in until Rita had let her out.

As time passed it seemed as if the worst effects of the oil had also passed (literally) as her frequent dashes to the back garden lessened. By late afternoon Rita felt confident that it was all systems go for dog training, but Jan, when she arrived home from work to discover what had happened, wasn't so sure.

'How much has she swallowed?' She asked Rita.

'About half a bottle I think.'

Beans was sitting in the middle of the living room, looking totally unconcerned. Jan wasn't convinced the bowel-loosening effects of consuming almost an entire bottle of oil had run their course.

'When did she last go out to the garden?'

'It was over an hour ago,' Rita replied. 'Before that, she was going out every half hour or so. She'd stand at the back door, squeaking frantically. I'd barely opened it before she was running out. God knows what the lawn looks like.'

'Oh Beans, what are we going to do with you?' Jan said to the errant dog.

The idea of all this happening in the car or the Scout Hall was unthinkable, but since it had been some time since one of Beans' dashes to the lawn, perhaps the worst was over, but, in the dark recesses of her insides hell was brewing – and would soon be unleashed.

Dog training classes fall into two distinct camps: there's the very serious class where everyone is aiming for possible Crufts standard, and the more relaxed friendly affair where the training still gets done, but everyone looks as if they are enjoying it – including the dogs. Beans' class was in the first category; the Boot Camp style of training accompanied by much shouting and telling off – and that's just at the owners.

Beans had already been instructed in the art of not pulling on the lead, thanks to some basic training from Bob, who'd handled dogs during his National Service days in the army. He knew exactly how to stop a dog from taking its owner for a walk. A simple but stern command of 'Beans; heel', followed by a firm, but not harsh, pull into the shin was all it took for Beans to quickly get the message. Although there was firmness and authority in his voice, he knew that a dog's hearing is very sensitive, so simply bellowing commands at Beans would have served no purpose whatsoever. Beans knew where she stood with Bob.

Beans' formal world of dog training had, however, been embarrassingly cut short, as I discovered when I popped over to Jan's later that evening. As I opened the door to the living room, it was obvious something wasn't right. Jan was sitting there, looking totally fed up and even Beans seemed more subdued than usual. She perked up when she spotted me and trotted over to greet me.

'How did the training go then?' I asked, trying to sound upbeat. Something was obviously amiss.

'It was a disaster,' Jan replied, 'an absolute embarrassing disaster.'

I wondered what could possibly have gone wrong. Perhaps Beans had scrapped with someone's prize-winning pooch. I checked her over; there were no marks on her, or patches where her fur had been pulled out. Maybe she'd been deemed untrainable and shown the door. I gave up.

'What happened?' I asked, in readiness for Jan's explanation. Then she told me why there would be no more dog training – well at least not at the Scout Hall.

Apparently, everything had been going reasonably well (although every time Beans did something wrong, it was Jan who got the telling off) until about half way through the session when the witches brew that had been simmering inside her released itself in an explosion of foul brown liquid all over the hall floor. Jan didn't stand a chance. As soon as the loud drawn-out *phaaaart* echoed around the hall, it was too late. The volcano that was thought to be dormant had erupted – with a vengeance. There was no time to drag Beans outside. She had brought the *Boot Camp* proceedings to a sudden and abrupt halt.

Sergeant Major Dog Trainer had no response to this most inconvenient interruption. Everything had suddenly descended into chaos.

'I'm sorry about this,' Jan said, looking at the rapidly spreading mess, 'she swallowed a load of cooking oil earlier today.'

'Really,' said the Sergeant Major, 'I'll go and find you a mop and bucket.'

Jan was helpless. The hall had gone silent – apart from some sniggers from the other dog owners – and further humiliation loomed as the trainer re-appeared with the mop. Despite Jan's protestations that she thought every last drop of oil had passed through Beans' system, it was clear what the trainer thought. Beans should have stayed at home.

'Will we see you next week?' the trainer asked, as Jan and Beans prepared to leave, carefully avoiding the large – and slippery – wet patch on the floor.

'We'll be here, won't we Beans?' Jan lied. In all honesty, she hadn't enjoyed the training classes. It was all so regimented. In her own way, Beans had done them both a favour. They would not be back.

Despite formal training being abruptly cut short, we didn't neglect this vital aspect of Beans' development. She would never be show standard, but so what; she was house-trained, walked to heel and, unless something more interesting (like a squirrel) was in her sights, she would come back when called. Short of stripping most of a dog's character away - which is what makes them so loveable - you can't ask for more. Just make sure that those tempting bottles of cooking oil   are   well   out   of   reach.

Travel Sickness

After the training class debacle we decided it was time to introduce Beans to the joys of car travel. This was essential if she was going to enjoy accompanying us on our many walks in the countryside, some involving a journey of an hour or more. In my experience, dogs will do one of four things in a car: bark continuously for the entire journey, jump around making a complete nuisance of themselves (whilst barking), throw up, or, if you are really lucky from the word go, sit quietly on the back seat.

In reality, you only arrive at the last category having gone through the trauma of the other three. We were lucky (or was it unlucky) in that Beans never bothered with categories one and two, preferring to go straight to the vomiting bit. I knew – and had to brace myself for the fact – that at some point I would be de-vomiting the car. It was only a matter of time. My dog-vomit initiation came around sooner than I expected. Beans made sure of that.

A nice moderate hike had been chosen to get her used to walking; the aim being to build up the length of the walks gradually. In the event, we needn't have worried about Beans not liking long walks; she took to it like a duck to water. After feeding her, we loaded the car with rucksacks, lunch and cameras and set off for Tatton Park, near Knutsford, a few miles away.

It was a Sunday and about the time when people would be starting to prepare the traditional Sunday lunch, so we assumed the (not unpleasant) smell that began to fill the car was the aroma from someone's oven.

'Hmm, that smells good,' I said to Jan. For a second, there was no reply.

'I think you'd better look at the back seat,' was all she said.

As I waited to turn right at the next junction I turned round to discover that the source of the smell was rather less appetising than I'd first thought.

'Oh no,' I said. I was looking at a fresh steaming pile of only partially digested dog food. Strangely, neither of us had even heard her throwing it up.

Perversely perhaps, I have always found it a fascinating – if not amusing – exercise, watching a dog go through the throes of vomiting. A dog seems to go about it in a much more businesslike, matter-of-fact way; something's down there that needs to come up, so let's get on with it. The face grimaces, the mouth curls and then the heaving noise starts: a sort of *uuuurph, uuuurph, uuuurph* followed by one big contraction of the stomach muscles, an *eeeearyk* as everything comes up, and then it's all over – back to business. How we hadn't heard any of this – even above the noise of the engine – was odd. Beans must have been perfecting the art of silent vomiting from an early age.

So as she sat there with a *there's more where that came from* look on her face, I gave thanks that I'd had the foresight to cover the back seat with a thick enough rug to absorb the meaty chunks in gravy. It was so fresh that it looked like someone had opened a can and then tipped the contents all over the back seat. The thought of a journey of several miles with that lot sitting on the back seat was more than I could contemplate. We turned back, removed the rug – and its contents – and replaced it with a fresh one. The clean-up could wait until later.

Lesson one: do not feed a dog immediately before travelling in a car. Lesson two: do not feed a dog before travelling in a car when the said animal has hardly ever been in a car. Lesson three: get the dog completely used to car travel and then feed beforehand at your own risk. Better still, ignore all this and feed dog at the end of the day when all car travel has ceased.

Despite this nauseating (but memorable) introduction to car travel, Beans didn't take very long to
adjust; a few more journeys and she was sitting on the
back seat as if there had never been a problem. She was
now a seasoned car-traveller, rocking from side to side
on the back seat, in tune with the motion of the car as it
rounded bends. She never did throw up in the car
again.

Obstacles

Beans loved her country walks with us and the
muddier and wetter they were, the better. Some dogs
are not too keen on venturing out in the wet, but not
Beans. In true outdoor adventurer style, she met
whatever the elements could throw at her with gusto.
Admittedly, if a shower turned into a downpour the
enthusiasm waned once the rain seeped through her
coat. By this stage, she simply plodded along, wet ears
flopping down, a rather pathetic sight. It isn't much fun
for us in such conditions, even if we are clad from head
to toe in the latest high tech outdoor gear.

In the Peak District National Park, where the vast
majority of our weekend walks took place, there are
some interesting, unusual, and at times, downright
difficult obstacles to overcome when crossing field
boundaries. Hedges, fences and stone walls all have
various constructions (or should it be contraptions?) to
enable the walker to pass from one field to the other.
This is certainly true for the country as a whole, but
each area has its own unique stiles or gates.

Many of the old stone walls in the Peak are crossed
by protruding stones on either side which can be
negotiated without too much difficulty, unless it's wet,
when the limestone, worn smooth by the passage of
many years of boots, can become slippery as ice.

Beans usually had no problem with these, bounding up one side of the wall, only to get stuck on the top when she realised that the drop on the other side was a little too high to contemplate jumping off, or the steps on the other side were less of an attractive proposition to come down than go up. After a year or so of walking she got better with wall stiles, but in the early days the poor dog would stand on the top of the wall quietly surveying her surroundings, waiting for help to arrive – in this case, us. If no amount of coaxing and gentle persuasion would budge her, more ingenious solutions had to be found.

Seeing somebody giving a dog a piggyback is probably one of the more unusual things you might encounter in the Derbyshire or Staffordshire countryside, but in our case it became a fairly regular feature on our Sunday jaunts. Beans was not a big or heavy dog, but it wasn't easy balancing on a wall trying to lift a helpless dog onto your wife's shoulders. It was a tried and tested method of dog transportation, but lost its appeal when Beans had just tramped through several wet, muddy fields. If the local cow population occupied the fields then the prospect of having to piggyback Beans was too unpleasant to think about. Beans just took all this in her stride, straddling Jan's back (or mine) oblivious to the stinking wet blend of mud and manure that she was plastering on our nice Gore-Tex jackets.

Ladder stiles are another common method of crossing the Peak District walls and fences and, in some cases, can be even more troublesome than step stiles, especially if the rungs are rounded, rather than flat. They aren't too difficult for boot-clad hikers, but present an almost impossible obstacle for a dog's paws, with the unfortunate animal slipping through the wooden rungs, unable to grip the smooth surface. Beans sometimes – but not always – managed to bumble her way to the top, but getting down was impossible. Cue the piggyback method again. More often than not we had to resort to the 'lift and piggyback' method if she couldn't manage the ascent.

While we negotiated these army-style assault courses, I couldn't help wondering how on earth people managed with dogs bigger - and heavier - than Beans. Come to think of it, you didn't see very many dogs much bigger than Beans in hiking terrain; they were mainly small terriers, spaniels or border collies. Those with larger animals could usually be seen standing helplessly at the foot of a daunting-looking stile, while a huge, lolloping, lumbering dog waited patiently, wondering how on earth they were going to get the animal over it. German Shepherds, as used by the police, are known for their agility at scaling walls and fences, but I wouldn't have wanted to be in the position of having to lift a more timid one.

The ideal solution, of course, is to have a dog that can be slipped easily into a rucksack when obstacles present themselves. I've seen many a happy, furry face peeping out of the top of a rucksack, though I suspect the look of contentment probably owed more to having just found and devoured the sandwiches in it.

Squeezer stiles, by their very name can be a problem for both man and beast. These very old methods of crossing walls are, in most cases, easier to negotiate than step or ladder stiles, since all you have to do is 'squeeze' yourself through the gap in the wall, which is narrow enough to prevent sheep or cattle passing through, but just wide enough for a human to negotiate.

Beans could slip through most of these stiles, but with some, the passage of time had narrowed the gap to such an extent that the two shorter stone pillars forming the wall supports almost touched each other, ensuring that she was able to get her front end through with no trouble at all, the problems starting when she tried to get her wider back end to follow. It was no problem for us, since all we had to do was perform a sort of 'vaulting' action using the pillars for support, or simply stride over the wider part of the gap.

Beans tried desperately to heave herself through the space, sometimes making several attempts before giving up with a rather forlorn look on her face as if to say: *you're going to have to help me.*

Sometimes, sheer determination – or just brute force – got her through, but more often than not we just stood there laughing as the poor dog's determined efforts ended in failure. If she couldn't climb the wall (which she often did) we again had to carry her through the gap, an experience I feel sure she found rather undignified, especially after such a titanic struggle.

Paw Prints on the Worktop

There's no doubt that dogs are opportunists. Leave any food item within easy reach of your canine companion and you can guarantee that when you return, the item will have been voraciously devoured. Your lucky dog (or unlucky for you, if he throws it all up on the carpet) will probably be sitting there with an *it wasn't me* look on his face, with a small, but tell-tale bulge in his belly; the only evidence of the crime that has been committed.

Even the best trained dog in the world will forget about its training when it spots a nice piece of forbidden cake. It's the classic 'stealing the link of sausages from the butchers' scenario. Beans proved this to us in grand style.

It was a summer evening and Rita had prepared plates of quiche and salad for our evening meal, which she'd left on the worktop in the kitchen. Beans had been out for her afternoon walk with us and we were all enjoying a cup of tea in the living room. She'd probably found herself a nice comfortable niche behind Jan's chair for a nap – or so we thought. Sleeping, however, was the last thing on her mind.

None of us had bothered to notice where Beans had been, but when, a bit later, Rita asked me if I would mind bringing in the food, I noticed the mischievous dog where I assumed she had been all along: behind Jan's chair. She wasn't asleep and the look on her face suggested to me that she knew I was about to discover the evidence of some furtive misdemeanour.

'Where's the quiche?' I called out to no-one in particular.

'On the plates.' Rita replied.

I stared at four plates of salad: lettuce; sliced tomatoes; salad onions; sliced hard-boiled eggs – but definitely no quiche.

Before we took Beans out for her walk I thought I'd noticed it on the plates, so I checked the fridge in case Rita had decided to put the slices in there. The fridge was a quiche-free zone.

'There's definitely no quiche here.' I yelled out again. By this time, of course, I was starting to put two and two together - Beans.

Rita came into the kitchen. 'I put it on the plates with the salad!' she exclaimed. As she was standing there, probably wondering whether her mind was going, I noticed a few crumbs and wet patches on the floor, below where the plates were. Then I spotted the faint dusty paw prints on the edge of the worktop. Realisation dawned; Beans had eaten all four pieces of the quiche - an entire family-sized one.

'I've just figured out our little mystery,' I said, pointing to the slobber on the floor and the paw marks on the worktop.

Rita's response was quite mild considering a large part of our evening meal was now inside Beans.

'Oh dear,' was all she could say.

It was a cheeky, but well executed act; so much so that I found it hard to be angry with Beans. When I confronted her (still lurking behind Jan's chair) all she got from me was, *Beans what have you done, you naughty dog* response, which was hardly likely to have her quivering with fear, especially as I was half laughing as I said it. So much for the dog disciplinarian. The only response from her was an ears back, doleful look that you just couldn't be cross with. Despite the demise of the quiche, it was hard not to admire the way in which she had carried out the theft. Beans was the *Stealth Bomber* of food theft; a *Nighthawk,* able to sneak in undetected by enemy radar, carry out her mission, and then return to base.

Each plate looked as if it had hardly moved and the remaining items were untouched, so she must have been incredibly careful to pull four pieces of quiche from the plates without dragging the whole lot to the floor. To accomplish all this without anyone in the next room hearing was even more of a feat. We wondered whether a round of applause was more appropriate than a telling off. Despite having all that cheese, egg, onion and pastry slowly digesting inside her, she did well to keep it all down, which perhaps wasn't surprising, given the fact that she'd had to accomplish the theft quietly and slowly. A plate crashing to the kitchen floor would have been the end of the mission.

Beans didn't have any tea that evening. As for us – it was prawn salads all round.

Snow and Ice

Dogs and snow practically guarantee first class entertainment. From the moment we introduced her to the delights of a wintry walk, Beans entertained us in grand style.

Beans' first taste (literally) of snow was in November 1988 on a visit to Tegg's Nose Country Park, near Macclesfield. Snow had fallen for several days, but the roads were passable, so we decided to head out to enjoy the snow-covered landscape while we could.

Tegg's Nose is a small country park just outside the much larger Peak Park, but what it lacks in size it makes up for with the views from its summit. On one side the Cheshire Plain sweeps away towards the distant Welsh hills, on the other the dark conifers of Macclesfield Forest gradually give way to the moors below Cheshire's second highest point, Shutlingsloe.

At any time of the year it is a splendid view, but that day it was even more spectacular. The snow adorning Shutlingsloe's distinctive pointed summit gave the whole scene an almost Alpine feel to it. Even from a distance of about two miles you could pick out the eroded path that led to the summit. With the help of binoculars, tiny figures of hikers could be seen, picking their way along the path, before making the final short steep climb to the summit trig point. In a field near the main road, happy, colourfully clad children hurtled down the hill on sledges and we wished we were doing the same. Beans, however, was providing us with some equally good entertainment of her own.

Dogs become child-like in the snow, bouncing and charging madly around in circles with the sheer joy of being alive. Jumping comically into deep drifts is even more fun, especially when there are exciting smells to seek out underneath. If they were able, I'm sure dogs would build snowmen or throw snowballs at each other. I've seen enough dogs playing in snow to realise they love it.

Beans bounced clumsily through the deeper drifts, quite clearly enjoying this new experience. As she tried to maintain her grip on the slippery and impacted snow, her legs had other ideas, sliding in all directions. It was like the famous sequence in Bambi where his mother tries to keep the little deer upright on the ice. This was great fun. At least on four legs she was making better progress than us, as we struggled pathetically to stay upright.

Naturally, before very long curiosity got the better of her, and she just had to try a mouthful of the icy substance, which resulted in very much the same reaction if I were to try chewing a mouthful of it. She shook her head uncontrollably as freezing snow found its mark in her mouth. After a few seconds though, she carried on eating it. All that ice must have completely anaesthetised her teeth, but heaven knows what effect it would have on her insides. Surprisingly, despite the fact that she'd shovelled a fair quantity down, nothing nasty happened.

Jan and I have never been ones for acting like 'grown-ups' or behaving as adults are supposed to do, and we weren't about to start now. Life's too short. We were going to have a snowball fight, and to hell with being 'grown-up.' Never one to be outdone when there was lots of fun to be had; Beans decided it was a great idea to join in. That snowball fight laid the foundations for a 'hobby' that she'd enjoy for the rest of her life: trying to catch snowballs.

When we started lobbing the snowballs at each other, she went mad, desperately trying to catch them in mid flight, leaping into the air in a vain attempt to catch the freezing missiles as they flew through the air. The height and velocity of them meant her success rate was virtually zero, so it was only right to weigh the odds a little more fairly in her direction. We threw the snowballs so that she could actually catch them, which she did very successfully. Catching is perhaps not really the right word, because when the snowballs made contact with her mouth they exploded in all directions, covering her entire head with a fine dusting of snow.

Beans leapt like a ballet dancer for one snowball after another. She would have carried on to the point of exhaustion – if we'd let her. By now, a layer of snow covered most of the rest of her and she stood there, poised and ready, looking more like a wolf in the snowy wilderness of Yellowstone, than a playful dog, waiting impatiently for the next lump of snow to hurtle towards her.

The winters of the late 1980s and early nineties were memorable for the amount of snow, so many of our walks were challenging. Snow and ice are not our favourite conditions for walking, because we like to play safe. Trying to negotiate icy, treacherous surfaces (even in good walking boots) is a reminder that *Homo sapiens,* at some point in its evolution, walked on all fours, and that it might have been better if things had stayed that way. Even ducks make a better job of staying upright than we do, assisted by their flat webbed feet. Beans, of course, had no such problem. If one leg slipped then at least there were another three to keep the momentum going.

Her first contact with ice produced some baffling behaviour. Everyone likes to kick their heels into fresh ice, that wonderful sound of it cracking underfoot. Beans' contribution to this winter fun was to drag out the broken pieces of ice with her teeth. What is it with dogs' compulsion to haul things out of water?

Out came the pieces of ice: small pieces, that were easily removed to be carried off and deposited with their companions and larger chunks that required more effort. This entailed using her teeth as crampons to grip the ice, lifting and dragging the jagged fragments from the pond, legs slipping in all directions on the unbroken ice. Her determination was remarkable.

Once the canine ice-breaker had shifted a few pieces, she had an icy pool to stand in, providing good anchorage for her paws. She was now in a position to try and break off the pieces as if she was eating some huge ice-lolly. After seeing her consume snow in vast quantities, I can only assume that dogs don't suffer from sensitive teeth. My own teeth ached at the thought of the punishment Beans was giving hers.

To anyone watching, this whole activity must have seemed a pointless waste of time; two people standing there, breaking ice, while a dog carried off the pieces. Pointless: probably; entertaining: definitely. I once read that dog-owners live longer because they get more exercise; to that I would add that it is probably because they laugh more. Beans certainly gave us plenty to laugh about.

A clue to her behaviour came whilst watching a television wildlife programme a few years ago. The film was about the lives of a family of wolves in Yellowstone National Park in the USA, depicting the cycles of birth, life and death. During one sequence a group of playful wolf cubs were captured doing exactly what Beans did with the ice. Happy memories flooded back as we watched this wonderful piece of film. After some joyous antics slipping and sliding around the ice, the young wolves proceeded to amuse themselves pulling out pieces of ice. There was no explanation as to why the cubs liked pulling the ice out, other than for the pure fun of it, but it didn't matter; this was the connection between dogs and their wolf ancestors.

According to the narration, dogs stay as puppies in their thinking – wolves don't.

So there it was: the answer to why our dog friends spend their entire lives wanting to play.

CHAPTER TWO

Sticks and Stones

Fun and Games

Beans now had a well-established routine of walks every Sunday and enjoyed her trips to the country with enthusiasm. As soon as the rucksacks appeared, together with all the other walking paraphernalia, she'd get excited, dashing around, tail wagging, in anticipation of the fun ahead. And as far as she was concerned, fun was the name of the game. The more equipment we piled up (boots, cameras, sandwiches and water bottles) the more excited she got. Things really heated up when I started to get her packed lunch ready – full of tasty dog treats.

Dogs amuse themselves with all manner of bizarre activities. Beans developed a whole range of them. Some, such as stick-throwing and playing 'tug' with a rubber ring are typical 'doggy' activities and Beans loved these as much as any dog, but the funniest were her unconventional pastimes.

Dogs and sticks go together like cheese and biscuits. Dogs running after sticks in the park; dogs running after sticks in the woods and then losing sticks and, finally, or in Beans' case, dogs pulling enormous sticks and branches out of rivers to the delight and amusement of the public.

Beans loved cooling off in rivers on hot days, and it usually took a fair amount of cajoling to coax her out of the water to walk on. If there was half a tree in the river that had to be removed from its resting place, then there was no chance of moving her on. It was Beans indulgence time.

I can't remember the first time she developed an interest in dredging rivers, nor can I imagine what was going through her mind when pulling some huge branch out of the water. One thing is certain: it isn't only humans who enjoy a challenge. We might go rock-climbing, sky-diving or bungee-jumping; Beans liked to pit herself against the submerged and partially rotten remains of trees.

Following her swim, she started searching for the most suitable branch poking out of the water. Once one had been found that fitted her requirements, it was then just a matter of working out the logistics of how to get it out. Sometimes, the branch would give in the fight relatively easily, but on other occasions, such as on one particularly memorable day in Dovedale, the tug of war between dog and branch became a titanic struggle of almost epic proportions: Lennox Lewis versus Mike Tyson.

Beautiful though it undoubtedly is, Dovedale has unfortunately become a part of the Peak District that could be described as a 'honeypot.' If you want peace and quiet, without the crowds, then avoid the Bank Holidays and summer weekends – especially around the southern section. Instead, choose a weekday or a winter day and the only company will be the odd passing walker, or the ducks and other birdlife who make the river their home.

As far back as Edwardian times Dovedale has been a major tourist attraction. A combination of stunning scenery, a beautifully clear river with the famous stepping stones over it, have made the dale one of the most popular places in the Peak District. The stepping stones themselves have been worn to a smooth finish by the passage of many thousands of feet over the years.

May and autumn are our favourite times of the year to enjoy the dale. Gradually, throughout April and then into May, leaves burst out from every tree and bush, transforming the dale into a vivid green paradise. It's a celebration of nature after the seemingly endless winter months. Blossom covers the hawthorns that line the dale, the air thick with its wonderful scent.

Colours of a different hue adorn the dale in October as autumn arrives. Choose a sunny day and the colours are stunning; the rich yellows, browns and reds glowing in the sunlight. In scenes reminiscent of a Monet painting, branches hang over the river, their leaves backlit and reflected beautifully in the clear water. How many people, I wonder, have taken up photography, once captivated by Dovedale's charms? This a place for stopping and looking, and patience is usually rewarded before long. Dippers or grey wagtails flit by, a flash of white on the dipper's chest or of yellow on the wagtail's, the first tell tale clue to the bird's identity.

Despite its popularity, nothing can detract from Dovedale's beauty – even on the busiest days. Walking from the car park at the southern end, following the river, the dale soon reveals itself in all its glory. The stepping stones lie enticingly across the Dove inviting you to cross over, although on a busy day there's usually a queue.

The Dove, at this point, isn't very deep, so Beans didn't bother with the problem of leaping from stone to stone; she just paddled across, while we attempted to negotiate the slippery rocks. Things got quite interesting if someone had decided to cross from the opposite bank; usually a child, who had to be coaxed back by the parents. Once across, there are two choices: head up the dale itself, passing the tempting ice cream vendor, or opt for a steep climb up Thorpe Cloud, towering over the head of the dale. Beans made it perfectly clear which way she wanted to go, and it wasn't up the hill. She loved this spot; paddling and messing about in the water.

We could have abandoned the walk, set up camp on the riverbank and she would have been happy for the rest of the day. But, as usual, there were miles to cover and exercise to be enjoyed, so on we went, through the steep-sided limestone gorge, passing the Lover's Leap viewpoint, where we paused to wonder at the Twelve Apostles; rock pinnacles that tower over the surrounding woodland. We passed more eroded rock formations at Tissington Spires, before reaching the cave at Pickering Tor, which Beans just had to explore. Across the river, sinewy climbers tackled the near-vertical sides of Ilam Rock, and we marvelled at their stamina and their courage.

On one idyllic summer walk along the dale, we'd stopped to let Beans cool off in the river. The water in the Dove is so clean and clear that if Beans wanted to retrieve anything, she would have no problem. She decided that this was a day for the challenge to beat all challenges. The gloves were on and the *Rocky* theme was playing.

Sticking out of the water was a huge broken branch that, to all intents and purposes, was a small tree in itself. The bulk lay in the water with a few straggly branches on the riverbank. The excitement mounted as she started hauling it from its watery grave. Preliminary underwater investigation revealed that the branch was snagged on the river bed by some large stones. A good deal of huffing and puffing would be required to free it. She started work, tugging at the small offshoot branches, which quickly parted company with the main branch, sending her catapulting backwards with a mouthful of twigs and rotting foliage.

The more the branch resisted her efforts, the more determined she became, pressing home a new attack on it with renewed vigour, tugging violently at the wood as if her life depended on it. She wasn't about to be defeated by a piece of old wood. Every muscle in her body trembled with effort, but the heavy branch wasn't going to give up without a fight. As I watched her tugging and straining, I wondered if she was acting out the aftermath of a hunt, imagining she was with a pack of tired hungry wolves, tearing and ripping at some fresh prey. Beans had no need to hunt, but that didn't mean the instinct to rip and devour wasn't buried deep inside her.

While all this had been going on, a small group of curious hikers had gathered behind us to watch Beans' display of strength. As we chatted and tried to explain our dog's obsession to the gathering crowd, Beans carried on her tug-of-war, at one point immersing her head in an effort to dislodge whatever was gripping the end of the branch. This seemed to do the trick because it slowly, but surely, started to move. Sensing that her struggle was nearly at an end, she grabbed the middle of the branch firmly between her jaws and with one more violent tug, heaved the sodden piece of tree onto the riverbank, to the accompaniment of cheers and claps from her audience.

Now the branch was out of the water, Beans' mission was complete and she had no further use for it, so we carried on with our walk, happy in the knowledge that our dog had provided some great entertainment completely free of charge.

Along with other aquatic activities, pulling sticks and branches out of rivers and ponds became a lifelong activity for Beans, but it soon became apparent that sticks and branches were not the only objects she was interested in.

Throughout the Peak District National Park, by the sides of rivers or streams, there can still be found, a short distance from the water, neat little piles of stones and rocks of not inconsiderable size. Some will have ended up there naturally; perhaps when the waters flooded; others however, will have been placed there deliberately, not by man, but by a dog. Beans had found another hobby.

When she wasn't avidly pulling sticks out of rivers, she had developed an obsession for plunging her head under water to pull out the largest and heaviest stones from the riverbed. These she carried to the riverbank, where they were carefully deposited in a place of her choosing. This strange piece of river-dredging would be repeated several times until there was a small cairn by the riverside.

The stones had to be of a particular type and size; pebbles simply would not do. Beans made sure she heaved the largest from the river, carrying them slowly and with great effort, to the riverbank. At times, she looked like those huge, muscular contestants in *The World's Strongest Man* competition, straining to carry heavy stone cannonballs, which they then have to deposit on some plinth. Okay, Beans wasn't the canine equivalent of Arnold Schwarzenegger, but the analogy does bear some comparison.

For what seemed like ages, she would have her head under water, attempting to wrestle a mini-boulder from its home. Once firmly grasped in her teeth, it would be unlikely to return to the water, unless, as happened on a few occasions, she had bitten off more than she could chew, and the rock had to be dropped. Sometimes, (which on reflection was probably a bit cruel, considering all the effort she had put in,) we would throw the stone back, which she promptly tried to retrieve, more often than not, successfully. This exercise in river-dredging was often done (as with the famous branch episode) for an audience.

Perhaps there is something to account for all these activities, but I have yet to discover what it is, despite watching several TV programmes on dog and wolf behaviour. If wolves ever did do something like this, what was its purpose? The dog experts need to do some work on this.

One of our favourite Peak District walks took us around the moors and dales connecting the picturesque villages of Eyam, Foolow and the tiny hamlet of Abney. It is hard to imagine that 340 years ago, Eyam was ravaged by a visitation of bubonic plague that was decimating London at the time. Tradition has it that a tailor, George Viccars, lodging in a cottage owned by Mary Cooper, inadvertently brought the deadly plague to the village in some cloth he had ordered from London. Within a short time, Viccars was dead and by the time the plague had burnt itself out the following year, another 259 had perished.

The villagers, led by their courageous vicar, William Mompesson, who was to lose his wife Catherine to the plague, instigated the first ever known quarantine, cutting themselves off to prevent the pestilence from spreading. Medical supplies and food were left at various points around the village, families buried their own dead near to their homes and all church services were stopped. There is a stone just outside the village, with an indentation in the top, known as The Plague Stone. It would be filled with vinegar to disinfect any coins left by the villagers for goods. Although weathered by time and the elements, it stands there by the footpath, a direct link to those terrible events long ago.

Although some recent scientific research has cast doubt on whether it was the plague that came to Eyam, there is no doubt that whether it was plague or some other virulent disease, many people died, and their poignant graves and memorials found in and around the village bear silent testament to this. Their selfless sacrifice ensured that the disease was contained. When I walk around this little village, busy as it always is with tourists, I look at the names of those who died, sometimes entire families, and wonder if such self-sacrifice would happen today in our selfish, every man for himself culture. Despite my cynicism at the modern world, I like to hope that it would.

Leaving Eyam behind to seek quieter surroundings, we usually stopped for lunch at an idyllic place known as Stoke Ford, where five footpaths converge at a footbridge across a stream called the Bretton Brook, where it meets Highlow Brook and Abney Clough. In summer it is a delight: birds flit through the trees, butterflies flutter and there is the constant, gentle, relaxing babble of the stream, the clear water reflecting the trees that surround it; everything in fact, that makes the Peak District the beautiful place it is.

We had what we called 'our spot' by a nearby wall where we always liked to enjoy our lunch. It faced the stream and was a good place to catch the sun, which of course meant it was popular with others. It was always a bitter disappointment if our stop coincided with that of a twenty-strong walking club and we saw someone else settled there. It's funny how we can get so possessive over something that, in all fairness, is there for everyone to enjoy.

One Sunday a volunteer ranger from the Peak Park was rebuilding a section of stone embankment near the bridge, to prevent the water from undermining the bank and making the bridge unstable. Some of the stones from the wall had been dislodged either by the force of floodwater or by children playing around, and these he was retrieving from the bed of the stream. Cue some timely intervention from Beans. She needed no encouragement and was soon hard at work, helping the man to move the stones. Those she managed to lift were carefully carried out and piled up on the bank for the grateful ranger. Naturally, Beans' wall-building knowledge was zero. As far as she was concerned this was just a fun game and the fact that she was helping with some important National Park conservation work was by the by. She had no concept of which were the best stones for the job; although, to be fair, she did try her best.

Naturally, anything pebble-sized was no challenge for her, so her offerings were, for the most part, useable. Any stones the man deemed unsuitable from this rapidly expanding pile were thrown back – to be promptly retrieved by Beans.

Another much-loved Peak District place we often ended up at was Milldale, a popular spot for tourists and walkers alike, where Beans kept ice-cream-eating adults and children amused for ages with her stone gathering antics. Milldale itself is little more than a cluster of picturesque cottages, the ruins of an old mill and a beautiful old packhorse bridge, known as Viator's Bridge, which crosses the River Dove. The bridge is a scheduled ancient monument and was mentioned in Izaak Walton's famous book on fly-fishing, *The Compleat Angler*, published in 1676.

With a little imagination, it isn't difficult to picture the trains of pack-horses, laden with goods, crossing the narrow bridge and then following the Dove as it made its way to the town of Ashbourne. It is a lovely place at any time of the year and seems to be one of those spots specially made for just stopping and picnicking. You are never alone there.

Nowadays, Milldale acts as a crossroads for walkers. Those coming from Dovedale cross the bridge before heading up Wolfscote Dale; some are heading for the delights of Dovedale or climbing the narrow lane that leads to the quiet village of Alstonefield. Tourists stop to picnic by the river and children amuse themselves by feeding the ever-present ducks. The National Trust has a discreet information point in a converted barn and a cheery café serves teas, cakes and ice-cream, along with pasties big enough to satisfy the hungriest hiker's appetite. It couldn't be more English. I love the place.

We'd stopped at Milldale to get tea and ice-cream, before pressing on with our walk. The Peak District is full of places like this and sometimes it's a wonder you manage to get any walking done. Sometimes, however, it's good to stop and soak up the scenery, relax and even indulge in a bit of people-watching, which at times can be just as entertaining as observing dog behaviour. Neither of us is the type of walker who ploughs on, head down, barely looking at the passing scenery, merely clocking up as many miles as possible in the shortest time. With so much to see in the countryside, who knows what you might miss: a heron perhaps, patiently hunting for fish; a dipper, hopping from rock to rock along the river, in pursuit of a meal, his white chest revealing him against the dark background; a buzzard, soaring gracefully overhead, its mewing calls filling the air. If, however, the birdlife eluded you, you might have been lucky enough to encounter a daft dog busying herself retrieving stones from the river.

On that day, Beans excelled herself for pure entertainment value. Stone after stone was carefully and methodically carried from the riverbed to be deposited in its new resting place, much to the amusement of the onlookers. Children especially, were delighted at her antics and there were many exclamations of: *'Mummy, look at that funny dog over there'* or *'Why is that dog carrying stones out of the water?'* Ice creams melted and dripped down clothing as their owners watched fascinated at the bizarre antics of our dog.

When your dog does strange things, you find it's a great conversation starter, even if it is difficult to explain to people why your beloved pet appears to derive such satisfaction retrieving stones from rivers. What's more, you soon find out about the things that other people's dogs like to get up to, some of which end in a trip to the vets. Thankfully, Beans never did develop a liking for swallowing golf balls, sweaty old socks or items of underwear.

Ultimately though, years of carrying stones was bound to have a detrimental effect on her teeth and they were soon mere shadows of their former selves. Those once-sharp gnashers were now nicely rounded at the ends. We had to make sure that this particular hobby was kept to a minimum. We didn't want accusations of dog cruelty because she couldn't use her teeth to chew properly. This never happened, of course, and her teeth were well up to the challenge of chewing various objects that dogs in their wisdom like to chew, but whether her blunted fangs would have been up to the challenge of tearing a fresh carcass to pieces can only be imagined.

Beans was never a vicious dog and the only time she tried to bite was when she was being groomed. I always thought that most dogs loved grooming, but not Beans. She hated it. Keeping her coat nice and sleek was a major operation - a two-person job: one to do the brushing - the brush monitor; the other to hold her head in case she whipped round with a fearsome bite - the head monitor.

In the end we resorted to applying a makeshift muzzle to minimise her biting ability, but it was always a major relief when grooming was over. By the time we'd finished, even the muzzle was coming loose, so determined was she to inflict harm on us. It was quite extraordinary to see a normally placid and good-natured dog turn into a salivating rabid beast at the mere sight of a grooming brush. It seemed a shame that what should have been a relaxing experience both for her and for us became a battleground. Poodle-parlours would have been queuing up to sue us.

Perhaps it was just as well that those teeth weren't as sharp as they should have been. We always joked that where Beans was concerned, it wouldn't be a case of 'severely bitten' rather, 'severely dented.'

Sticks

In January 1989 Jan and I became engaged, after being together for eight years. If I had been less of a coward, this proposal would have taken place the previous autumn on top of the somewhat less than romantic-sounding 'Tom Heights' in the Lake District. The Lakes are glorious at any time of the year, but in the autumn they're even more beautiful. The Lakeland Fells, resplendent in their autumn hues, tower magnificently over the lakes, such as Buttermere, Ullswater and Derwentwater. It is the land of William Wordsworth, who immortalised the area in his poems; of Beatrix Potter, who wrote her famous stories of Peter Rabbit and Mrs Tiggy-winkle; of the other great poets, Coleridge, Southey, De Quincey and Keats. It is a place for romance.

But, on top of Tom Heights on that beautiful autumn day, surrounded by such stunning scenery – the romantic part of me had gone on a holiday of its own.

It was the ideal time and place to pop the question and yet for some reason I just couldn't open my mouth to say those four simple words. Instead, I waited two months until a cold winter's day in Deepdale, in the Peak District, to ask Jan to marry me. Talk about plucking up the courage.

Whilst on Tom Heights that November day I had taken a photograph of Jan, with the magnificent Langdale Pikes in the background. Naturally, she was in full hiking garb, so I thought I'd try to get it published. The photograph turned out to be a good one, so I sent it off to the walking magazine and waited...and waited....and waited. I had almost forgotten about it until, one day in January 1997, a complimentary copy of the magazine dropped through the letterbox. Inside, gracing the cover of the pull-out walking routes supplement was Jan, looking happy and relaxed, on that glorious autumn day in the Lake District. Every time I look at it now, I am reminded of the day when I should have proposed – but didn't.

Beans had now been a part of our lives for nearly two years and, while we both went out to our respective jobs every day, she was quite happy living with Bob and Rita. Now we had started on the house-hunting trail, our thoughts turned to what would be the best option for Beans while we were at work. Wherever we eventually ended up living, we knew it was certainly not going to be in Wilmslow. House prices had rocketed, leaving people like us who had spent most of our lives there, unable to afford even the cheapest properties. The net was cast further afield.

After looking at several areas and properties, we found the best we could afford was a one-up, one-down terraced cottage in nearby Macclesfield. After the homes we'd been used to, it was quite a shock to the system. No garden, just a shared rear yard; no central heating, a bath but no shower and a toilet that hadn't seen so much as a whiff of bleach in years. Looking back, I cannot imagine what possessed us to even think about buying such a crumbling pile of bricks and mortar, let alone parting with hard earned cash for it.

With hindsight, I would not even look at such a place, but everything seems a bit of an adventure when you are starting out on the property ladder. Besides, wouldn't it be fun to get the place just as we wanted? Maybe at the start perhaps, but after the year of hard work that it eventually took, fun is not the word I would have chosen. Nightmare would perhaps be a better description. I am no stranger to DIY and I tackle any job I feel is within my limited capabilities, but total renovation – no thanks. If I have to do anything like that again I hope there will be enough cash in the bank to pay someone else to do it.

By necessity, the year that it took to make the house habitable was to severely curtail ours and Beans' walking activities at the weekends, which became a tedious ritual of scraping, sanding, filling, cleaning, painting and wallpapering. Some jobs (such as re-plastering and installing a loft hatch) were sensibly passed to a builder. The cottage itself was about 150 years old and, for most of its life would have had a real fire burning, which would have produced soot. A very large quantity of it had collected in the roof space and there it would have remained, safely out of sight, had we not been advised, by reason of fire safety, to install a loft hatch.

The next time we met the builder he told us about the moment he and his mate removed the piece of ceiling. A torrent of thick black soot erupted from the hole in the ceiling like a pyroclastic cloud from a volcano, enveloping them both and billowing out into the rest of the house. Soot that hadn't seen the light of day since Queen Victoria was on the throne now covered every nook and cranny of the cottage.

'It was a right old mess,' he said. 'We looked like miners after a day down the pit.'

'How the heck did you get cleaned up?' I asked, knowing full well that there was no hot water – or a shower – in the house at the time.

'We had cold baths,' he replied, in a tone of voice that suggested being covered from head to toe in the stuff was an everyday occurrence.

'You must have been freezing,' I said, looking at the enamel bath and imaging them trying to get soot out of every pore with no soap and only cold water.

'Well at least it's not winter,' he laughed. 'I think we might have been tempted to drive home looking like we did.'

Although trying to remove soot from the house was a less than pleasant experience, I am so glad I wasn't the one who cut the hole in that ceiling.

While these tumultuous events were taking place at our cottage, Beans' life in Wilmslow carried on much as normal, the only exception being that we couldn't spare the time to go on our regular trips to the Peak District. Lindow Common, a piece of rare lowland heath in Wilmslow, was just a short walk from Jan's house and during this time it became Beans' main playground. It was at the Common that she developed her passion for stick chasing.

Like most dogs, Beans loved to run after thrown objects, such as balls and rubber rings. She would carry on until almost exhausted, enthused with the sheer joy of living, each throw of the particular object awaited with eager anticipation. Dogs seem to be blessed with a joy in just being alive that could be a lesson for all of us.

I remember the comedian Billy Connolly, describing what a great life dogs have (at least those with decent owners) when all they have to do is sleep, get fed, chase cats, catch balls and relieve themselves. It was a simplistic but hilarious view of a dog's life, told in typical Connolly style, which had me doubled up with laughter. It was also bang on in its description. Lucky dogs really do have a great life.

Our regular walk to the Common was a very sociable affair as far as Beans was concerned. On the way we would usually bump into some of her many chums, passing the time of day with their owners. It was what you might call a 'dog club' of regulars, all stopping to meet and greet. Whilst we got chatting to the owners the dogs would busy themselves with the ritual of mutual bottom-sniffing. Daisy and Delta were two of Beans' best friends, along with a cat (whose name I cannot remember) who – unusually – accompanied the dogs on their walk. None of the dogs bothered the cat – everyone got on just fine, which was good news for the cat. With pleasantries exchanged we carried on, passing the field where the donkeys (Noddy and Eeyore) lived.

Beans loved donkeys, and always made a determined effort to introduce herself to them. Despite the size differences, there were never any incidents. Dog and donkey gently nuzzled each other as if they were old friends, though sensibly, she stopped short of trying to sniff their bottoms. Even the most chilled donkey would have taken exception to that.

This adoration of all things equine extended to any ponies and foals that she came across on her travels. Horses though, were carefully avoided. They were much too intimidating. Crossing a field with horses in it was always a major undertaking, as we tried to make a detour around the field, Beans creeping along, low to the ground, her tail between her legs, hoping the horse hadn't noticed her.

Noddy and Eeyore, in true donkey fashion, were two of the most laid-back creatures you could possibly meet. We would stand at the gate next to their field and wait to see if they might grace us with their presence. Sometimes, they would be grazing near the gate, so it wasn't too much of an effort for them to wander over and greet us. If they were at the far end the wait could be considerably longer, because, friendly though they were, Noddy and Eeyore were lazy. If they didn't feel like making the long and arduous trek across the field, there was little you could do about it.

Sometimes, persistence and calling their names out paid off, but the wait while they ambled slowly across the field could seem like an eternity. They never took the direct route to us. Instead, they'd take a meandering course across the field. When they saw us, waiting patiently by the gate, their pace did quicken a little, but as far as breaking into a trot was concerned, that was too much.

There's nothing unusual about dogs chasing sticks, and I suppose Beans' stick activities were no different to other dogs, but she built up a complete series of stick - related activities that didn't just involve running after and retrieving them. There was the 'leap as high as you can to grab the stick' game; the 'how the hell do I get this two foot long stick through the squeezer stile' game and not to mention the 'how many sticks can I pile up on Bob's lawn before he tells me off?' game.

Her trip to Lindow Common was not complete without a series of little games and rituals that added to the fun. There was the 'chewy tree,' which we transformed into a source of instant delight for Beans, by placing some of her favourite hide chews in various recesses and then standing back and watching the fun unfold, as she tried desperately to dislodge the tasty treats from their hiding places. Her high-jumping ability, coupled with her canine sense of smell, meant that not many chews were undiscovered.

And then, on the way back from the Common, there was the 'lead tree,' a marker for the point at which her lead had to be attached as we neared the road. After her first few trips to the Common, she would instinctively know at which point on the path to stop and wait there for us.

Years later, the authorities decided that Lindow Common had to be restored to its former status as lowland heath, which meant that many of the so-called 'invasive' trees had to be removed. Sadly, two of the casualties were Beans' trees. It felt like a part of our lives had been removed with them.

Dogs, when playing sticks, either retrieve the stick then deposit it at your feet to be thrown again or they retrieve it, run back with it and then stubbornly refuse to hand it over, at which point you have to play tug-of-war until either you or the dog gives in. The dog's making sure that he isn't the only one doing all the work.

'You want this stick? Then fight me for it' is what they are saying.

Beans liked to work us hard where stick-throwing was concerned. There was a seemingly endless supply of broken branches on the Common to keep her going for ages. Stick after stick flew through the air as Beans sprinted after them, leaping over clumps of heather and splashing through puddles in a kind of mad headlong charge to try and get to the missile before it landed. Luckily, she was never that fast, but we had a few near misses where dog and stick almost collided. After hearing about dogs that had been seriously injured during this activity, we had to throw them hard enough so they would land before she reached them.

In order to keep the momentum going, we made sure there was always another stick in reserve, because hell would have to freeze over before she'd let you have the one she'd brought back. It was only fair to let her win the tug of war game now and then, but if we did then the stick would end up being chewed to bits and completely useless for any more games.

Beans' athletic prowess really came into its own when leaping. Had anyone ever decided to hold an Olympic Games for dogs then I'm sure she would have won gold for the dogs' high jump. If the object you were holding was a nice stick, then the more determined her efforts became. You could see the concentration and determination in her face as she prepared for that one giant leap for dog kind and then, as if her whole body was made of elastic, she leapt into the air, mouth open - her entire body stretched from nose to tail. Of course, this didn't always result in a successful catch, but she carried on jumping until we gave in out of sympathy and lowered the stick, or she got too tired and gave up. At the end of her marathon session she calmly set about reducing it to matchwood.

Naturally, some sticks were just too good to chew up, and these were carried back home with the utmost care and determination. Not for Beans were the smaller, easier to carry in one's mouth variety, for she made sure that the sticks she carried home were the biggest and best - a good piece of wood that she could feel proud of. These were ones that proclaimed to other dogs: 'Look at the size of my stick; I bet you'd like this one'.

Carrying such large sticks home was not without its problems. After a vigorous exercise session she would be puffing and panting and hardly in a fit state to be carrying a heavy item in her mouth for the best part of a mile. She had to ensure that she carried the stick so that one end wasn't heavier than the other, causing her to overbalance. This entailed several failed attempts to pick the thing up, but once satisfied, off she trotted. You could tell by her determined gait that one way or another she was going to get that stick home.

At regular intervals she stopped to pant properly, and then carried on in the same determined manner. Other dogs with their owners walked past, but Beans ignored them. The friendliest dogs were given no more than a cursory glance; others, who were probably more interested in trying to relieve her of the stick, were met with a warning growl. Squirrels could have stood at the side of the path pulling faces and carrying placards with *'catch me'* written on them, but she would have taken no notice.

There was, however, one major impediment to Beans' odyssey: squeezer stiles. The bane of her progress through the Peak District now became an even more seemingly insurmountable problem. Although the stile in question, a wooden one, was wide enough for her to get her body through, the problem was she couldn't figure out that her width had actually increased - at least at the front end. She trotted purposefully towards the gap, oblivious to the fact that her progress was going to be abruptly cut short.

Both ends of the stick slammed into the posts on either side of the gap, sending Beans bouncing backwards with such force that she dropped the stick, and was left standing there, dazed and confused. Dogs are intelligent creatures, but in this situation Beans was not the sharpest knife in the drawer. Once she got over the shock of realising that the stick was not a bendy piece of rubber that would have yielded nicely as she passed through the gap, she picked it up again with the same predictable result. A couple of aborted attempts later and she was no nearer to solving the problem, and probably nursing a bad headache. Just as we were wondering whether to intervene or not, the penny finally dropped. She picked the stick up at one end and then dragged it through the gap. Job done.

We couldn't resist rewarding her problem-solving with lots of pats and exclamations of, 'What a clever girl!' It seemed unfair not to reward such perseverance, though we knew that come next time, the entire process would be repeated.

Once this major obstacle had been negotiated, Beans was on the home run. Perhaps realising that her destination was not far off, she gained her second wind, covering the remaining few hundred yards with ease. Nothing would stop her. Cars parked by the side of the road narrowly missed having their paintwork scratched, walls were scraped and people darted out of the way to avoid being kneecapped. We could have been sued.

With all obstacles successfully overcome, Beans' stick was soon deposited with several other companions of similar size on Bob's back lawn. Quite what her purpose was in creating a woodpile in the back garden remains a mystery. Perhaps they were presents for Bob, who didn't take too kindly to his prize lawn being covered with bits of trees, but whatever her purpose was, she was immensely proud of her growing pile of sticks. Some were occasionally picked out and chewed, but, after all the effort expended on getting them there, she had no further use for them.

Dogs' minds are a mystery, so perhaps it's as well that we just enjoy their funny activities simply for what they are. Long after we'd left Macclesfield and moved to Congleton, Brereton Heath Country Park became one of our favourite places to take Beans. On one particular visit she'd pulled a large branch out of the lake and hauled it up the side of the bank where she proceeded to roll on it. She was totally carried away, grunting and growling with pleasure, her legs waving in all directions.

Quite what was on this particular stick to warrant such frenzied aerobics I don't know, but she was oblivious to the fact that both she and the branch were starting to slide back down the bank towards the water. Even as the branch gained momentum, she continued to roll on it, losing all sense of dignity and decorum as she slid, headfirst, down the wet grass, the stick at first acting as a sort of ski, before it finally parted company with her, just short of the water. Looking decidedly unsteady after her dry ski run, Beans regained her composure, leaving us in fits of laughter.

On another occasion during a walk in the Todd Valley she spent ages desperately tugging at a branch sticking out of the Todd Brook, only to discover that the branch was in fact still attached to the tree, which grew very near to the bank. Even Beans couldn't bring that down.

Memories like that will stay with us forever.

After a year, the cottage in Macclesfield was ready to move into. We may have done very little walking during that period, but we'd made up for it with all the hard work and sweat we'd put into the place.

In May 1990, we got married. The wedding day was perfect, despite some last minute panic with my car, which had decided that the ideal time for its entire speedometer unit to pack up was a few days before the wedding.

Jan would have liked Beans at the wedding, but I don't think the vicar would have been too keen on the idea. It would have been great if she could have walked up the aisle with Jan and posed for photographs with us, but she did have one very important role to play on the morning of the wedding. Jan hadn't been able to eat properly for days; not, she said, because of nerves, more out of excitement, although nerves undoubtedly played a part. There was only one thing to do to try and relax and that was to take Beans out for her morning walk – a familiar routine on a day of the unfamiliar. After a good walk up the bridleway towards the Common and around the woodland paths, she was feeling far more relaxed. Beans had played her part.

The wedding day will stay in our minds for several reasons. There was a country fair at the reception venue to raise money for wildlife conservation, together with a troupe of Morris Dancers, who had been entertaining the crowd – it was too good an opportunity for the photographer to miss. He persuaded the Morris Men to pose with us for the photographs. We didn't need any persuading.

'Support Cheshire wildlife – wedding thrown in for free,' shouted one of the Morris Men, as we all lined up for the photograph; a bizarre mixture of the bride in her wedding dress, me in my morning suit – and the Morris Men with their painted faces and comical outfits. People stopped to watch the proceedings, but we didn't mind; it somehow seemed to add to the fun of the day, as all those pre-wedding nerves were banished by laughter. This was a day for everyone to enjoy.

After months of sometimes soul-destroying work on the house, we made sure our honeymoon was a relaxing one. Two weeks in Scotland was just what we needed. Two weeks of walks, sight-seeing, boat trips and wonderful pure air was the start of a love-affair with Scotland that will never end. It is a place to lift the spirit. After months of breathing in dust, paint fumes, soot and paint-stripper, coupled with a severe lack of walks; it was bliss.

Cat and Mouse

With the wedding and honeymoon over, Beans came to live with us in Macclesfield. We knew from the outset that this wasn't going to be the ideal situation. We both worked, the cottage only had a shared rear yard, so Beans had lost her garden to play in, and there was little in the way of countryside on our doorstep, so we would just have to make the most of our new situation. It was a big change – for us and Beans.

On Saturdays we'd head over to Wilmslow with Beans. She still loved her walk to the Common for a spot of stick-throwing and the chance to meet some of her old doggy pals. After tea with Bob and Rita it was back to Macclesfield and the promise of some good hiking the next day in the Peak District. We didn't travel over to Wilmslow every Saturday, but since we didn't have a back garden, it was a good excuse to go where there was one – especially in the summer.

Chasing after objects, whether Frisbees, sticks or rubber rings is normal for a dog, but Beans proved once again that she needed more challenging, although sometimes worrying, activities. Vanishing into the night to seek out foxes and playing cat and mouse with Bob and Rita were two favourites. Doing a disappearing act was nothing new to Beans. The summer after we brought her home from the rescue kennels, we drove up to the Lake District for a much-needed two week walking holiday, leaving her at what soon became known as her Wilmslow bed and breakfast establishment: Bob and Rita's. Those summers of the 1980s always seemed to be sunnier, if our many photographs of holidays spent in the Lakes are anything to go by.

Some of the higher Lakeland Fells involve quite difficult walking on narrow ridges, requiring the use of hands as well as feet, together with tricky ascents and descents on loose rock, known as 'scree.' We didn't feel confident enough to take Beans to such terrain, so it was decided that she would stay in Wilmslow. She would have tackled the walking easily, but the thought of hurtling down a mountain behind her, as she pursued one of the native Herdwick sheep, fellow walkers desperately trying to avoid an avalanche of rocks and boulders, was too frightening to contemplate.

At breakfast one morning, in the guesthouse where we were staying, Jan was reading one of Rita's letters she always sent to us when we were on holiday. They were usually more about what Beans had been up to. As I munched down my cornflakes, Jan started laughing.

'What's she done now?' I said, through a mouthful of cereal.

'Gone missing,' Jan replied, without taking her eyes from the letter.

I couldn't quite figure out what was so funny about Beans going missing; unless there was more to it than that. She'd obviously been found; otherwise Jan wouldn't have been laughing.

'Where?' I asked, hoping for a bit more information.

'On the Common,' she said, before carrying on reading.

Once she'd finished the letter, Jan told me that Rita had taken Beans out for a walk over towards Lindow Common and somehow, between home and the Common, Beans had decided to go off on an adventure of her own. We got more details when we got home, but the letter gave a pretty good account.

Beans was off her lead at the time and had wandered away from the main path, so Rita soon lost sight of her in the trees. The area around the Common is wooded and criss-crossed with paths. There are also numerous fox and badger trails and it was one of these that Beans

59

had obviously decided was well worth following. She could be let off her lead quite safely and would usually stay close, but like any dog, instincts took over where scents were concerned, to the exclusion of everything else.

Jan's early morning walks with Beans took them over many of the paths and tracks that the wayward dog was probably now exploring, including a mysterious area known as Lindow Moss. For many years, peat has been dug from this place forming deep channels where the ancient material has been gouged out. After heavy rain, they fill with water and the unwary could find themselves in trouble if they fell into those dark trenches.

On autumn mornings mist shrouds the Moss, and you could be a million miles away from the residential area only a few hundred yards away. On 1st August 1984, something happened that put Lindow Moss in the spotlight. Men cutting peat discovered a body.

All they found initially was a leg, but later, when the police were called, further investigations revealed a human torso in the peat. The lower half of the body was missing, together with the other leg, but what made things even more exciting was the condition of the corpse. The peat had preserved the body so well that the skin, although leathery, was intact. The face, complete with red hair and beard, was clearly visible.

Tests showed that the body was that of a man, aged about 25 from the Iron Age; at least mid 1st century AD. This was a major archaeological find. Lindow Pete, as he was nicknamed, had now joined the ranks of those other ancient 'bog bodies' that had been discovered in similar places around Europe. There was, however, a grisly twist to the story. The police weren't entirely wrong with their first assumption that they had a murder victim on their hands – Lindow Man had been ritually – and brutally – killed.

His head had been struck twice with a heavy object, and then he received another blow to his back, breaking one of his ribs. Next, he was probably garrotted with the piece of cord that was still tied around his neck, before finally having his throat cut. His body was then left face down in a pool in the bog, where it lay undiscovered until that day 2000 years later. Lindow Man eventually went on permanent display at the British Museum in London, but every now and again he's allowed back up north to go on display at Manchester University Museum.

When Beans arrived on the scene three years after that amazing discovery, we often wondered if her keen sense of smell and delight in digging would one day unearth another bog body on Lindow Moss, but despite many walks around the area Beans was not destined to have her face on the front of the local newspaper, alongside another preserved body.

The worry now was, had she wandered over to the moss and got into difficulties in one of those deep trenches? The thought of Beans' well-preserved 'bog dog' corpse being unearthed in the distant future was too awful to contemplate. But, it was summer and it had been reasonably dry, so even if she was following some interesting scent through the peat channels, she should hopefully be able to haul herself out.

Rita started to panic, calling out for Beans in the vain hope she would respond. She didn't. Whatever had caught Beans' attention must have been interesting, because, despite hours of searching, there was no sign of her. It's a horrible feeling when your dog disappears, a feeling of dread that something awful has happened. Then there's the worry that the dog is panicking as well, when it realises its owners are nowhere to be seen.

Panic, though, was probably the last thing on Beans' mind. She'd walked to the Common countless times and would be quite capable of making her own way home. For now though, something far more interesting than a walk with Rita had compelled her to go off piste. The scent trails of badgers or foxes would have been irresistible and could have taken her miles from Rita. However good a dog's hearing, she may well have been unable to hear Rita's anxious calls. Once her interest had waned, that would have been the point when she would have panicked. Instinct would then take over and all those lovely scent trails would lead her back, albeit in a meandering fashion, to safety. They didn't, as it turned out, lead her back to Rita.

After fruitless searching and name-calling all she could do was head for home, hoping that Beans had retraced her steps. Dark was some hours off, so there was still time to get Bob to help with the search. Maybe she would spot Beans on the path, trotting for home. Perhaps another passing dog-walker had seen her. Perhaps Beans, who had no road-sense, had been hit by a car as she crossed a road and was lying injured – or worse. She tried to put that idea out of her mind, but nevertheless it was a horrible possibility. What would she do about breaking such upsetting news to Jan and Mart? Wait until they'd got home from holiday or tell them now? No, it would be fine; Beans would be safely back at home. There would be no frantic calls to the vet. But as much as she tried to block that scenario out, it wouldn't go away.

Back at home, Bob was on the verge of calling out a search party for Rita. It had been hours since she'd gone out on what was supposed to be just a short walk, so what had happened? At that moment he got his answer.

'Where *have* you been?' he said, as she staggered into the garden.

'I've lost Beans,' she exclaimed.

'She's here,' said Bob, as if there was no reason to expect that she shouldn't be.

The words had hardly left his mouth when a calm and relaxed-looking Beans wandered out of the house, tail wagging, to greet Rita as if nothing had happened. Rita stood there, dumbfounded. She'd just spent the best part of an afternoon traipsing every path and track around the Common worrying herself sick and now here was Beans, looking quite unfazed by the whole affair. To her it had probably been a jolly afternoon's adventure.

'I've been looking for you for hours,' she said to Beans, who was pleased to be reunited with everyone. Despite the worries, she wasn't coated from head to toe in ominous black peat.

Apparently, Beans had decided, after her adventure had run its course, to make her own way home some hours before. Unable to find Rita, she'd simply retraced her steps. After all, it wasn't as if she didn't know the way home. She'd done that route so many times with Jan and Mart. Quite why Rita had decided to do a disappearing act on her she'd no idea, but, despite a thorough search for her it seemed the best course of action was to go home and hope that Rita had made her way back home. Why do humans always manage to get lost?

Little did Beans realise that if Rita had not returned when she did, the whole scenario would have become farcical, with Bob searching for Rita, searching for Beans, while the villain of the piece relaxed at home, unconcerned.

Mud Mud Glorious Mud

Where mud, water, bogs and otherwise filthy unpleasant conditions are concerned, dogs fall into two camps: they love it or they don't. Benji refused to venture out in anything other than drizzle; such was his aversion to getting wet. My first dog – a Beagle named Judy – was a little better; you could at least walk her in the rain, though she hated swimming. Benji hated both.

Beans, however, was from the SAS school of outdoor endurance. It would take driving, horizontal, freezing rain to 'dampen' her enthusiasm for all things wet. For a dog accustomed to the great outdoors this is no bad thing.

The terrain in the Peak District can be challenging; particularly the northern section, known as the Dark Peak. Not surprisingly, the southernmost section is known as the White Peak, the two terms deriving from the darker gritstone of the north and the lighter limestone of the south. Areas such as Saddleworth Moor, Kinder Scout and Bleaklow in the northern section, may seem bleak and uninviting to some, but they have a sense of wilderness so vital in this modern age. The moors stretch as far as the eye can see, dotted with wind-sculpted gritstone rocks, the only prominent landmarks in a vast featureless landscape. Cotton grass sways gently in the breeze and the call of birds such as red grouse and golden plover fill the air. It is a place to enjoy nature – *Big Sky country*.

Dark Peak has always seemed to me an apt name for that part of the Peak District. Not so much because of the dark gritstone but more the fact that it contains large areas of bog and moorland. Huge areas of peat, intersected with deep channels, known as *groughs* will test the most experienced of hikers. In the summer (or more particularly during a drought) the terrain is easy to cross with the aid of a good map and compass, but in the autumn and winter when the ground is sodden after weeks of rain, only the fittest and hardiest of walkers (and dogs) can attempt to traverse it.

The peat becomes a waterlogged, boot-sucking morass; a quagmire that reduces progress to a snail's pace. It helps if you have a sense of humour; especially when you find yourself up to your knees in the stuff. To some this would be a place to be avoided, somewhere hostile and dangerous, which it can be at times for the ill-prepared. To those in the know however, it is a place where nature is untamed, that the modern world cannot touch. No houses or roads can be built here; no sprawling business parks or industrial estates. It is somewhere to switch off the mobile, forget the emails and submit to the mercy of the elements. Instead of the challenge of how to survive the world of office politics, it is a place where you have to try and work out a way of crossing a seemingly impassable stretch of oozing, black, cloying gunge.

It is also a terrain where you come across the stark reminder of the fragility of life. Many aircraft have come to grief on these moors and perhaps none are more poignant than the B29 Superfortress that crashed near Higher Shelf Stones on 3rd November 1948. The aircraft was on a short twenty-five-minute flight from RAF Scampton in Lincolnshire to USAF Burtonwood, near Warrington in Cheshire. On board the ill-fated aircraft were 13 crew, sacks of mail for USAF staff, and the payroll. All the crew on board the B29 were due to return home to the United States in three days.

The pilot was told that he could expect broken clouds between 2000 and 4000ft and visibility of between four to six miles. Did he encounter these clouds and become disorientated, so tried to get below them to see where he was? Did the aircraft's instruments fail and he thought he was at a higher altitude than he actually was? The answer to that question died with the crew as their huge aircraft slammed into the ground north of Higher Shelf Stones.

The ensuing explosion and fire killed everyone on board instantly. Although search and rescue teams soon arrived at the crash site, it was clear that nothing could be done for those on board the aircraft. Rescuers found a wristwatch belonging to one of the crew in the wreckage – the time had stopped at 11am.

Although most of the wreckage was cleared away, even now, sixty years later, pieces of the aircraft can still be seen. There was even a report of a ghostly sighting of the plane's young pilot, Captain Langdon P. Tanner, although a small service and blessing some years ago seem to have finally put the poor man's spirit to rest. A small memorial to the dead young men was erected by 367 Squadron RAF Finningley in 1988. No matter the time of year, it is always surrounded by poppy crosses.

However small a piece of wreckage you come across up here (and not just that of the Superfortress) it is still tangible evidence that for someone, death came suddenly and violently. In the midst of our enjoyment of such wild landscape, we are reminded, in those twisted pieces of wreckage, of how abruptly life can be cut short – and how important it is to live it.

It was into this wild, lonely, beautiful, tragic terrain that Beans came - and she loved it. I've seen dogs gingerly tiptoe around the smallest puddle, but not Beans. She splashed through puddles, pools, bogs and sloppy mud like a toddler trying out his first pair of shiny new Wellington boots. The pleasure was doubled, on a warm day, if she wanted to cool off, because she'd head for the first convenient patch of water and dive in. It didn't matter how smelly or filthy the water was. If it was cool and wet she was in there, wallowing like a hippopotamus on the *Maasai Mara*. She emerged from this primeval ooze, unbothered that she was half-caked in black muck. It had done its job by cooling her down, so that was all that mattered. The fact that some of this filth would end up in our car later, or that we would have to spend half an hour cleaning her up back home, was of no concern.

Muddy boots can be removed and kept in a plastic bag until ready to be cleaned. A dog, on the other hand, cannot be conveniently placed in a carrier bag and then cleaned a day or so later. Mind you, it was tempting.

Although we took towels and covered the back seats with umpteen layers of plastic sheets and old blankets, inevitably we came home with a still-dirty dog, a couple of wet, black towels and the familiar, though strangely not too unpleasant odour of damp dog filling the car.

A few minutes into the journey home and a soft, rhythmic sound came from the back seat. The gentle *slurp slurp* of Beans, trying to lick herself clean. It was a satisfying, almost comforting sound, as if she was saying, *'I've had a wonderful day, and I will try to clean myself up.'*

Night Exercises

When Beans was in Wilmslow, she enjoyed night-time adventures on her evening walk with Bob. This walk would usually be around 11.30 at night, since it was his routine to visit his local pub about 10 – 10.30 for last orders, and then take Beans out before bed. Never one for turning in early, this routine suited him well. Beans however, made sure that he was up well into the small hours.

His nightly route took him around the well-lit roads as well as part way up the unlit track leading to the Common. Beans was usually off her lead but stayed by his side, such was her obedience. We weren't too happy about this, but he insisted she was fine and didn't run out into the road, so we were surprised and secretly pleased when we found out that she wasn't *that* obedient.

Beans had developed a liking for following the night-time calls of the foxes who lived near the Common.

All training and obedience evaporated the moment the foxes' eerie screams pierced the night. With Bob standing helplessly by, unable to attach her lead quickly enough, she would disappear into the darkness to heaven knows what adventures. She may well have resembled a fox, but there the similarities end. Dogs and foxes do not belong to the same family; a fact I found hard to believe when I first discovered it. This fact didn't matter to Beans; although quite what the foxes thought, if she ever did meet them, can only be imagined.

Finding out your dog is disappearing at night can be quite disconcerting, but, as it turned out, we needn't have worried. Beans' homing skills were obviously better than anyone had believed. Once he had lost her to the night – and the foxes – Bob would return home, and so, eventually, would Beans - about three in the morning.

A short tell-tale bark would rouse Bob from his armchair slumber, and there, at the front door, would be Beans, fresh from her nocturnal pursuits, with, no doubt, some fresh fox excrement ingrained into her fur, just behind one of her ears.

CHAPTER THREE

Broad Beans and Rotting Jellyfish

Broad Beans

Dogs will have a go at eating any tempting-looking treat or scrap offered to them – regardless of the effect it might have on their insides. After all, a dog doesn't know that eating too much of something is going to have the same effect on its bowels as an overdose of laxative. The pleasure is in the eating, never mind the consequences. The fact that a well-fed dog snatches cold chips, half-eaten bits of pizza and other takeaway detritus from the pavement, has more to do with their scavenging nature than being hungry. Even so, it's still galling to see your dog devour a grubby, stale piece of *Margarita,* having just been fed on the best dog food money can buy.

Beans was never treated as a four-legged dustbin; but she did enjoy occasional little treats. Small pieces of cheese and the odd crisp were some favourites, together with slices of raw carrot. She never seemed to know what to do with carrot; rolling it around in her mouth without chewing, spitting it out, playing with it, picking it up again and then taking the plunge and actually biting into it, at which point she must have decided that carrot was okay. If it didn't re-appear a few seconds later as a half chewed mess, then it could be safely assumed it had passed the Beans taste test.

Some foods however, have such a drastic effect on a dog's internal workings that the food is returned to the world in truly spectacular fashion, as the appalling effects of the cooking oil demonstrated. It is a stomach-churning learning curve of clean ups and stained carpets. Dogs too, can get stomach upsets, despite keeping the little treats to a bare minimum, and when a dog has to go, it has to go. Unless a dog can be trained to both climb on to, and sit on, a toilet, then I'm afraid the carpet is going to bear the brunt. Sometimes, you really only have yourself to blame if something you have quite innocently given to your dog, comes back to haunt you. Take broad beans for example.

We had finished our evening meal and, as is often the case, overdone it on the vegetables. Beans was doing her best to procure one or two tasty offerings left on our plates. It's an effective technique; just sit there quietly, put on a pleading face and fix your gaze on the plate. Before long the drool will well up at the side of your mouth and release itself in a steady, continuous stream onto the carpet, where it forms a small pool. Before very long – if you are lucky – they'll capitulate and your patient, almost dignified vigil will be rewarded with a few tasty morsels. And so it was with the broad beans; small, kidney-shaped vegetables, also known as fava beans. They couldn't possibly harm a dog – could they? Wrong.

I offered one to Beans; she took it, chewed a couple of times, and swallowed. She liked it. I gave her another, then another, then another. In retrospect I should have stopped at two, but between us we must have handed over at least ten of the beans. Nothing reappeared on the carpet (thank goodness) and all seemed well. I took Beans out for her evening walk and nothing untoward happened. If anything was going to happen, surely it would have done by now. We went to bed.

Sometime during the night, I gradually became aware of a persistent, though not loud, squeaking whining sound, which penetrated my subconscious, awakening me from my sleep. I hadn't dreamt the noise; it carried on, only louder as I became more awake. I turned over to see the shadowy outline of Beans, sitting patiently by my side of the bed, obviously in some sort of distress. The squeaking definitely had a sense of urgency about it; she needed to go out – now.

I stumbled out of bed trying to feel my way in the darkness until my eyes adjusted. The street light outside provided enough illumination for me to locate the landing light switch, which I flicked on, to see Beans, trotting quickly downstairs. Following as quickly as I could in my half awake state, I tried to calm her by saying 'It's alright Beanie, I'm coming, hold on,' but she had disappeared into the living room. Almost flying headfirst over an armchair, I picked my way through to the kitchen without switching the living room light on. As the realisation of what was probably about to happen dawned on me, I half expected to step into something soft, warm, and extremely unpleasant, but I made it unscathed to the kitchen, to find Beans, still squeaking, at the back door.

'Almost there,' I said to myself as I fumbled with the locks on the door. I cursed aloud as one bolt stubbornly refused to move. Living in the middle of town, with a shared rear yard and an unlocked access gate, security was paramount, but at that particular moment in time I would have given anything for one lock and one key.

The door opened to let in an icy blast of cold night air. Beans had barely waited for the door to open fully and was somewhere at the back of the yard before the night chill had even registered with me. Considering we were near some main roads, it was strangely quiet outside, apart from the occasional sound of a drunken late night reveller, somewhere far off in the distance. I'd lost sight of Beans, who had vanished into the darkness at the end of the yard.

As I stood there shivering, I listened to the only other noise to pierce the air that night - the sound of Beans' bowels, exploding onto the cold flagstones of the yard. I could almost feel her relief myself. Heaven knows how she had managed to hold on to that lot before being able to wake me.

The beans had done their job – with ruthless efficiency.

I got up very early the next morning for the clean up; before any of the other residents. Whatever horror lay waiting for me, I wasn't about to share it with them. I needed to remove the evidence – quickly.

Armed with rubber gloves, a bucket of hot water and several newspapers, I ventured forth. At the top left corner of the yard lay an amorphous green mass; a hideous pile of slop that didn't resemble conventional excrement at all. As if it was saying, *'serves you right,'* it could almost have been broad bean shaped. It certainly was in colour.

Casting my over-active imagination aside, I gingerly cleared away the revolting pile of puréed broad beans, giving thanks that I had had the foresight not to have an early breakfast. I gagged as some of the slop fell out of the scrunched up newspaper. I needed a heavy duty Sunday broadsheet, not a weekday tabloid.

It would be a long time before I could look a bowl of guacamole in the face again.

Many years after this episode we discovered that – like dark chocolate – broad beans are harmful to dogs. Beans had got off lightly – and we'd learnt a valuable lesson.

The Seaside

It had never been part of our plan to start married life living in the middle of a town, but when your ideal home and location is out of reach, inevitably you are settling for second best. Because of our less than perfect location, we escaped to the countryside as often as we could, mostly to the Peak District, but sometimes to the coast for a dose of fresh sea air to blow the town cobwebs away. Beans always enjoyed her trips to the seaside, although I have yet to see any dog not having a good time there; running at full pelt along the firm sand, digging holes, playing games, running into the sea – and drinking it.

Prestatyn, on the North Wales coast was the location for Beans' introduction to the wonders of the seaside. This was a whole new wonderland to explore and it was great fun to see her reaction to it. If dogs could talk, you could almost imagine her saying, *'oh yeah, this is great; let's come here again!'*

She would charge along the beach, the wind in her hair, sometimes just for the hell of it, or if we threw something for her to catch. The sand fascinated her, because she would suddenly stop the mad races and commence some major excavation work on the beach, her head disappearing into the sand, front paws frantically digging for whatever she thought was underneath. Knowing her taste for hauling out stones, we gave her something to aim for, and buried one in the sand, which she promptly dug up.

She didn't quite know what to make of seaweed, apart from giving it a thorough investigation with her nose. If it warranted further attention, it would be picked up, carried a short distance and then abandoned. After the purgative effects of the broad beans it was just as well that it failed the taste test. Had she taken a liking for it, I feel sure it would have reappeared later – most likely in the car on the way home. But it pays not to be complacent. Some years later, we were horribly reminded that it's not just the things dogs eat that result in unpleasant situations. Beans had other plans in store for us.

We wondered what the reaction would be when Beans inevitably took her first sip of seawater. We weren't disappointed. After a few hours running around on the beach, digging holes and licking seaweed, she was thirsty. Sure enough, curiosity got the better of her.

The moment the first drop of water passed into her mouth, she shook her head violently from side to side and then did that shaking of the whole body thing that dogs do to dry themselves. The sides of her mouth curled up in a grimace, as the brine found its mark. As if she had just ingested the hottest chilli the chef could muster, she ran from the sea, still shaking her head, completely and utterly baffled as to why *this* water tasted so awful.

Now she had had an ingestion of brine (and heaven knows what else was in the seawater) she was thirsty again, even though only a small amount of sea had passed down her throat. Guess what; as if the first dose had never happened, she headed back to the sea for a drink – with the same inevitable results. The second dose must have got the message through that this stuff was definitely not fit for canine consumption - she didn't repeat the experience a third time. She lapped up the fresh water we'd brought with us as fast as we could pour it into her bowl. Soon, there were just a few drops left in her bottle.

This combination of seawater ingestion followed by gallons of fresh water was going to have a dramatic effect on her bladder. In between her fun and games on the beach, she spent the remainder of the afternoon squatting to do the longest pees I think I have ever seen. For what seemed an eternity, a huge pool of urine spread out behind her, neatly forming its own little channel in the sand. At least it probably wasn't much different in consistency to the stuff it was slowly trickling away to join.

Jellyfish

New Years' Day 1991 was cold, but beautifully sunny; fresh and invigorating like only a sunny winters' day can be. Whatever else the weather had in store for us that year; it was starting on the brightest note possible, with a cloudless blue sky and clear views, unspoiled by the heat haze of summer.

We could have gone anywhere that day; the Peak District would have been beautiful, with views that photographers beg for, but we felt that a trip to the seaside was just what the doctor ordered. There's something about being beside the sea in winter that draws you there, just like the migrating birds who find a home on Britain's coast during the winter months. It's probably down to all those negative ions in the sea air, making you feel good. The same feeling you get sitting near a waterfall or a fast moving river.

Hoylake, on the Wirral peninsula, was our destination that day. The Wirral is a strip of land jutting out into Liverpool Bay, separating the estuaries of the rivers Mersey and Dee. Across the Dee Estuary lies the North Wales coast, while a short ferry or tunnel ride across the Mersey Estuary lies the City of Liverpool. It is a fine area for expansive beaches and wonderful bird watching sites.

Hoylake was busy on that crisp New Years' Day; day trippers, dog walkers, joggers, a man working out with weights on the beach – no I'm not joking – and the odd horse rider. Everybody was out enjoying a beautiful day.

Beans too, was enjoying herself, galloping along the beach and investigating every pool, channel and strange object she could find. When a dog's world revolves around hearing and smell, it's difficult for us to imagine quite what it must be like to have these senses so finely attuned, but I reckon dogs have a wonderful time with them. Beans must have added miles to her walks, as she constantly doubled back, following this trail and that.

Deciding to give her some freedom, I nervously removed her lead. I knew instinctively that this was going to end in trouble of one sort or another, but hey, she needed to run and besides, it felt cruel denying her the freedom of all that lovely sand to run on. She could have chosen to have a scrap with another dog, chase after a child's football, or try to nip the heel of a passing jogger. Thankfully, none of this behaviour was in Beans' repertoire, but she wasn't about to leave us unscathed.

Among my many photographs of Beans there is a shot of her at Hoylake, silhouetted against the beach, her nose obviously investigating something in a shallow pool. Seconds after that picture was taken, she found something else nearby on a drier patch of beach that really grabbed her attention. With hindsight, I suppose we should have realised that she was about to dive headlong into something foul, because the warning signs are obvious. Sniffing that lasts longer than a few seconds, and examining the source of the smell from every conceivable angle are pretty good indicators that the dog isn't just looking for somewhere to pee.

In the blink of an eye there's the sudden dive into the stinking mess. Dogs seem to have the annoying knack of being able to do this before you have time to pull them away; I've been caught out many times. My sprint across the sands was not fast enough to stop her from plunging the side of her head into the mystery substance.

I was shouting as I was running, 'Beans, no!'

I should have saved my breath for running. She was in full swing by now; rolling on her back, legs in the air, in what to her was probably pure ecstasy.

Oh please don't let it be another dog's crap, I thought.

The favourite place for rolling seems to be the side of the head, just behind the ear. This is the doggie equivalent of splashing on aftershave, or a quick spray of perfume to the neck. To Beans this was *Chanel No.5*. A male dog would no doubt consider it to be his *Lynx* or *Armani*. Theories abound as to why dogs do this: to disguise their own smell when hunting, by rolling in the faeces of their prey or even (in the case of rotting carcasses) to let the other pack members know that there is food about. It seems our canine companions indulge in activities left over from their wolf or wild dog ancestry.

As I stood over Beans, getting my breath back, the stomach-churning reality of what she had rolled in revealed itself in all its glory. I was looking at the stinking, putrefying remains of a dead jellyfish. What wasn't left on the sand, was attached to Beans; rotting tissue ingrained into her fur. The stench was indescribable.

And I was hoping it wouldn't be another dog's crap.

I wanted to put her lead back on in case she had any ideas of a repeat performance, but to my horror discovered that some of the jellyfish was smeared on her collar, shreds of putrid flesh dangling off it. *Bloody hell, Beans, why did you have to do this?* Any attempt to grab the collar would transfer some of the mess to me and anything my hands came into contact with. I stood there helplessly, wishing that I could just throw her into a large bin bag and put her in the boot of the car. Dismissing that particular thought as quickly as it came into my head, I carefully managed to clip the end of the lead onto the ring of her collar, which was positioned – thankfully – where I could see it, without getting any decomposing jellyfish on my hands. Gagging, with my stomach doing somersaults, I quickly pulled her away from the necrotic remains of the jellyfish.

No way are you diving into that again, I thought. Beans looked quite pleased with her performance. Who she was hoping to attract by smelling of a decomposing sea creature, I can't imagine.

By now, Jan had caught up with me. 'What's that horrible smell?' she asked, her nose crinkling up.

'Rotting jellyfish. Beans has just adorned herself with it.'

'Is that what's on the bottom of your jeans?' she said, pointing to my feet.

We wondered whether a dip in the sea might be enough to clean Beans up, but short of a paddle, she refused to go any deeper, having taken a dislike to the waves that threatened to cover her every few seconds.

'Go on Beans, you love the water usually,' I said pathetically.

'Not this water I don't; I'd rather smell of rotting jellyfish, if that's okay with you.'

We tried to enjoy the rest of our day at Hoylake, keeping Beans at a safe distance, but the thought at the back of our minds was that sooner or later we were going to have to put her in the car. It was cold, the windows would be up and the car heating on; not the best combination when you have the creature from the black lagoon sitting on the back seat, stinking like the bottom of a septic tank.

There was also the small problem of how we were going to get her cleaned up and sweet smelling again. We were still living in Macclesfield at the time and the only hot water we had was from an immersion heater that took an agonising hour to do its job. Beans needed industrial cleaning, not a sprinkling with a bit of cold water. Besides, we didn't have a garden, so there was no need for a watering can or hosepipe. Plonking her in the bath and using the rubber shower attachment was one possibility, but quickly abandoned when the thought of Beans shaking herself in the bathroom came to mind, not to mention trying to lift the fetid dog into the bath. In the end we decided on a detour via Jan's parents where there was constant hot water and hosepipes in abundance.

The memory of that journey to Wilmslow will go with me to my grave. Gingerly loading Beans onto the back seat of the car (thankfully well-covered), we left the Wirral in the late afternoon sunshine and headed for the motorway. The smell emanating from the back, even before the heaters kicked in, was nauseating. Once the heat had cooked the mess on my jeans, the atmosphere in the car was unbearable. The two of us sat there, gagging and trying to hold our breath, desperately trying to inhale as little of the stench as possible.

'Oh this is horrible,' I said, reaching for the window handle. 'I don't care how cold it is, get the windows open.'

'It's too cold to have the windows open,' Jan pleaded.

'I don't care, I'd rather be cold than breathe in any more of this.'

So we zoomed down the M53 motorway with both windows open, freezing January air rushing in, laughing our heads off, which was really all we could do. My hands were virtually frozen to the steering wheel and my hair was developing an interesting bouffant style of its own as the 70mph gale ripped through the car.

On the back seat all was calm. Beans lay curled up, fast asleep, every now and again uttering a deep, satisfying sigh. She'd had a good day.

Beans the Model

During the late 1980s I was in the process of trying to make a career (and a bit of extra money) out of photography and writing. I had always liked writing and had enjoyed photography since childhood, so it was the ideal way forward for me. That was the easy part; what wasn't so easy was actually getting published. However, salvation was at hand in the form of a magazine named *Country Walking* and two able and willing models – Jan and Beans.

Walking and photography have always been good companions to me, whether it's walking in the country or strolling around an interesting town or city. My stack of photographs had been building up for several years, so walking magazines seemed the ideal outlet for them, especially when a lot of my pictures included a walker – Jan – wearing the appropriate outdoor clothing. I felt confident that Beans was bound to appeal to any sensible magazine editor. As with most creative enterprises, it took perseverance and determination before the months of sending out dozens of photographs bore fruit. I suppose targeting just one walking magazine wasn't exactly pushing the boat out, but the pictures they used were the type of photo I took, so I stuck to my guns. They weren't, in retrospect, anything special, just nice picture postcard views of the Peak District with the odd dog and walker thrown in. Despite inundating the magazine with my work, it would be nearly a year before any of my pictures saw the light of day.

It was worth the wait.

I'll never forget the first time that a complimentary copy of the magazine with my photographs in it dropped through the letterbox. Even before I opened the A4 manila envelope, I knew what was inside; for one thing the package was magazine thickness, but what really gave the game away was the postmark with the magazine publisher's logo. My confidence that I was published was not cruelly dashed when I peeled open the envelope; inside the magazine, which I eagerly flicked through, were two of my photographs. To say I practically leapt onto the table with joy would be overdoing things, but needless to say I was on a high for the remainder of the day. Mum, Dad and my sister Pam were just as delighted as I was as they eagerly asked to see the pictures. This felt good, and I wanted more of it.

Hot-footing it down to *WH Smiths,* I gazed at the magazine on the shelf, before picking up a copy and flicking through it. Sure enough, my photographs were inside, though why I thought they might not be, I don't know. Delighted and re-assured that I wasn't just imaging the whole thing; I left the shop with another two copies of the magazine, no doubt leaving the bemused assistant wondering why I'd practically cleared the shelf. There was, however, method in my madness. The complimentary copy would remain as it was, for reasons best left alone, in its envelope; a reminder of the day my first published work popped through the letterbox; one copy would be carefully cut up and the pages placed in my pristine brand new portfolio case, while the other would be the well-thumbed copy that got shown around my family and friends.

At this point I feel it would be wise to offer my sincere apologies to those people in Wilmslow who were disappointed to discover that copies of their favourite walking magazine – dated January 1989 – had disappeared from the shelf quicker than they had perhaps expected.

After this, things got better and better, and my next publication, in the April 1989 issue, was even more exciting; my first photograph of Jan and Beans was used to illustrate a Peak District walk. I was over the moon, even if it was only a rear view of them heading down a lane towards Hartington village. Over the next year or so I had further successes culminating with the crowning glory, a cover shot, showing Jan atop Red Pike in the Lake District. Thrilled though I was; published shots with Beans in them were conspicuous by their absence - it was time to step up a gear. My two models would have to do a bit of work to get published.

I once read in a photography magazine that getting someone to wear red, or some other brightly coloured clothing, would increase the chances of the photograph selling – at least to those magazines who liked colourfully-clad walkers in their pictures. This approach wasn't going to get my work published in magazines specialising in serious landscape photography, but I enjoyed it and I could do it whilst pursuing my other great love – walking. If a magazine wanted to use a photograph of my wife – and my dog – on its cover and pay me for the privilege, then that was fine by me. It was a good way to get published and a terrific thrill to see one of my photos used to sell the magazine.

I started seeing every viewpoint we stopped at in terms of whether it would make a good cover shot, picturing the scene before me on the front of a magazine. Looking back, it was bordering on obsession. Our walks started to take longer as every location was checked out for its potential. If it fitted the bill, then Jan and Beans would pose for me while I took the photographs. I could have been taking photographs for an outdoor clothing catalogue. Another missed career opportunity.

'Move a little further to the right,' I would shout.

'Is this far enough?'

'No, just a few more steps and look at the view, not at me,' I replied, trying not to get exasperated.

'Have you taken it yet?'

'Just a couple more shots for back-up.'

Perhaps it's just as well that the walking magazines didn't want happy holiday snaps with people grinning inanely at the camera, because by the time I had finished messing around I don't think Jan would have been in the mood for smiling. This was long before the arrival of digital photography, so as a failsafe I ended up taking three or four shots for every one I took. My models' patience was running out.

Beans was tolerant up to a point, but sometimes even she gave up, flopping to the ground and refusing to resume a more dynamic pose. By the time she had been cajoled into standing up again, the sun had disappeared behind the largest cloud in the sky. I could have hurled my camera into the nearest river. I'm not really a fan of digital cheating, but, had Photoshop been available back then, I can imagine lots of stock shots of Jan and Beans superimposed on nice, suitably lit landscapes.

Just imagine – all that frustration avoided with just a touch of digital manipulation.

Over the next ten years Jan and Beans appeared in print regularly, including two front covers. Beans' status as a model was confirmed to me when a one-time editor of the magazine told me what a nice-looking dog she was, following one of her cover appearances. Ever the professional, Beans took it all in her stride. She wasn't going to let success go to her head.

The thrill of opening a magazine and seeing photographs of them both inside never diminished. Not only did I have a portfolio of published work, but also a treasured reminder of the happy times we spent together on our walks.

Not all our memorable – or those moments we'd maybe prefer to forget – were captured on film. I think Jan would have cheerfully thrown my camera into the nearest river if I'd sneakily taken a snap of her undignified soaking that day at Chatsworth Park. I do however, have my standards, and this was not something that needed immortalising on film, even if now, all these years later, we can laugh about it.

Chatsworth House, together with its gardens and surrounding parkland, is one of the most beautiful – albeit man-made – parts of the Peak District. To me, it is a prime example of man adding something of great beauty to the landscape, without destroying it. The present house and grounds date mainly from the eighteenth century and are a delight for the eyes. The gardens and park were designed by the great Lancelot 'Capability' Brown.

Brown created some of the finest parks in England during the great 'Classical' period of the eighteenth century. He was indeed 'capable' of transforming the countryside surrounding stately homes into elegantly laid out parks befitting the needs of the wealthy owners. Chatsworth was no exception.

The walk from Bakewell, up through Manners Wood and then down towards Edensor village, is surely one of the finest in the Peak. As you head down across the pastures and through the deer park, a glorious scene unfolds. Chatsworth House lies ahead, with the River Derwent to the front, whilst behind is the wooded Dobb Edge, forming a perfect backdrop. In autumn, especially if the house is front-lit, the view is even better, the autumn colours of the wood complimenting the honey-coloured stonework of the house perfectly. I am not normally a photographer of parks and stately homes, preferring wilder landscapes, but with Chatsworth I have to make an exception. One view in particular is so wonderfully photogenic that it could almost have one of those rather tacky Kodak *'Photo Opportunity'* signs erected by it. Thank heavens it hasn't though.

Walking into the park from Edensor village you arrive at a splendid bridge across the Derwent, built by James Paine, a contemporary of Capability Brown. Instead of crossing the bridge, head left down towards the river and a brilliant *'Kodak Moment'* awaits you. The house, bridge, river and the woods beyond are all laid out perfectly, as if those eighteenth century men were anticipating the needs of photographers or painters. It is perfect. All you have to do is frame the scene with one of the riverside trees – and wait patiently for people to move from the bridge and cars to stop crossing it. If you can manage that (and have some good light) the only effort required is to press the shutter release. No wonder this view has appeared on countless calendars.

Although Brown by necessity changed and altered the landscape – even the course of the river – he was able to create something equally beautiful; planting great trees where there had been none before, which have now reached full maturity, some 200 years after they were first planted. I wonder what he would make of the situation today; where whole swathes of our beautiful countryside are being butchered for yet more roads, housing estates or out-of-town shopping developments? Unlike the 1760s, when he was creating his magnificent parks and gardens, there is little that could be considered elegant today. Roads are carved through pristine countryside, ancient woods are lost forever and then what happens? Trees are planted along the road to 'minimise' its impact on the environment.

Elegance was in short supply the day we started our walk from Chatsworth, following the Derwent through the park. Rain had fallen steadily for several days and in parts the river had burst its banks, leaving several large pools along the riverbank where the water had receded.

Apart from when we were walking across rough and difficult terrain, Jan had always been in charge of Beans on our walks, but that situation was about to change. Some ducks had decided that the pools made a pleasant alternative to the river and were happily going about their business undisturbed – until Beans spotted them. While Jan was busy talking to me and trying to avoid the muddiest patches, she hadn't spotted the ducks. Beans had.

One minute Jan was at my side, the next there was a scream and I turned to see her being dragged along head first by the duck-crazed Beans through the water. Jan water-skied for several yards before managing to bring Beans under control. For a few seconds she lay on her back in the brown water, with a dazed expression on her face, before getting to her feet. Most of her top half had been immersed in the churned up water and mud. It was not a pretty sight. Her jacket, jumper and one trouser leg were soaked, and half her face was streaked with mud.

At this point, bearing in mind that Jan was now cold and wet, the best option (and the most chivalrous) would have been to abandon the rest of the walk and head back to the car. I looked at her standing there, dripping, rucksack covered in mud and then uttered the immortal line:

'You'll soon dry out; let's carry on with the walk.'

I came out with the usual unhelpful 'are you okay?' nonsense, but in retrospect my first statement wasn't the best. Jan certainly wasn't okay, but there were no injuries (only to her pride) or broken bones, so there seemed no reason not to carry on. But then again I wasn't the one who'd just suffered the indignity of being dragged through a load of water by a dog.

Jan was in no mood for my cheerful take on the proceedings, as I stood there laughing at her.

'You look like you've just done an army assault course,' I said, trying to be witty.

'It's not funny, I'm soaked,' she snapped, looking on the verge of tears. She took out a handkerchief from her pocket to try and clean her face, and then swore as she discovered that it too was sodden and useless.

'It was from where I was standing,' was my less than sympathetic reply.

'Oh shut up.'

I didn't think she was going to see the funny side in this, so I gave up on the wisecracks.

Beans had no interest in Jan's predicament; she was too busy looking for the ducks, who had long since scattered to safety.

Despite the fact that Jan had lost interest in continuing with the walk, to my eternal shame I insisted that we carried on. I've never been forgiven for making her do another seven miles in wet clothing. Thick woollen jumpers do not dry out quickly.

Not content with getting Jan thoroughly soaked at Chatsworth, Beans' fixation with our feathered friends was to lead to even more trouble for her. By a strange twist of fate, the next incident took place not far from Chatsworth, on the road to Pilsley (an attractive village which is part of the Chatsworth Estate) and, as if they were waging some personal war against Jan, ducks were involved.

This was history repeating itself; only this time, instead of water, Jan almost nose-dived into the road. Beans suddenly did an about turn in the direction of some ducks hiding in the long grass at the roadside. I hadn't spotted them and neither had Jan. She had no time to even think about reigning Beans in – or stopping herself from falling. With a scream, she was violently twisted round, just having time to put her hand out, which slammed into the road, then to be dragged along the tarmac as Beans aimed for the ducks.

The panicked ducks shot into the air with a flurry of quacks and feathers, Beans barking furiously at them for having the audacity to fly away again. This duck-catching business was so frustrating. Why couldn't she be just let off her lead and why was there so much shouting and swearing just because she'd run after a few ducks? She just couldn't understand it. Time for the, *oh dear, what have I done* look.

Jan looked down at her bleeding hand, now completely useless for Beans-control, telling me in no uncertain terms that Beans was now firmly my responsibility. She still has that scar on her hand.

That might have been the end of Beans' attempts to cause injury to Jan – albeit unintentionally – but she still had one more trick up her sleeve.

Although I was now permanently in charge of Beans, there were times when I had to hand the lead over to Jan, especially when negotiating stiles or gates. One day, when I was trying to get myself through a squeezer stile, the ideal opportunity arose for Beans to get up to her old tricks again. She wasted no time in seizing the moment.

As I used both hands to get myself, my rucksack and camera bag through the squeezer stile, Jan walked ahead across an undulating field towards the next wall. She'd only gone a few yards before the tell-tale yell told me that Beans had done it again. Just as I'd extricated myself from the stile I looked up to see Jan hurtling across the field, seemingly out of control. Some thirty yards ahead of her I saw the unmistakeable shape of a hare, disappearing over the top of a small rise. I always enjoy seeing one of these beautiful animals, with their long ears and legs, so perfectly adapted for hearing and running. The hare's ears would have picked up Beans' approach from several fields away, but even if it had been caught unawares its legs would surely have outrun Beans'. Even if she'd been off the lead, Beans hadn't a hope in hell of catching the hare, but it didn't stop her trying – this was something new to chase.

In all the excitement I hadn't noticed that Jan was holding her shoulder and grimacing. Once I caught up with her she told me what happened. It was the same old story. Barely had I handed the lead to her than she was wrenched around, almost dislocating her shoulder. It was a wonder the lead hadn't snapped; such was the force of Beans' sprint towards the hare, who neither of us had spotted. We'd been caught out again.

Jan's shoulder was painful for some days after Beans' encounter with the hare. I wondered what other damage she could inflict on my hapless wife.

CHAPTER FOUR

Funny Birds and Donkeys

Funny Birds

Walking, to us, was not just an enjoyable pursuit – it was a way of life. Not being able to escape the confines of our little cottage and the town on a Sunday would have been unthinkable, and there wasn't much that would prevent us from heading off to the wilds of the Peak District. Important family functions or snow-blocked roads were the only things that kept us away.

Exercise has to be enjoyable – no matter what you choose to do. It's whatever rocks your boat. Some people prefer the communal exercise of the gym whilst others pound the streets or do yoga. Walking, however, seems the most natural thing in the world. You cross the land at nature's pace, absorbing your surroundings as you go, taking in all the sights and sounds. It's what humans were designed to do.

Dogs certainly seem to subscribe to this philosophy and relish the outdoor life with their masters. Taking a dog for a walk through the country is surely one of life's pleasures – especially if that dog is highly attuned to the sights and sounds. Beans was to prove that she was very much a walker and a wildlife enthusiast, although the enthusiasm for the wildlife had more to do with the fact that she would have liked to eat it – given the chance.

The moors of the Peak District are home to a rich variety of wildlife, carefully managed by the Park and the National Trust to maintain their rich diversity. Birds such as the curlew and golden plover inhabit this landscape, their enigmatic calls a delight to the ears. A lucky wildlife spotter might see the rare mountain hare, his blue-grey coat turning snowy white in winter to blend in with the snow-covered landscape.

One of the other birds that thrive in this landscape is the red grouse, a rather comical-looking game bird with an even more comical but distinctive 'go-back, go-back, go-back' call. When I first heard these odd sounds I had no idea what bird was making them. It was finding out what bird it was that began an interest in bird-watching on a more serious level, rather than the 'I wonder what species that was' approach I'd used previously.

Beans was enjoying her first 'proper' hike with us as we followed the route from the attractive town of Hayfield in Derbyshire, as it wound its way up past Kinder Reservoir to the moors, with the huge plateau of Kinder Scout dominating the surroundings. This is real Dark Peak country, where narrow paths follow the route of streams that tumble down from the plateau, with the unexpected delight of a waterfall as the path rounds a bend. Friendly walkers greet each other as they pass.

We climbed above the reservoir and struck off across the moors towards a place called Stony Ford. It was here we first became aware of the unknown birds with their strange calls, flitting around the heather, or suddenly flapping up in front of us as our approach startled them. As they flew off in a flurry of flapping wings and 'go-back, go-back' calls, Beans went berserk, barking and straining on her lead to get at these strange things that had just appeared in front of her. She wasn't a huge dog, but I had one hell of a job to stop myself from being pulled over and dragged through the heather by a normally placid dog who had suddenly turned into a powerhouse of straining muscles.

Beans was foaming at the mouth – all her doggy instincts that had lain dormant had suddenly erupted into life. This was Beans the hunter. She wanted live prey and the fact that I was in danger of being towed to the very base of Kinder Scout was way down her list of priorities. From that day onwards back in late December 1987 it became her mission in life to catch a red grouse. Though she never would – and we weren't about to let her either – she had great fun trying.

She did calm down eventually once the birds and their calls had disappeared into the heather. At that point we started to speculate as to what species they were.

'What were those funny birds?' I said, as I tried to stop Beans from heading off again.

'I'm not sure,' Jan replied, 'do you think they were grouse?'

'Could have been,' I said, trying to sound knowledgeable, 'I'll have a look in the bird book when we get home.'

They were indeed red grouse, as my book confirmed, but even though we now knew what they were, they would be forever known as *'funny birds.'*

As well as being the place where Beans was introduced to the delights of red grouse, Kinder Scout is more famously remembered for being the site of the Mass Trespass of April 1932, when hundreds of ramblers from the surrounding towns and cities, tired of being unable to walk in forbidden areas took to the hills, defying the gamekeepers and, in some cases, ending up in prison as a result. It was thanks in part to these brave people that we now have the new 'Open Access' areas throughout the country, although it has been a long and difficult campaign against the vested interests of wealthy landowners and those who believed that vast swathes of wonderful walking country should only be for the privileged few, who wanted nothing more than to have it to themselves for the purpose of game-shooting.

Beans' introduction to wildlife on her Peak District walks was the start of a lifelong fascination she had with anything that flew, flapped, ran, squeaked, howled, bellowed, or, in fact, made any sort of noise. As the months passed and we headed anywhere where there were grouse, the mere mention of 'funny birds' was enough to make her ears prick up and tilt her head in recognition of the name. Inevitably, if we were on a 'grouse-walk' I would spend a large portion of the walk being towed along as soon as Beans spotted her first prey of the day.

Running in walking boots is not much fun – but that is what I spent most of my time doing. The downhill stretches were the worst, especially if a whole flock of the birds suddenly shot up from their hiding place. How I never went head-over-heels or twisted an ankle, I don't know. It was no good expecting any consideration from Beans either – she was having far too much of a good time to be bothered with obedience. Shouting at her to stop or slow down was as useless as it was embarrassing, as I shot past my fellow walkers, with this grouse-crazed dog hurtling along in front. It was like those ghost stories I used to read, where packs of howling dogs ran ahead of headless spectral figures across Dartmoor under the light of a full moon, except this was the Peak District and it was broad daylight.

All I could do, if I thought I was likely to take a tumble, was to dig my heels in and haul her back. I soon learnt that it was better to have her on a short lead rather than the freedom of her extending one; it was easier to rein her in and keep my balance. I'm sure it saved quite a few grouse from ending up between Beans' teeth as well.

Before I incur anyone's wrath for disturbing wildlife, I should point out that Beans was *never* off her lead on any of our Peak District walks, and on stretches where there were likely to be grouse, her extending lead was drawn in. However, there was little we could do to stop her going bananas every time she saw one, but we weren't irresponsible. Much of the Peak District is privately owned farmland where sheep and cattle graze, but people are allowed to cross this land on sometimes very old rights-of-way (as is the case elsewhere) which brings with it a level of responsibility on dog-owners. It incenses me when I see people allowing their dogs to run loose when sheep are about. Apart from the obvious danger to the animals, the owner runs the risk of having their dog shot by the farmer, who is quite at liberty to do so, if he thinks his stock are at risk, especially during lambing. Needless to say, sheep were on Beans' list of preferred animals, but she never got quite as interested in them as she did with grouse.

The shiny, round, dark brown droppings they produced were, however, of great interest to her and these she devoured as if they were chocolate-coated raisins. Left to her own devices, I feel sure she could have cleared an entire field of sheep droppings. To see the way she shovelled them down her throat, you would think we were starving her. It was like letting a child loose at *Cadbury World*. Despite trying to pull her away from the tasty currant-like droppings, I never managed to stop her from grabbing a mouthful.

There is no getting away from the fact that excrement-eating is the rather distasteful side of dog ownership, and a lot of dogs indulge in it. Thankfully, Beans drew the line at eating her own (though some dogs do) but everything else was fair game. Sheep droppings were the favourite, but cow, horse and even deer – quite a rare one for her – were all on the menu. The fresher the better. In fact, if the steam was still rising off it, then that was *haute cuisine* of the finest quality. Old, dried up droppings would not do.

The Peak District could be described as the 'lungs' of the area, surrounded as it is by major towns and cities such as Manchester, Sheffield, Chesterfield and Stockport. Was it any wonder that people who spent the week toiling away in mills and factories should want to escape to the fresh air and open space?

Nowadays, the mills and factories have been replaced by stuffy computer-filled offices, but the need to escape from it all is no different than it was seventy years ago. I am pleased the Peak District was designated the first National Park in 1951, because for those people who took part in the Trespass nearly twenty years before, it must have seemed that their efforts had finally been recognised.

Throughout her hiking life Beans was to enjoy many more walks in this dramatic part of the Peak District. We had our favourites of course; some of which we must have done umpteen times over the years. The classic round from Grindsbrook Booth in Edale, following the Pennine Way up dramatic Grindsbrook Clough and onto the plateau was one route we never tired of. Once on the plateau, the route passes through some truly amazing wind-sculpted grtitsone boulders, known as The Woolpacks, before a spectacular finale down a knee-jarring path called Jacob's Ladder. At the bottom, where the path crosses a stream by a lovely old packhorse bridge, Beans quenched her thirst and we gave our tired legs a rest before the final stretch back to our start. If we had timed things right, a welcoming cup of tea awaited us at the café.

The Pennine Way (England's longest long-distance trail at 276 miles) begins its odyssey along the backbone of the country at Grindsbrook Booth, and, although I have never walked it, I pride myself in having at least tackled the first portion several times. It's a dramatic start; the path leads you into a false sense of security as it gently follows the delightful Grinds Brook, twisting and winding past pools and waterfalls. Before long, however, the ascent changes dramatically and you find yourself losing the path and scrambling over rocks and boulders before the path re-appears and there is a temporary respite from the scrambling.

Beans loved this terrain, tackling it with ease, although my job was significantly harder as I tried to keep hold of her lead and use both hands to haul myself up the rocks. Thankfully, this was a relatively grouse-free zone, so Beans responded obediently to my calls to wait, but there were some tricky moments near the top when the scrambling got harder and the temptation was always there to release her from her lead. It took the sudden chatter of a group of the birds near the top to remind me that this would not be a good move. The sudden increase in tension on the lead was another very good reason - Beans had switched to *'funny bird'* mode.

Despite our many trips to Kinder Scout, there was (and still is) another place nearby that will always be special. Middle Moor, also above Hayfield, is a heather-covered stretch of land in the care of The National Trust. It featured on another of our favourite walks in the area and was also one of Beans' first walks in the Peak District. Much to her delight, it was also well-stocked with grouse.

Personally, I don't like game-shooting; I'd rather the grouse were left in peace to go about their business, rather than ending up on a plate, though it has to be acknowledged that the landowners do preserve the moors for other wildlife as well as grouse.

The shooting fraternity have a little white-painted cabin on Middle Moor, to use when the weather takes a turn for the worst. As shooting takes place mainly in August, the cabin remains locked for most of the year to keep out undesirables. The steps in front of it were a convenient place to sit and enjoy our lunch, in glorious surroundings with the ever-present calls of the grouse. It was Beans heaven.

We always packed some snacks for Beans with our sandwiches, but there wasn't much eating going on when she was on grouse patrol. No sooner had she bitten in to a biscuit than the familiar cackles of the grouse would resonate from somewhere in the heather. The food was promptly dropped and all grouse detection systems were set to red alert, her ears so erect, I was convinced they actually increased in length the more she tuned in. This was no time for eating – she was after something far more interesting. She stared intently in the direction of the noises, nose twitching, eyes ready to pick up the slightest movement. Her head moved in sudden jerks as she picked something up from another direction. She wasn't the only one who was on red alert though. Suddenly, everything would get too much and she was unable to contain herself any longer, launching me, my sandwiches and herself in the direction of the grouse. Hot coffee flew in all directions and the sandwiches hit the deck as she went from 0 to 60 in four seconds – at least that's what it felt like to the arm that was attached to her lead. Although I tried to be prepared for Beans' sudden lift off, she caught me out *every time*.

Once I had satisfied myself that my shoulder hadn't been dislocated by this sudden violent wrench, I attempted to bring my wayward dog under control, which was a bit like trying to separate two very angry men intent on killing each other; the only difference being that Beans was the only angry contestant in this contest. The grouse (perhaps a little annoyed at being disturbed) were long gone to a Beans-free part of the moor.

To add insult to injury, as we returned to the steps she promptly grabbed the remains of my lunch - devouring the soiled sandwiches within seconds.

Now that Beans' interest in grouse was firmly established, I resigned myself to the fact that any walk in 'funny bird' territory would not be a very relaxed affair. There was to be no let up in her enthusiasm; if anything, it grew to encompass a whole variety of wildlife. Pheasants - who also have a distinctive call and a habit of making themselves invisible to all but a dog, became another firm favourite. These were more of a danger to the integrity of my shoulders than grouse, because they thought they were sufficiently well camouflaged to remain undetected by the Beans radar systems – which was a big mistake. There were no warning calls from the birds or that tell-tale tension on the lead as Beans spotted them, just sudden explosive barking and the blurred outline of a pheasant as it shot up from its hiding place, only inches away from her.

Although the birds managed to hide themselves behind the smallest of thickets, I rarely saw them before Beans. If I didn't end up face down in a load of thistles, my arm was yanked in a direction I never thought possible.

Despite my being towed at breakneck speed over most of the Peak District's moors by the grouse-obsessed Beans, and hurled into stinging nettles and stabbing thistles, I managed to come through without any serious injuries. The only injury was to my pride, as fellows hikers saw me heading for yet another dive into the ground.

Hard Times

In January 1991 I changed jobs. My new job at the Town Hall was now only about ten minutes walk away, so it was goodbye to tedious car commuting. Best of all, I could now come home to Beans at lunchtime – much to her delight. This was a much better situation.

There was more time in the morning too; I could pop down to the nearby country park in the car with her to do the necessary and have a quick walk. When I commuted to my previous job, Beans' welfare was left largely to Jan, whose journey to work took minutes, compared to the hour that mine could sometimes take. Evening walks were largely down to me.

That year after our wedding in 1990, was to be our *annus horribilis*. Barely three months into 1991 and Jan was made redundant from her job as a graphic designer with the company she had been with for seven years. Apart from losing a job she liked, it was a hell of a blow to us, coming as it did only a year after getting married and starting our new home. Beans, however, was absolutely delighted by all this – she would have Jan there all day, and me at lunchtimes as well. Despite the fact we worked to put food both on the table and in her bowl, she was blissfully free of all the financial worries.

This agreeable state of affairs didn't last long. Jan used a few contacts to pick up some freelance work with some local companies, and then, by a strange twist of irony, ended up doing freelance work for the company that had made her redundant – the irony being that she was able to charge them freelance rates, which was more than they'd ever paid her when she was an employee. Served them right.

Jan's freelance work was sporadic, so she was often at home during the week and able to take Beans on longer walks than I could at lunchtime. She would sometimes take her on a car trip, or over to Wilmslow for the day, but quite often the two of them would head down the road to Riverside Park. The park is the start of the Bollin Valley Way and it is possible to follow the river all the way from Macclesfield to Wilmslow, although in all the time we lived in Macclesfield we never walked it. A herd of Old English Longhorn Cattle reside in the park, who, despite their gentle nature, Beans was always careful to avoid. We were relieved the cows weren't on her list of interesting animals, because those horns could have done some serious damage.

As it leaves the visitor centre, the path follows the river on one side, with the railway line over to the right. Although close to built up areas, it is an attractive place, with woods, ponds and wildflower meadows. Trains leaving Macclesfield pass through a short section of tunnel before emerging to overlook the park. At this point in their journey they are only just picking up speed, so the passengers have a good view of the park, together with anyone walking in it, as they pass alongside.

Jan usually allowed Beans off her lead along this stretch, unless the cows were about. Beans would be busy sniffing, investigating the river or socialising with other dogs, but if she heard a train, a remarkable transformation took place. All activity was abandoned, other dogs ignored, ears pricked up at the sound of the train. Before the train had even left the tunnel its horn would usually sound, at which point Beans hurtled off down the path in an attempt to gain a head start on it. Jan was left standing there helplessly, the realisation dawning that our daft dog had added another activity to her list.

The train was going slowly enough for Beans to keep pace with it, but inevitably its speed increased. At this point she started to bark at it out of sheer frustration. This wasn't right; the train had an unfair advantage, but Beans wasn't about to give up. Dog and train were now neck and neck, but by the time she'd reached the wildflower meadow and the electricity pylon, the train was well in the lead and she reluctantly had to admit defeat and give up the chase.

Although thankfully separated by safety fencing, the trains are close enough to the path to see the passengers. Before Beans became a speck in the distance, Jan could see the laughing faces of people at the train windows, pointing at Beans and telling fellow passengers to take a look out of the window. She must have brightened the morning of many a weary commuter. It was definitely more entertaining than trying to ingest the latest stock prices in the Financial Times.

Jan eventually caught up with a by now heavily panting Beans at the wildflower meadow, the train now long gone. The look on her face said it all. She'd enjoyed every minute of that madcap chase after the London – Manchester express, and could she do it again next time please? There would be plenty of next times too – and many more entertained smiling commuters.

Despite the fact Jan was not always at home, I was still coming home to Beans at lunchtime. The welcome I received was always enthusiastic and it was so good to be able to escape work and the office, even if it was only for an hour. The problems of a difficult morning evaporated once I'd had the Beans welcome. Dog 'experts' say that our interpretation of this jumping up

102

and wagging as being a welcome is no more than the dog exerting its dominance over you, and asking for food – but I'm not so sure. Beans would bounce over to one of her many squeaky toys, run round with it and then promptly deposit it at my feet, as if saying 'thanks for coming home and look what I've brought you.' The experts would probably say that this was merely a throwback to some wolf-like behaviour; maybe, maybe not, but who cares – it certainly feels like a wonderful welcome.

Despite this ideal situation, a problem had arisen that was going to need a fair amount of patience (as well as legwork) on our part. Beans liked to do all her 'business' on grass; that was the way we had trained her and it was a very rare occurrence when she did her duties anywhere else. Where we lived however, grass was in very short supply. There was the odd grass verge somewhere over the main road, a few patches down some side alleyways and a few pathetic tufts sprouting between flagstones - but that was it. By any stretch of the imagination it was not ideal for a dog accustomed to plenty of the green stuff. Trying to find somewhere for her to 'perform' became a nightmare.

We traipsed the streets, desperately trying to find the odd blade of grass for her to pee on. Given the limited time I had during my lunch breaks, it was a frustrating and, at times, infuriating business. It was hardly fair to be cross with her, although at times it was hard not to be. We had brought her up that way after all. There are plenty of people around whose dogs are allowed to foul the pavements, so we were naturally proud of Beans' fastidious standards. If there were any 'accidents' they would be promptly removed.

I soon got to know those places where Beans would get down to things, and, to her eternal credit, she would manage to pee on even the smallest patch of grass. Sometimes, after a particularly lengthy search for that perfect spot, I would give her a congratulatory pat and a hug. Then she'd jump up at me as if to say 'thanks for being so patient with me.'

Trying to get Beans to pee was, as it turned out, the very least of our problems. It was trying to get her to do the other that became a daily problem. There was nowhere within a few yards of our home that was suitable, so a lunchtime 'performance' was out of the question. This left either end of the day, so I resorted to an early morning drive down to the park armed with poop-scoops. This wasn't too bad in the summer, but winter was another matter. Getting up even earlier to scrape the ice from the car just for a short journey was not much fun.

Evening number twos (apart from in the summer when we could drive out to the country) involved a walk to a couple of far-flung grass verges that felt miles away. Even then, it was pot luck if we got a result.

Dogs' antics, when they are preparing to get down to business, have always rather fascinated me – which isn't to say I make a habit of studying every dog doing its business. There's the endless sniffing, the circling, the false alarms and the pacing up and down to find the perfect spot. No doubt there is a reason for this behaviour when preparing for 'bombs away,' otherwise it would just be find the nearest grass and drop – never mind all that palaver. Beans was the absolute master of the 'I'm going to keep them waiting as long as possible' approach, so there was always a great sense of 'relief' when we returned from a successful mission.

We were in no doubt that our dog was a keen birdwatcher (well of two varieties at least) but her interests were beginning to widen to encompass other species from the animal kingdom. Squirrels in particular were a firm favourite. Wanting to catch these cute little creatures is nothing out of the ordinary for a dog. I've seen many a desperate dog barking furiously at the base of a tree, while a squirrel sits way up on some branch, taunting the infuriated dog. If dogs could climb trees, there would be carnage within the squirrel population – but a lot of very happy dogs.

One of the places we escaped to for our walks was the National Trust-owned woodland at Alderley Edge, just a few miles away. The woods at Alderley Edge have long been a favourite of ours. I have cosy childhood memories of blackberry-picking trips with my grandparents, spending hours following the woodland paths, coming across the overgrown remains of the old quarries and then standing on Castle Rock gazing out over the Cheshire Plain. Alan Garner, the local children's author, used the location in his classic novel *The Weirdstone of Brisingamen* which I must have read umpteen times as a child. It is easy to see how he was so inspired by some of the more mysterious corners of the woods.

Beans, however, had far more important things on her mind than classic literature. They were grey, had four legs, and bushy tails that they liked to flick excitedly. They also had the infuriating ability to be able to evade her in most situations, which owed more to the presence of a convenient tree than it did to speed. A few, however, were very nearly sent to that great wood in the sky; only narrowly escaping Beans' jaws.

Alderley Edge was one of the few places where we could safely let Beans off her lead, without worrying about any livestock that might be around. There were plenty of other dogs, but (thanks to Beans' placid nature) we had very few scraps. Of course, if another dog decided to take against her she did her best to retaliate, but more often than not instant submission was her preferred course of action. Sometimes she let out a heart-rending yelp and we felt sure that something nasty must have happened. A quick inspection revealed that there was no damage and the yelp was more from fear than pain. Beans was not a fighter. Of all our trips to the vets, thankfully none were due to injuries from fighting.

There was a spot in the woods where we released her from her lead, which was sufficiently far enough away from the car park and roads. The mere mention of the word 'squirrel' and she was off, as fast as her legs would carry her. It didn't matter that word had got round the local squirrel population that a dog was on the prowl (and not just Beans) because there was always the remote possibility that one would be surprised, lurking behind a tree. Most were safely up trees, pulling faces and making rude gestures at all the frenzied dogs below.

Beans had done 0 – 60 in two seconds and was lost from view; the only indication of her presence being sudden barking as she spotted a squirrel on open ground. Every now and again we saw a beige blur as she bolted in hot pursuit of one of the little animals and then more frantic barking as it made it to the safety of a tree. At that point it wasn't difficult to find her: we just followed the direction of the barking and she could usually be seen standing at the base of a tree, eyes glued to the upper branches, desperately wishing she could climb it.

Occasionally we lost her altogether; only finding her when we reached the Beacon; a ruined building, which is all that remains of a structure built at the time of the Spanish Armada in 1588, one of a chain that were built across England to warn of the impending invasion. Once the Spanish fleet had been spotted and invasion seemed imminent, the first beacon would be lit, followed by the others, so alerting the populace. Its only purpose now however was to provide a meeting place for us and Beans – once she'd finished hunting squirrels.

Autumn, when the squirrels would be gathering acorns and burying them, was the best time to be in the woods. It also meant that Beans was so well camouflaged against the fallen leaves that even we had a job to spot her sometimes. She could have used this to her advantage, but it was the usual mad charge into the depths of the woods hoping that a squirrel would meekly surrender itself to her mouth. Thankfully, we never had to witness the bloody sight of her mangling a squirrel - but on one occasion we came very close to it.

Beans had already exhausted herself charging around the woods in all directions, so we had made our way to the viewpoint at Stormy Point, overlooking the Cheshire Plain. This outcrop of sandstone, worn by the elements and crossed by mysterious fissures that invite exploration, is a piece of open ground backed by trees; not the sort of place you would normally expect to find a squirrel.

Beans found one; it could have been no more than fifty yards away, making its way across the rocks towards more woods to the left. Like a rocket, she bolted towards the squirrel (which hadn't spotted her) leaping over the deep clefts in the rocks, with one purpose only on her mind. This squirrel was out of luck; the trees were some way off, and the edge fell away quite steeply towards more woods below. This was payback time for all that taunting from high up.

Just as we were thinking that Beans was about to catch the squirrel, it spotted her and fled towards the edge of the rocks. We were now more concerned for Beans' safety than that of the squirrel; the drop, although not vertical, could be a potential disaster for an animal travelling at speed. We had visions of broken legs as Beans caught herself in one of the clefts. Shouting at her to come back was useless; all thoughts were on the squirrel, not the fact she was about to hurtle into the abyss.

At the last moment, the squirrel made an abrupt left turn and headed for the trees to the left. This sudden change of direction was enough to check Beans and prevent her becoming airborne, but she was still only what seemed like inches away from the squirrel - I swear her teeth almost made contact with its tail.

The squirrel was running for its life. Just as it seemed like Beans' luck was in, it made it to a tree and safety. Beans collided with the tree as the squirrel scampered up the trunk. Incredibly, she didn't knock herself out. It was like something out of a *Tom and Jerry* cartoon. I half expected to see one of those cartoon impressions of her in the tree, as she slid slowly down it, legs outstretched, with a silly look on her face – in true cartoon fashion.

Jerry, meanwhile, was somewhere up the tree, counting his lucky stars.

The common grey squirrel, found throughout the UK, is not a true native of the country. In fact, it was brought here from North America by some misguided Victorians, released, and then spread like wildfire, forcing our native red squirrels into small pockets of the country, where they continue to cling on. The greys, apart from outnumbering the reds, carry a disease that the red squirrels cannot fight off, so their numbers have been decimated. Plans are in hand to save the reds, which, unfortunately, will probably entail culling, but this may be the only option to prevent the extinction of an animal that, until only seventy years ago was still common in this country.

Perhaps the conservation groups should consider the fact that there is an army of ready and willing dogs out there, who would be only too happy to assist in the removal of the greys. The only problem with this suggestion is, of course, that dogs, to the best of my knowledge are not conservationists, and in their zeal to hunt down the squirrels would make no distinction between red and grey; all would be fair game.

At present, the red squirrel survives in only a few widespread areas of the country, namely: The Lake District, Anglesey, Northumberland, The Isle of Wight, Scotland, Brownsea Island, a tiny portion of the Yorkshire Dales and a National Trust-owned reserve at Formby, on Merseyside.

The reserve at Formby is open to the public, who are also allowed to take their dogs, which must of course be on leads. The whole area, as well as the portion owned by the Trust, is an important nature reserve. The squirrels inhabit a delightful wooded area of Scots pines, where they are relatively safe from any encroaching greys. The land behind the reserve is largely flat farmland, with little tree cover, or is built on, acting as a wonderful 'buffer-zone' to keep the greys out; although this doesn't mean that there are none around. Any that do try and enter this forbidden zone are swiftly dealt with. Bordering the woods, and reached via some of the finest sand dunes you will see, is Formby beach, a wonderful piece of coast that stretches for miles in either direction. On clear days, Blackpool Tower can be picked out further up the coast and in the autumn and winter months migrant wading birds, such as sanderlings, can be seen at the water's edge. The very lucky might spot one of the rare Natterjack toads who live here.

I've often thought Formby must be a pleasant place to live; nature on your doorstep, a fantastic beach for bracing dog walks and all that invigorating sea air. Judging by some of the imposing-looking properties hiding away behind large security gates it seemed many people agreed with me. As we passed house after house on the reserve approach road, with Mercedes and BMWs on their drives, it was plain that house prices in this area were well out of our league. With Liverpool only a short drive away, could this be the place where its famous football team's wealthy players lived? It certainly looked like it.

We made the first of our many visits to Formby in 1993. Beans always seemed to enjoy trips out to new and exciting places, but I don't think she realised just *how* exciting this one would turn out to be. The moment you park up squirrels can be seen; dozens of them, running here there and everywhere. You buy a little bag of peanuts in their shells at the entrance to the car park and the relatively tame squirrels will feed from your hand. This is a magical experience, enchanting to adults as well as children. Despite their long sharp claws, which they need for tree-climbing, the squirrels gently push your hand down to reach the nuts, take one, scurry off to either eat it or bury it, and then come back for more!

As we followed the trail through the pines, Beans couldn't believe her luck. Fancy being brought to a place where there were squirrels in abundance *and* dogs were allowed – this must be dog-heaven. With Beans beside herself in squirrel ecstasy, trying to enjoy the experience ourselves was trying. One of us would take her to a place where there were fewer squirrels, while the other got on with feeding them. No squirrel is going to take nuts from someone's hand with a slavering dog only inches away, nor was it fair to the other visitors without dogs. It would only have taken a few complaints from some disgruntled squirrel-feeders for us (and our dog) to be escorted off the reserve. Not a very good advert for the Trust's dog-tolerant approach.

Sadly, in the last few years the red squirrels of Formby have been stricken by that awful virus, probably brought in by a grey that had managed to avoid being caught. There are now only a handful of the reds left. It is hoped that soon a vaccine will be found and, once again, these delightful little creatures will be back where they belong.

At Formby I first noticed that not all dogs are squirrel-obsessed. Some barely gave them a second glance. Although I didn't want to lose any of my dog's character, I suppose I was secretly envious of those people who didn't have dogs that lunged after anything that flapped, scuttled or made any kind of strange noise.

Despite Beans' best efforts, the red squirrels of Formby were safe. I even managed to squeeze in some half-decent photographs of them during those brief moments when she'd calmed down. A dog can have too much of a good thing, so we left the squirrels in peace and made our way over the dunes to the beach. Pooches of every variety were having a rare old time, chasing each other, their owners or just simply running for the heck of it. All thoughts of bushy tails were soon forgotten when Beans saw this wonderful playground. Now she was back in familiar dog territory that all dogs love: digging holes in the sand and forgetting that yes, seawater does still taste horrible.

They say owning a dog is the best stress reliever and I wouldn't disagree. Boy, did I need my dog. Problems at work, coupled with an increasingly intolerable situation with the neighbours, were beginning to take their toll on my mental health. Heavy Metal music blasting through our thin walls at three in the mornings was starting to put me in a murderous frame of mind.

After several visits to the doctor, anxiety was diagnosed and I was given a programme of relaxation techniques. Because the stress affected my stomach, I was on drugs to combat excess acid. It was not a happy time.

I couldn't believe the effect stress could have on the body. My heart was skipping beats so often I became convinced there was something wrong with it, despite constant reassurance to the contrary from my doctor. After each visit, I went away feeling happier only for my heart to start jumping around again and I was back to square one. *Remember what the doctor said*, I had to keep telling myself; *everyone's heart misses a beat now and then; it's nothing to worry about, you're just producing more adrenalin, that's all,* and then: *besides, your heart isn't really missing a beat or stopping, it just pauses a little to make up for the two quick beats.*

Despite repeating the doctor's mantra to myself constantly, I couldn't stop worrying – and that just made matters worse. The more I worried that my heart was about to pack in, the more it palpitated. I was trapped in a vicious circle. The worry made my stomach worse and I was given stronger drugs that had unpleasant side effects. Sometimes, I could actually feel a sudden *explosion* in my stomach, which I was told was the adrenalin and, guess what, the adrenalin made my heart jump around even more. I read somewhere that the stomach weeps when the mind isn't at peace – mine must have been shedding bucket loads. Every morning I awoke to a lurching stomach and nausea so bad I could barely eat any breakfast. Not surprisingly, my appetite waned and I started to lose weight. Talk about dropping a dress size; I dropped a waist size.

The panic attacks were a new and unexpected nightmare for me. The first time one hit me, I thought I was about to die and nothing would have convinced me otherwise. Waking from a particularly bad dream, with my heart racing and jumping all over the place, I lay there with a terrifying feeling of impending doom closing in on me. My stomach felt like it was being squeezed. I wanted to be sick, but couldn't. No wonder I thought I was having a heart attack. Instead of calming down and going back to sleep, my heart seemed to beat ever faster and I started to shiver. My *you're not having a heart attack* mantra didn't work either. *Come on, you're only 33, your heart has been checked out, your blood pressure is only slightly raised, you're a fit hill-walker – you're not having a heart attack!*

By now, Jan had been woken to the sound of me pleading with her to call an ambulance, convinced I was dying. Despite all the reassurance she could give, nothing would calm me down.

'Have you got pain in your chest or arms?' she asked.

'No, but my chest feels weird and my heart won't stop beating fast,' I replied with such desperation in my voice, I felt sure she would dial 999.

'Try and calm down, it's not a heart attack; you've had a bad dream that's all.'

This would go on for what seemed like hours, before my heart eventually slowed down and I had warmed myself up by standing in front of the convector heater. Exhausted, I would sink back onto the bed and let sleep drift over me again.

Then the alarm would go off and the stomach-churning would start again.

My lunchtimes with Beans became an oasis of calm in my world, which had suddenly come apart in ways I had never thought possible. I didn't have cancer; there was nothing wrong with my heart – despite thinking there was, and I had no other serious illness. Despite this, I felt like hell most of the time. I knew that somewhere along the line I would be free of it all – I just didn't know when. I felt unjustifiably guilty for feeling like I did when so many people suffer with serious and life-threatening illnesses, but it helped that the doctor said I had nothing to feel guilty about. If it hadn't been for Jan's help and that wonderful, enthusiastic, tail-wagging welcome from Beans every day, I would have been a whole lot worse.

It was another four years before this 'cloud' lifted from me completely. Part of the recovery involved our decision to put the house on the market in 1993. Neither of us was happy where we lived and to move somewhere with a garden and space around us was something we both craved. I was starting to feel increasingly trapped in a place that should have felt more like home than it did, so much so that on my days off work I felt unable to stay in the house and headed to Wilmslow with Beans, either to my parents or Jan's. We were desperate to escape. Jan's health hadn't suffered in the way mine had (despite her redundancy) but the strain of having to handle the unreasonable neighbours was beginning to take its toll on her.

Within weeks of our decision, there was a for sale sign outside the house and we started to feel that things were moving forward. It felt like we only used the house for sleeping and eating, since we spent so little time in it. Maybe if the neighbour problem had been resolved we would have waited a little longer until our finances were more secure, but it wasn't going to happen. Jan now had a new full-time job so there seemed no better time than the present.

Our walks in the Peak District with Beans became even more important and there were very few weekends when we didn't head for the hills. House-hunting took up most Saturdays, so that left Sunday for walking. My stamina had taken a bit of a knock because of my reduced appetite, but I was determined that I wasn't going to let a neighbour's selfish behaviour ruin the only thing that helped us switch off. We had to boost ourselves up with thoughts of new homes, nice walks and holidays.

Any hopes we had of a quick sale were soon dashed. We bought the house during the boom period of the late eighties and were now selling during the slump of the early nineties; people wanted a bargain and were prepared to put in the most derisory of offers. This coupled with the fact that the house had been over-valued, forced us to change estate agents when it became apparent that people were looking – but not buying. In June we had a lovely, relaxing holiday in Devon, while Beans went on her own holiday to Wilmslow. Two weeks of glorious beaches, walks on Dartmoor and plenty of cream teas had the energising effect we had hoped for, and we felt more positive about the house sale. A change of agent, with a lower (but more realistic) value on the house, gave us more hope that a buyer would soon be found.

Summer gave way to autumn, autumn gave way to winter, and before long we were in the new year with still little sign of a serious buyer – it was back to thinking of holidays again. We needed an away-from-it-all place, but not somewhere too expensive. The Isles of Scilly, just twenty eight miles off the Cornish coast, were the ideal destination. Accommodation was found and booked, travel arrangements made and Beans looked forward to another two weeks of lazy days with Bob and Rita. We felt hopeful again.

The Scillies were fantastic: we could have been in the Caribbean, rather than an archipelago, twenty-odd miles from Land's End. The beaches were beautiful, the sun shone and all thoughts of house moves and nasty neighbours were soon banished.

Coming home from such a holiday was awful, but we always had the thought of our reunion with Beans to look forward to. I will never forget those special welcomes Beans always gave us when we returned from holiday. The moment she saw our car draw up at the side of Bob and Rita's house, she went berserk. She would run back in the house as if to say 'they're here' and then, just as we managed to shut the gate, she ran out again barking, squeaking and frantically jumping up at us. Then it was back inside, only to return with one of her many toys in her mouth, which she dropped enthusiastically at our feet. After several minutes, and much barking, she calmed down. Nothing could beat that Beans welcome.

As the taxi dropped us off outside our home, the Scillies could have been a million miles away. The *For Sale* sign looked down on us as if saying 'welcome back to reality.' There was also no food in the house, so it was down to the supermarket for provisions – more reality.

My spirits couldn't have been lower as I browsed the magazine stand in the supermarket. As my eyes drifted over gloomy newspaper headlines and endless diet and fitness titles, I suddenly remembered that *Country Walking* should be on the shelves about now. *Something to cheer me up,* I thought to myself, scanning the magazines for the leisure titles. I suddenly stopped dead in my tracks. There in front of me was the July 1994 issue of my favourite magazine – with Jan and Beans adorning the front cover! Back from holiday gloom evaporated in an instant as I excitedly picked up the magazine, before shouting to Jan to come and look, oblivious to the bemused shoppers around me. As Jan joined me, I hurriedly turned to the inside page for the credit; there it was: *Windgather Rocks in the Peak District. Photograph by Martin Johnson.*

I still have the copy I picked up from the magazine stand that day; as pristine as the day I bought it. Of course, I was duly sent my complimentary magazine and bought a few copies for the family, but in a way, that original copy seemed to signal the start of good things to come. Three months later we had a buyer for the cottage.

Now that all the legal and other practicalities of house-moving were taking place, it felt that at last things were beginning to move. I even started to feel better in myself. Part of this recovery was due in no small part to my discovering the delights of Billy Connolly. During that period between finding a buyer and moving, the BBC screened his *World Tour of Scotland* series, an immensely entertaining blend of travelogue and clips from his legendary one man shows.

Although I had seen clips of his shows over the years, I had never actually sat down and enjoyed his humour properly.

What have I been missing all this time, I thought to myself as I lay doubled up with laughter on the settee one evening. By the time the show had finished, half an hour later, my stomach muscles were aching. This was just what the doctor ordered. I soon began to love Billy's take on life and found myself agreeing with the things he came out with.

'*Do these things,*' he said, talking about schoolboy pranks such as stretching cling film over the toilet pan. It was time to bring a little more devilment into my life and the house move would provide the perfect opportunity. The question was: would I have the guts to do anything?

Some people behave like considerate, rational human beings when negotiating a path through the minefield that is moving house – our buyers' sole mission in life seemed to be to make our move as nightmarish as possible. They were the house buyers from hell. Our estate agent had never encountered anything like it in his entire career.

It would be no exaggeration to say that I hoped the house would fall down around them. When people go back on their word to you, feelings run high. To add insult to injury they even asked what exactly we had done to improve the house, just because our finances had precluded installing central heating. As the memory of the years' work – almost right up to the eve of our wedding – came back, I was tempted to call the whole deal off and ask them to please get the hell out of my house, but the thought of waiting months for another buyer to come along was too much to contemplate.

The temptation to secrete a bag of prawns in some hidden recess of the house, before we left it for the final time, was overwhelming, but I contented myself with hammering down the carpet tacks so they couldn't be re-used, hiding the spare keys on top of a cupboard in the kitchen and making damned sure that every last light bulb was removed. Jan was still dying to pull the rotting prawns stunt and I must admit I was tempted – remembering Billy Connolly's advice – but it was time to cut our losses and get the hell out.

By October we were happily installed in our new home in Congleton. Beans seemed happier too, as she bounced out the back door to explore her new garden. We had turned the corner.

Beans and Other Animals

Near the beginning of the Mel Gibson movie *'Maverick'*, there's a hilarious sequence where the star of the film rides into town not on a trusty steed (as in true western style) but on a very noisy mule, which he soon manages to offload.

A few months before we left Macclesfield we'd gone to see this great film – twice – at the cinema. Jan has always been a Mel Gibson fan so the video of the film was soon added to her collection. Little did we realise that Mel also had another adoring fan – Beans.

We knew she was a keen wildlife spotter, but this interest was not just confined to the outdoors. She liked to watch television – animal or wildlife shows in particular. I have always loved wildlife films such as Natural World, Survival, or anything by David Attenborough. I feel I am missing something special if I don't watch one of these films, much to Jan's amusement. Although she likes them as well, she doesn't hurriedly reach for the recorder button if there's the slightest chance of missing one. Beans just took whatever was on offer. She liked anything from *Animal Hospital*, to *One Man and His Dog,* where the skills of the sheepdogs were of great fascination to her, matched only by her interest in the sheep themselves.

It's one of the funniest things in life to watch a dog watching the television, and seeing Beans suddenly dart around the back of the set in pursuit of them, after following their every movement around the screen, is a memory we treasure. It must have come as a terrible disappointment to her to discover that there were, in fact, no sheep lurking behind the set, but she never remembered this, so the next time the whole scenario was repeated; much to our delight – and Beans' frustration.

If we thought this was funny enough, little did we realise what her reaction to the beginning of 'Maverick' was going to be. One evening, a few weeks after we'd moved into our new home, we settled down to watch the video.

As the film soundtrack started and Mel rode into town on his mule, which was braying vociferously, Beans walked up to the set, her head twisting from side to side at this strange sound – and started howling. At first it was quite a low, almost mournful howl, but the louder the mule became, the louder Beans howled, drowning out both Randy Newman's stirring soundtrack and the mule.

As the call of the wild filled our living room, the whole scene became almost surreal; the braying mule, bleating goats, music and Beans' howling becoming a bizarre mixture of sounds. While we sat there doubled up with laughter, she was in full swing; head held aloft, ears swept back, looking like a true wolf. It was like a western version of *Old McDonald's Farm.*

It would be easy to say that Mel Gibson's noisy mule had awakened some primal instincts deep within Beans; a throwback to the distant past when the ancestors of dogs roamed the wilderness, but if my own experience is anything to go by, it might be more a reaction to certain sounds, although, as we discovered later, Beans was certainly attuned to the calls of her wild cousins.

When I was a boy I had a harmonica which I used to play and play until my lips were sore. I will never forget the reaction of my first dog, Judy, the moment I started playing it. She howled and howled along to my (rather bad) playing until I stopped. The moment I played just a few notes, she started again. It was great fun. Had I been enthused with some entrepreneurial spirit, I could have earned a packet from busking on the streets; me, my beagle, and a harmonica – who knows where it might have taken me.

Beans demonstrated that she too, had an ear for music. Not long after we'd moved to our first home, Bob decided to buy an organ; not one of those portable ones, but a big, full size one, which took up a large portion of the living room. He enlisted the services of a tutor and before long became a competent player. He hadn't however, bargained on Beans' reaction to this strange new addition to her home, which made some equally strange noises. She howled at it.

There was never any pattern to the howling; it would be whenever she felt the need, usually at some critical part of a new tune he was learning, completely throwing him off course. Although the poor dog's attempts at accompanying him were usually met with cross words, everyone enjoyed Beans' musical abilities. I often wonder what her reaction to a mouth organ would have been. The sound of a full size organ, a mouth organ and a howling dog would have soon had the neighbours complaining.

Beans was a confirmed TV addict – of that we were in no doubt. Her list of favourite programmes was steadily growing, although the preferred subject matter was still the same: dogs, cats, wolves, grouse, nature and wildlife films, in fact anything that moved or made a noise. Braying donkeys or howling wolves received the full Beans howling treatment. Her reaction to any film about wolves – and there were many – was so spectacular that we even recorded one especially for her. My notion that she was merely reacting to certain sounds was tested when I saw her howling along with an entire pack of wolves. There was definitely more intensity to her howling; more of a haunting call-of-the-wild feel to it. She was answering the wolves and for that moment was a part of their pack – a part of their world. For a few moments, a domestic dog – a pet – became a wild animal.

How strong the connection is between dogs and wolves became very apparent to us when we had the opportunity to visit a wolf conservation centre. To see these magnificent creatures up close and personal – even walking with them – was amazing and strengthened my belief that they should be protected from persecution at all costs.

Wolves have always been one of my favourite animals. To me, they represent the wild. When *Two Socks,* the wolf Kevin Costner befriends in his magnificent *Dances with Wolves,* was killed, I was in pieces for days.

The forests of Europe were alive with them before they were hunted to virtual extinction by superstitious people, convinced they were harbingers of doom or mass killers of people. The plains and mountains of North America were the dominion of the wolf, revered by the Native Americans in their legends and folklore, but then despised by the settlers, who slaughtered them in their thousands and persecuted the indigenous people into virtual oblivion. It was the destruction of a centuries old way of life. Wolves hunted the buffalo and so did the Native Americans, but the balance of nature was maintained. There was plenty for everyone; until the buffalo were exterminated and the settlers brought in thousands of cattle, who had no defence against the marauding wolves. That spelt the end for these magnificent creatures.

As we watched the wolves at the conservation centre, we realised we were watching an animal that had been around at the time of some of the earliest humans, a time when man first realised he could befriend and domesticate a wild animal. When we discovered that one of the wolves was also partial to a bit of cheese – one of Beans' favourite treats – we figured that there wasn't that much difference between them.

After that wonderful day with the wolves, I made it my business to find out more about them and what was being done to bring them back. I learned about efforts being made in the US to return them to the wild; the fact that they were still being persecuted in those parts of Europe where they clung on, and the work being carried out to protect them.

I learnt about Ernest Thompson Seton, the English-born nineteenth century naturalist, writer and artist, and hunter of one of the few remaining wolves in New

Mexico – 'Lobo' and his tragic mate 'Blanco.' The killing of Lobo and Blanco affected Seton so much that he spent the rest of his life in defending wolves and the wild landscapes they lived in. Thanks to Seton, the world was set on the course of nature conservation and the creation of national parks across the US and later the rest of the world, including our beloved Peak District, where our very own little 'wolf' liked to roam.

Whether wolves would share in Beans' television-watching antics was debatable, but given their shared delight in the taste of cheese and playing with pieces of broken ice; more than likely.

Top of Beans' TV charts was undoubtedly *'One Man and His Dog'* with its ideal blend of sheep and sheepdogs, but *'Animal Hospital'* came a very close second. Filmed in one of the RSPCA's hospitals, this wonderful show followed the vets as they treated a variety of animals with equally varied complaints. The series – which has now sadly finished – was both heart-warming and at times heart-breaking, when tearful owners said farewell to much loved pets. Beans always got a special cuddle during those sad bits.

The show did not shy away from showing the dreadful cruelty inflicted on helpless animals, both domestic and wild. The notion of Britain being a 'Nation of Animal Lovers' was sorely tested when neglected and emaciated dogs and cats were brought in for treatment. There was always a positive note to the show when these animals were shown months later, restored to health and with new, caring owners. Having endured such cruelty, it was amazing to see how these animals bounced back. If an animal is loved and looked after it will – perhaps not straight away - respond in kind. Maybe there's a lesson for us there.

Beans never ceased to delight us with her ability to recognise moments in TV shows where an animal was likely to put in an appearance. The soap 'Coronation

Street' was a good example. Britain's longest running soap opera was, until not long ago, famous for its cat, that made an appearance in the opening title sequence as it walked along a wall behind the famous terraced houses of the street. Beans had an uncanny ability to make sure her gaze was well and truly fixed on the screen at the precise moment the cat appeared. It didn't matter where she was; in her bed, in the kitchen hoping for some scraps, lying down in front of the TV, or playing. Even when she was older and a little deaf, she still looked up at the screen. As soon as the cat ambled along that wall, she was there, staring intently at it. It took us a while to figure out what prompted her to be there every time, until, one evening, I noticed her ears prick up at the exact moment in the theme tune when the cat appeared. Maybe it was just a coincidence, so the next time I made a point of watching whether the same thing happened. Sure enough, it did.

Eventually, the title sequence changed and Beans' cat was sadly no more, to be replaced by a handful of pigeons. Beans never quite warmed to those pigeons, although some chirping budgies in the sponsor's film before the main show did arouse a fair bit of interest. Despite the absence of the cat she still lived in hope that it would once again walk along that wall. For months, she continued to look up at the same point in the theme tune. It was strangely sad to see her looking in vain for her favourite cat.

Help was at hand however, for the bereft dog, in the form of a clever television whisky advert.

With a brand name of *Famous Grouse* I suppose it was inevitable that at some point Beans and their brand advertising grouse would meet. Bottles of the company's whisky had long been adorned with a picture of Beans' favourite bird, but when they started a television advertising campaign in 1996 featuring a red grouse, things really heated up. The grouse was depicted in various funny situations such as ice-skating and tap-dancing, accompanied by an amusing little staccato tune. It was a brilliant piece of advertising – and the best TV present Beans could wish for.

When we first saw the advert we quickly called Beans to the TV. She couldn't believe her luck; a grouse in her living room - this was too good to be true. She ran at the set so fast that she almost head-butted it. Barking, head twitching from side to side, she followed the grouse around the screen until it finally disappeared. Then followed the usual trick of trying to find out where it had gone. Perhaps it had walked behind the set or was lurking in a corner of the room, waiting to flap out in front of her. Sadly, it had joined the sheep, the dogs and the various other animals in that mysterious place where TV animals go. With the advert finished, a confused and frustrated dog looked at us as if to say *where's it gone?'* and then pace the room trying to find the grouse. It was funny, but at the same time almost heart-rending, watching her look in vain for the bird.

The advert appeared mainly at Christmas, but Beans always recognised the music that accompanied it, despite it being absent from the screens for a year. She even woke up when the music started. Just as she did with the Coronation Street cat, there she was, plonked in front of the set, waiting for the grouse to appear. When the grouse developed an interest in music and wandered across the screen to a jazzed-up version of the tune, she was delighted, because it meant the bird was around for a little longer than it usually was, before it vanished. I wonder if the company realised just how much pleasure their grouse advertisement gave a dog. It may not have encouraged her to go out and buy whisky, but in terms of entertainment value, it was a great success.

What with TV grouse, sheep, sheepdogs, donkeys and a whole menagerie of other animals to follow around the screen – or to howl at – you would think that the radio would not have much to offer Beans, but even that did not escape her attention. Sarah Kennedy's early morning show on Radio 2 proved to be a great favourite.

Early mornings, prior to another day at work are not everyone's favourite. I am probably *Number One Grump* at this time of the day, muttering about another dreaded day at the office or some loathsome customers whose lights I would dearly love to punch out. Thank heavens for the radio and the friendly banter of the DJs to brighten things up. Terry Wogan and Sarah Kennedy have cheered up many a dreary morning.

Beans' reaction to Sarah's show made things even more bearable. Every now and again she played a variety of animal noises to accompany her chat, and it wasn't long before Beans had cottoned on. Moose, cats and a cockerel, amongst others, soon attracted her attention.

The cat, needless to say, became her favourite. An invisible cat, miaowing somewhere in her living room was simply more than Beans could take. As soon as the sounds emanated from the radio she hurled herself in their direction, in the vain – but always hopeful – chance that the cat would be there, standing on top of the radio, pulling its tongue out at her.

She sat by the radio as the miaowing continued, tilting her head from side to side - waiting to pounce. Sometimes it all got too much and she had to carry out a thorough search of that end of the room, just in case the cat was lurking somewhere. The chance of her actually finding a cat was not totally stretching the bounds of possibility, but to see her trying to locate a fully grown moose in an English living room was.

Despite her regular morning searches for the moose, Beans' dream of finding a cat in her house was soon to become a reality.

CHAPTER FIVE

Trains, Caves and Rabbit Burrows

Cat Trouble

For several months after our move to Congleton we were in a state of disarray. Our old cottage could only support a limited number of books, ornaments, photo albums and all those other bits and pieces collected over the years. When we moved to our first home we had to leave a lot of our belongings with our parents, so now they had all been gathered up and dumped in our spacious new home. My old bed went in the spare room, Jan's desk found a convenient niche in the box room at the front and now we had lots of wall space to hang all those pictures and photos that had been in hibernation for four years. Beans was happy: she could spread her growing collection of toys liberally throughout the house.

The small, cottage-size settee was sold to a work colleague, leaving us with nothing to sit on but a few garden chairs and recliners until our new suite arrived. I quite enjoyed watching the TV relaxing on my favourite garden recliner.

Boxes filled with belongings of every sort were piled up in the living room. The trouble was; we couldn't be bothered to unpack them. To suddenly have all this space, as well as all those belongings we'd forgotten we had, was a bit of a shock to the system. We didn't know where to start.

We decided the best approach was the gradual one. Clean the place up; unpack the stuff which had come from Macclesfield and then decide how many cabinets we needed for the surplus. This approach wouldn't be for everyone. I've seen people move in, start decorating straight away and then get the builders in for an extension or a new porch – all within a few weeks. A couple of years later and the house is on the market again. What a waste of time and money. I hate living in chaos and I at least want to be sure I'm going to stay in a place before I start spending money on it. Each to his own I suppose.

The previous occupiers of our new home owned a cat called 'Monty' who, judging by the smell of it, must have spent most of his time in the garage, coming and going through a cat flap. The first time I opened the back door to the garage, my eyes watered at the overpowering smell of cat pee. We knew the cat did come into the house, because we saw him one day when we came for a viewing, but most of his 'business' was obviously conducted in the garage. As I recoiled from the garage to gulp some fresh air I wondered what Beans' reaction to the strong smell of cat would be. I had visions of her searching every inch of the garage desperately trying to find the cat. It would drive her mad. The garage had to be cleaned up – fast.

'This is going to need some industrial-strength disinfectant,' I said, unscrewing the top from a bottle of *Jeyes Fluid*.

'I don't know which is worse, that or the cat pee,' Jan replied, as the nose-unblocking reek of the fluid filled the garage.

By the time I'd finished cleaning out the garage, I was beginning to think she was probably right. The disinfectant was bringing on my asthma. The smell lingered for weeks – but at least the smell of cat pee had gone.

Cats are creatures of habit and Monty soon decided that he didn't like his new home. Luckily for him it was only a short distance away from his old one. I opened the back door one day to find him sitting there asking to come in. Shutting the door quickly before Beans caught his scent, I did my best to persuade him to go home. But as far as he was concerned this was home. I felt awful, having to send him away.

'You wouldn't like it here now, there's a dog living here,' I said, as if he would understand.

He finally got the message that there was no room at the inn and walked dejectedly away. Hoping I'd convinced him that coming to live with a dog was not a good idea, I thought that would be the last I'd see of him. Monty, however, was not going to give up that easily. This was his home and he couldn't understand why he wasn't allowed there anymore.

Over the next few months he made repeated visits to us. Sometimes he wandered into the garden; on other occasions he made himself comfortable on the front doorstep, relaxing contentedly in the sunshine. Unfortunately he was about to make a big mistake that would scupper his plans to move back in. It happened the summer following our move.

Despite Monty's regular visits, Beans had only met him a few times, greeting him in her customary way with a cold wet nose up his backside. Monty's response was as swift as it was predictable, his loud hiss sufficient to send Beans packing. Any garden confrontation was, as always, swiftly ended by Beans and all we would see of Monty was his tail disappearing rapidly over the fence with Beans barking madly behind. It was *Tom and Jerry* again, only Beans had changed sex and become *Spike,* the bulldog arch enemy of Tom. The only difference being, she didn't have a kennel with *'Killer'* written on it.

Despite being regularly seen off by Beans, Monty still had designs on moving back in. He'd made friends with a cat-loving lady up the road who took it upon herself to feed him, which obviously made him feel even more like staying in the neighbourhood. Quite what his owners thought about all this, I don't know, but they never came looking for him. That suited Monty just fine. He'd have something to eat and then pop round the corner to try and ingratiate himself with us a little more.

The summer of 1995 was a memorably hot one; it reminded me of that glorious long summer of 1976 – the year I left school. The year of the great drought and water standpipes, when Elton John and Kiki Dee topped the charts with that summer's anthem: *Don't Go Breaking My Heart.* The year The Rolling Stones played at Knebworth and the year I got so sunburnt on holiday in Cornwall that I couldn't lie down for days.

We'd left the back door open to let what air there was circulate through the house. Jan was busy upstairs and Beans had come inside to cool off. While I'd been busy outside in the garden I hadn't spotted our feline friend calmly trotting into the house and making himself comfortable on our settee.

I came in to get myself a drink of water and stuck my head around the living room door to see Monty, sitting on the settee with a look of pure contentment on his face. I did a double take. How he had managed to get past the door without Beans spotting him was a tribute to his determination to regain his proper home.

I must have disturbed Beans from her nap, because her head suddenly popped up at the end of the settee. It took a fraction of a second for it to register that a cat was literally inches away from her face. It was all the time Monty needed. He was off that settee like a bullet.

A brown shape flashed past me, followed instantly by a beige blur, accompanied by much barking and a desperate shriek from Monty. All I could do was hope that Beans hadn't caught him. He was lucky. Beans may have been close enough to grab some tail fur, but no more. In a chase it's rarely the dog who wins.

This was the final straw for poor old Monty; he'd tried and failed to get his home back, but it was time to admit defeat. There was no way Beans was going to let him stay. For the next few years he contented himself with the odd visit, but gradually became adopted by a lady up the road called Sue, who'd become his unofficial owner. Apparently his real owners had been unable to stop his daily excursions and decided to let him move in with Sue. This was probably for the best – a very busy main road lay between Monty and his preferred home.

We still saw him around, but it was sad to see old age and infirmity gradually taking its toll on him. He was also going blind. Despite this, it was good to know he was being well cared for, with people who loved him, even if he couldn't move in with us.

One day when we'd taken Beans for a quick walk around the block, Sue was outside her house – but without Monty, who, because of his failing eyesight, was always near at hand. It was then that she gave us the sad news that he had passed away.

Trains

There's a great café at Grindleford Station, in the Peak District's Hope Valley; a proper 'hikers and bikers' café, where the tea comes in huge pint-sized mugs, cakes are cut into proper 'man-size' wedges and, if you want, you can have chips with everything – smothered in tomato ketchup. It's wonderful, just-what-you-need-after-a-hike fare that replenishes all that lost energy – good, honest carbohydrate with a little bit of stodge thrown in for good measure. To find the place is still open when you return from a days' walk is like coming across an oasis in the desert, only instead of camels, palm trees and cooling water, there are those big mugs of tea and mouth-watering slices of cake waiting.

Hikers queue up with leather-clad bikers and lean muscular climbers, fresh from a days' climbing on nearby Froggatt Edge. Sometimes the queue stretches out of the building, everyone patiently waiting their turn. I always felt particularly sorry for the poor bikers during the summer, standing there in their heat-absorbing black leathers. They may not have been exerting themselves in the same way the walkers and climbers had, but I bet that tea was just as welcome. There is a feeling of friendly camaraderie about the place, and conversations are inevitably struck up about favourite walks, best climbs or ideal biking routes.

The café's outside seating area is literally next to the main Manchester to Sheffield railway line, where it enters Totley Tunnel. A raised embankment and cutting separate customers from the trains, but even so, they do pass uncomfortably close. For a keen train-spotter eager to note down those vital numbers, it cannot be bettered.

For one train-spotter in particular the café was ideally located. But, instead of binoculars, notebook and essential guide to the rolling stock of Great Britain, this one came equipped with nothing more than extremely good eyesight, enthusiasm bordering on the obsessive, and a cold, wet nose. Beans had found the perfect place to indulge her new-found hobby.

Woe betides if all the tables at the side had been taken. A seat anywhere else was all well and good, but it wasn't exactly in the thick of the action. Beans needed to be able to put her front paws on the fence and peer over to watch the trains. If we couldn't get our usual spot, her ears would still prick up at the sound of a passing train, but it could never beat being able to see them properly.

There was one small problem to dog train-spotting at Grindleford: the tunnel. Beans' excitement as a train approached from the Manchester side was abruptly cut short as it was swallowed by the tunnel. This was a source of perplexity to her; she simply couldn't understand the concept of a tunnel. One minute the train was there; the next it had gone. If a train appeared out of the tunnel going the opposite way, that really confused her. You could almost see the puzzlement on her face when she turned to look at you, turning back just as quickly in case another train should appear. On the rare occasion when two trains appeared, going in opposite directions, she was beside herself with excitement, barking and jumping at the fence. This tunnel was a curious thing; it swallowed the trains and then, moments later, spat them out.

Maybe this was just over-active imagination on our part and Beans didn't really give a stuff about the tunnel, our perception of her confusion being no more than excitement on seeing the trains. In the end, we cannot really know what a dog is thinking all the time – only take an educated guess.

As with Beans' other outdoor activities, there was always a ready audience for her train-spotting antics at the café. All conversations stopped and mugs of tea and bacon sandwiches were momentarily forgotten when her performance started. The bikers thought it was all very amusing, as they sat there grinning at Beans' desperate attempts to find out why the Manchester-Sheffield Cross Country Express had disappeared.

'That's a very funny dog you've got there,' said one biker who was sitting near us.

'You should see her when she's chasing them,' I replied, and then went on to tell him about her express-chasing antics when we lived in Macclesfield.

'Nice to have a dog with a bit of character,' he said, taking a sip from his pint mug of tea, 'good-looking dog too; looks a bit like a dingo.'

Beans momentarily stopped her train-spotting to take a welcome morsel of cake the friendly biker offered her.

I laughed. 'Yes, we've got a train-chasing dingo.' I'd always thought she resembled one of those tough Australian dogs, despite other people saying she was more fox-like.

There was something else about trains that fascinated Beans – their whistles. If we were anywhere within earshot of a railway line, all activity was halted as her ears picked up the sound.

The Sheffield line runs through the beautiful Edale and Hope valleys, overshadowed on one side by the massive plateau of Kinder Scout, and on the other, by the Great Ridge of Mam Tor, Hollins Cross, Back Tor and Lose Hill. Win Hill guards the head of the valley. Legend has it that a great battle was once fought near here; the losers encamped on 'Lose' Hill, the winners on 'Win' Hill.

It never mattered which side of the valley we happened to be walking on. We might be climbing the rocky track to Back Tor or negotiating the steep muscle-aching path up to the strangely named Ringing Roger. If Beans heard a train down in the valley far below, that was it; we had to stop. Her ears were able to pick up the merest sound of the engine or the wheels on the track. If it sounded its horn as well, that was an added bonus.

It was impossible to continue our walk until the train had gone. Once Beans had spotted it, the train's progress up the valley was very carefully followed, pausing as it stopped at Edale station and then resuming as it headed up the valley. Only when it had completely disappeared from view had we a chance of carrying on. It was best to position yourself behind her when she was locked onto a train and watch her head slowly turning from left to right (or vice versa) as she followed it. There was real concentration in the motion of that head, with its alert erect ears.

It wasn't just modern engines Beans liked; the steam variety were just as good – perhaps more so. They had one thing the others hadn't got: a loud, good old-fashioned whistle. Thankfully, there are still many of these lovely old steam engines running in Britain, lovingly restored and operated by true enthusiasts. Several are in, or near, the Peak District, at places such as Darley Dale and Cheddleton.

The Darley Dale line runs below Stanton Moor, another of our frequent walking spots we try and visit regularly. It is only a small heather moor by comparison with others in the Peak, but what it lacks in size it makes up for in quality. There is an ancient stone circle known as *The Nine Ladies;* a distinctive stone, called the *Cork Stone,* which has steps cut into it if you feel the need for a spot of climbing, and the *Earl Grey Tower,* named after Earl Charles Grey, perhaps best known for the tea that carries his name.

With a careful choice of lunch stop we had a good view of the railway below, which delighted Beans. There were no grouse on Stanton Moor, but watching Beans train-spotting while trying to eat her lunch was a bit like watching her grouse-spotting; take a bite, stop and look up when train whistled (or grouse called), resume lunch, stop and look up again. It was a wonder she ever managed to finish her food.

We often wondered what Beans' reaction would be if she encountered a train at close quarters. Watching them from a safe distance is all well and good, but up close and personal could be quite frightening to a dog. We got our answer one day at Cheddleton station. They were holding one of their special *Thomas the Tank Engine* days, so all the trains would be decked out with faces from the famous storybooks. The question was: would Beans be impressed by Thomas?

We'd chosen a walk away from our usual stomping ground of the Peak District, which very handily passed the steam railway centre. It was worth a detour – or so we thought – to see the trains in action, but if we thought Beans was going to be thrilled with the idea then we were very much mistaken.

A train was just about to depart as we walked onto the platform, Thomas' colourful smiling face adorning the front of its engine. People were milling about, carriage doors shutting and guards shouting. Beans seemed a little uneasy, but that wasn't too surprising, given the noise and crowds. Suddenly, the train's whistle blew and a loud blast of steam was released. It made me jump, but Beans' reaction was even more unexpected.

I have never left a railway station so fast in my life. The moment the whistle blew Beans bolted from the platform like a sprinter off a starting block as I – attached to her lead – attempted to keep up. She couldn't get away quick enough. People waiting on the platform jumped out of the way as Beans forced her way through them, panting with fear. I noticed that most people were grinning as I hurtled past, shouting my apologies. I suppose it added a bit more fun to the proceedings.

Perhaps I should have realised that being so close to a train might well have ended the way it did. The whistle was loud enough to me, so what it must have been like to Beans, with her enhanced hearing, I can only imagine. Knowing Beans' interest in all things locomotive, I couldn't help but feel a little sad at seeing her reaction, but it didn't put her off watching them – from a distance.

Our Caring Dog

A year after moving into our new home it felt that at last we had room to breathe, after the claustrophobia of a small cottage. All those extra belongings had long found homes; we had some new furniture and started some re-decorating. There was space for Jan to do her painting and space for me to write my articles and sort my photographs. There was space around us too; countryside within easy walking distance and a garden to relax in. It's a bit of a cliché, but it really felt like a fresh start for us.

We'd already found the best local dog-walking routes not long after moving in. The canal towpath was literally yards away and following it in either direction brought us to some nice rural countryside. The bridleway led past the local golf club towards Astbury, one of the most attractive Cheshire villages, returning over fields and through woods back to the canal. We could walk up to Mow Cop; a mock castle folly, overlooking the Cheshire Plain on one side and the Staffordshire Moorlands on the other. Best of all, we could, if we wanted, walk to Bosley Cloud without using the car; a good seven mile walk – right from our front door. We could even see it from our back window.

It would be unfair to say we didn't have equally nice places to go to when we lived in Macclesfield; it's just that they weren't quite as accessible. Riverside Park was within easy walking distance, but that was it. Everywhere else involved the car. Now we could walk without taking the car at all, but that would mean abandoning the Peak District – something we could never do – so we still motored off to favourite Peak haunts on Sundays.

We discovered new places we'd never been to before as well. Gun Moor, Brereton Heath, Biddulph Country Park and Tittesworth all became favourite dog walking spots. Beans was delighted with all these new areas to explore. Even more agreeable was being able to trot out the back door for a pee. They say that bitch urine turns grass brown, but luckily for us Beans' didn't; although quite what was different about her pee to other dogs is perhaps a scientific mystery. Despite constant squats by Beans, our lawn remained nice and green. In fact, the grass grew longer in those places where she peed regularly, so there's another mystery. Perhaps I should have bottled her pee and sold it as lawn-restorer – another entrepreneurial opportunity missed. Beans' pee could have been famous; a gardening phenomenon. Just imagine: self-made millionaires – from selling bottled dog pee.

History is full of stories of dogs' devotion to their human masters. The story of *Greyfriars Bobby* is probably the most well known. Bobby was a Skye terrier who lived in nineteenth century Edinburgh with his policeman owner, John Gray. When Gray died, Bobby kept a fourteen year vigil by his beloved master's grave in Greyfriars Churchyard, refusing all attempts to move him. Eventually he was befriended by the keeper, James Brown, who discovered Bobby's talents at rat catching. Bobby became a much-loved Victorian celebrity and after he died, a statue was erected in his honour, near to where he lived. He lies somewhere in Greyfriars Churchyard near the master he loved. A memorial tells his story.

Jan and I had always been well aware of our pets' capacity to recognise when we weren't well, or feeling sad. Both Judy and Benji used to sit on my bed when I was sick and Jan's cat, Crockett, always knew when she was feeling down, coming to sit with her. There's a bond between people and their pets that is almost supernatural. We could feel this with Beans.

I remember reading about a little boy who escaped the dreadful carnage of the Allied bombing of Hamburg in 1943, reaching the Danish border clutching a suitcase, which contained the dead bodies of his little sister - and his pet rabbit. In the midst of such appalling violence he'd gathered up the two things he cared about most. Whatever the cynics may say; pets matter to us.

One Saturday afternoon in September, almost a year after we had moved to our new home, we had a phone call from Bob; Rita had been taken ill. As Jan came off the phone, the look on her face told me this was serious.

'What's happened?' I asked.

'Mum's had a brain haemorrhage,' she replied, her voice shaking, 'she's unconscious in intensive care at Macclesfield hospital.'

Apparently she'd had a bad headache for a couple of days, but on the Saturday morning, things had taken a turn for the worse and the ambulance had been called. A scan soon revealed a bleed in her brain.

'We'd better get over there,' I said, hugging Jan.

'No, you stay here and look after Beans, I'll be okay,' she insisted. I knew she obviously wasn't okay.

As she drove off, several minutes later, I looked down at Beans; she was standing by the door, squeaking; she knew there was something wrong. Why had Jan gone so suddenly? This wasn't right.

I found myself talking to her: 'It's alright Beanie,' I said, stroking her head, 'everything will be okay.' After a while, she moved away from the door and settled down.

A few hours later I noticed Beans starting to get agitated, crying softly and looking up at the door or the front window, as if there was something there. I wondered whether Jan was back from hospital, but there was no car on the drive. Beans was restless and acting as if someone had arrived.

'There's nobody there,' I said, as if she would understand.

About ten minutes later Beans repeated this performance, but this time there was someone there. Jan was home. I hadn't heard the car, but Beans had. It was uncanny, but she'd obviously known Jan was nearly home, although she couldn't possibly have heard the car. You can cover a fair distance in ten minutes drive, so some unknown sense that we can only imagine had told Beans that Jan wasn't far away. Beans had most probably acted like this before, but we just hadn't been aware of it. From then on, every time one of us went out without the other, she did the same thing, becoming unsettled and pacing, several minutes before we arrived home. I've heard that dogs can see and sense things that we can't and I wouldn't disagree with that.

Beans greeted Jan in her usual way, jumping up, squeaking madly and running to find the nearest toy as a welcome home present. Jan did her best to reciprocate, but her red eyes were telling me things were not looking good. She walked over to her armchair and sank into it. I asked her what the prognosis was.

'She's being transferred to the Manchester Royal Infirmary tomorrow,' Jan replied, 'they're going to have to operate as soon as possible.' She burst into tears.

Beans walked over to her and immediately rested her head on Jan's knee. I followed, and the two of us did our best to comfort her.

Although Rita had survived the initial haemorrhage, she was in a critical condition, her only hope of survival being a major operation to remove the bleed, a process which in itself was incredibly risky. It was going to be touch and go.

Jan barely moved from her chair until it was time for bed. Every now and again she would start crying as the enormity of the situation overcame her. She was facing losing her mother and there was little I could do or say to her, other than to hold her and say that everything would be okay. I felt helpless.

Beans kept up her vigil at Jan's side for most of the evening, breaking only to eat her meal. As she calmly sat by Jan's side, we realised what a wonderful dog we had. This is the special bond that exists between dogs and their owners that non dog owners will never experience, or, perhaps, understand – the fact that a completely different species is capable of sensing the feelings of another.

We phoned into work the next day, told them what had happened and that we weren't coming in. That afternoon we headed for Manchester with Bob.

The doctors laid everything before us at the hospital. Rita was stable and the operation was scheduled for the next day. They told us that although she was undoubtedly in a critical condition, she was lucky. Very few people survive a brain haemorrhage. Many are usually dead within minutes. The fact that she was still holding on, nearly two days later, was hopeful. All we could do now was put our trust in the skills of the surgeon.

There was no point staying off work the next day, although it was hard to concentrate. All we could do was wait for the call to say the operation was over. Just before lunch Jan phoned me to say Rita was out of theatre and that the operation had been a success. That was one obstacle cleared, but we were not out of the woods yet.

At the hospital later that evening the doctor put us in the picture. They had successfully removed the bleed, but the operation had unavoidably caused a stroke, which meant Rita was going to be permanently disabled. Her speech was fine, although she would need support for walking. Her left arm was severely incapacitated which meant that everyday tasks were going to be very difficult. It was going to be one step at a time.

Following the operation, Rita was transferred to the rehabilitation unit at Macclesfield Hospital. It wasn't going to be a quick recovery. Day after day of just lying in bed was making her depressed, so when the nurses finally told her she could start moving about, nothing was going to stop her. If there was one thing Rita had in abundance it was stubborn determination, so nothing was going to stop her heading for the little covered area outside the unit.

At least there she could make friends with the other patients, have a chat and enjoy the sunshine. When we told her that Beans would be allowed to visit – as long as we didn't bring her on the ward – her face lit up. This was just what the doctor ordered and Beans was the ideal tonic.

Rita and the other patients looked forward to Beans' visits and I'm sure the interaction with an animal helped them all recover quicker. The smiling faces as they stroked and petted Beans said it all.

After a few more weeks of intensive physiotherapy – and Beans' regular welfare visits – Rita came home. It was now a case of getting used to various bits of apparatus to help her lead as normal a life as possible.

It took some time, but gradually she learned to work around this new way of life. Despite the disabilities, she knew she had been lucky to come through such a traumatic event.

Making Friends

We always felt bad about it, but since the move we'd had no choice but to leave Beans on her own every day while we went to work. Unless one of us could again find a job within walking distance – or work at home – there was little else we could do. It would also be unfair to leave her with Bob and Rita. They now had enough to cope with.

Strangers coming into the house had always unnerved her, so we decided against getting a dog-walker. Anyone coming into the house was met with much barking and a certain amount of mistrust, although thankfully she never bit anyone. It would be too unsettling to introduce another person into her life, but we were determined that she would not be neglected.

After her morning walk with me, she had to wait until we came home from work for the main walk of the day, but we always ensured it was a good long one, followed by another before bed. It was rare for us to come home to wet (or soiled) carpets. Beans would have a little water after her breakfast, do all her bodily functions on her morning walk and then shut down – sleep – for the rest of the day. In fact, if I ever had a day off with her, she spent most of the day asleep anyway, apart from when I took her out for her walk. It didn't make leaving her every day any better, but at least we knew she wouldn't want to go out every few minutes. Provided we gave her some of her favourite 'leaving snacks' before we left for the day, we felt she was okay.

She knew those nice chewy sticks meant we were coming back.

Here's the deal: make sure I'm well stocked with lots of nice doggie snacks before you go, and I'll forgive you for leaving me. Forget the snacks and I'll pee all over your carpet – or worse.

Of course, it wasn't an ideal situation, but then again neither is being confined in a rescue kennels. I know plenty of people who don't work, own dogs and the animals never see anything but the back garden, so which is worse? Whatever your situation, you owe it to the dog to give it the exercise it deserves. Anything less and why bother having a dog at all? To the dog experts who say those who work shouldn't have dogs; I would say that for many people dogs are valuable companions. They provide a focus; something to love and care for throughout its life. An animal that is totally dependent on you for water, food, exercise and healthcare. Dogs are good for us as well. What could be better after a day's work than a good long walk in the countryside with your four-legged friend? It beats a sweaty gym any day.

Beans was very well house-trained and any accidents she ever had could be counted on one hand, but when they happened, you had to admire her attempts to minimise the damage. We put newspaper down in the kitchen just in case she needed to 'go,' but the paper was invariably unused when we got home. We never chastised her for any accidents; that would have been unfair. Even when we let her in the garden, after all her enthusiastic greetings, she'd spend several minutes sniffing, before having a pee – so she wasn't exactly desperate. It was what she did in the bathroom upstairs that showed us what an intelligent dog she really was.

Coming home one evening we opened the door to be greeted by a barking wagging Beans – and an appalling smell. Preliminary searches downstairs revealed nothing. The newspaper in the kitchen was undisturbed and there was nothing nasty lurking in some hidden recess, but that smell wasn't going away.

Trying to blot out what horror could possibly be waiting for me, I made my way upstairs. The smell was getting stronger. I checked both the bedrooms – clear; I checked the box room – clear; that just left the bathroom. I peered around the half-open door with a certain amount of trepidation, although why, I don't know. Whatever it was, it was hardly going to leap out and bite me.

Next to the toilet bowl, as near as she'd been able to get, Beans had left a deposit on the carpet. Something she'd eaten that morning – probably grabbed off the pavement – had gone rapidly through her. Short of actually sitting on the toilet, which she obviously couldn't do, she'd tried to minimise the damage in the only way she knew. She must have realised this was the place humans go and had made a determined effort to do the same herself. How could anyone be cross with her?

In that year since leaving Macclesfield Beans had got to know a whole new circle of doggy friends, as well as the ones she still knew in Wilmslow. That didn't mean that her friends in Wilmslow would be neglected, because we still visited regularly.

Over the years she'd gathered quite a group of canine chums around her, who she'd meet on her walks. Not only were the dogs all friends, but friendships had been struck up with their owners. That is one of the good things about dog-walking; it is a very social activity. You can pass people in the street, or even in your own neighbourhood, and never say a word, but a put dog into the equation and it's a different story.

If the dogs are intent on hating each other, then sometimes things can be different. I've noticed that some people take it very personally if your dog has a go at theirs, scowling at you as if it's your fault. Dogs will be dogs and if one takes against the other, there's little you can do, other than to make sure the dog is always on a lead. Even more bizarre are those people who never have their dog on a lead and wonder why it gets barked at or attacked when it charges up to some poor unsuspecting pooch trotting along on a lead.

Luckily, there was very little trouble when we took Beans out. Everyone was very well behaved. These friendships had been built up over nearly six years and, though Daisy and Delta were her favourites, there were several other dogs who later joined her little circle of friends. There was friendly Mr Thomas, with Badger, his faithful Jack Russell; Peter, the Boxer; Ears, the deaf Cocker Spaniel and, of course, the mystery cat who tagged along for the walk. These were just the Wilmslow dogs, so when she moved to Congleton, the circle grew even bigger. To it were added: Toby, the Miniature Schnauzer; Jack, the Border Collie; Ben, the Alsatian, and another Boxer, whose name I cannot remember.

The Boxer's owner liked to take the dog for a walk quite late at night, not long after we'd gone to bed. We always knew when the dog was walking past, even with the windows closed, because Beans' ultra-sensitive hearing picked up the jingle of his collar as he walked past. Sometimes, as I lay there, on the verge of sleep, Beans, who often slept beside our bed, would start growling very quietly. At first I thought we had an intruder, but then as I listened for the slightest sound, I would hear the familiar jingling of the collar. If I said the word 'boxer' she'd growl a little louder. I found this nightly routine strangely comforting. It was also sleep-inducing, because my hand was usually dangling down at the side of the bed, stroking Beans as she lay there, growling softly.

Very soon, sleep would overcome me.

I'm certain that Beans' excellent hearing saved us from being burgled late one night. Being violently woken from sleep by a barking dog is not the most pleasant of experiences, but you can bet that when a dog does this, there is something afoot.

So as I lay there with my heart pounding, scrabbling for the light switch in the early hours of one Saturday morning, I hoped that whoever was creeping around outside had been scared off. This was not Beans' usual barking; it had more of a sense of urgency and fear about it.

With the light on, I wondered what to do next. Beans was downstairs, still growling and giving short, sharp barks. By now, the barking had woken Jan.

'What's the matter?' she muttered.

'I think Beans has heard something outside,' I replied, getting out of bed.

'Where are you going?'

'Downstairs to switch the lights on. If there's someone out there it might scare them off,' I said nervously.

With any luck Beans' barking would have been enough to see the prowler off, but I needed to make sure there were no signs of tampered locks or broken windows. Beans had now come upstairs and I could see she was on full alert. Every now and then her ears would prick up and she'd growl, turning to look in the direction of the landing window.

'What's up Beanie?' I said, stroking her head to try and calm her.

I walked onto the landing, switched the lights on and headed into the back bedroom. Peering out into the night, I could see nothing lurking in the garden, even with the light provided by the nearby street lamp.

Beans followed me downstairs into the living room, my faithful dog ready to protect me from danger. Turning the kitchen light on, I stood there for a few minutes listening for any sounds outside. There was nothing. Satisfied that everything was okay, I went back to bed. Sleep, however, was a long time coming. I lay awake for ages listening for the slightest sound, before sleep overcame me. Beans had stopped her growling and pacing too, although she spent the rest of the night by the side of the bed.

Next morning, as I took Beans out for her first walk of the day, I looked down near the back door. There on the ground was a cigarette end. As I walked around the front of the house, there was another by the garage door. Neither of us smokes, so the butts must have belonged to the midnight prowler. I praised Beans for saving us from a potential break-in.

'You clever girl,' I said, giving her a hug.

She jumped up at me, her tail wagging enthusiastically. She'd done a good job.

On the way back, I bumped into my neighbour, Andy, out walking his own dog.

'Have you heard about John and Margaret across the road?' he asked me.

'No, what's happened?' I replied.

'Their shed was broken into last night. They've had a few things stolen.'

Andy said he'd been woken in the early hours by the sound of a dog barking in the distance, and then saw the police arriving sometime later. John had told him the thieves had tried to force the back door, but gave up when he put the lights on.

As I told Andy it was Beans he'd probably heard, I realised what a lucky escape we'd had. The thief, put off by her barking, had gone over the road to take his chances there – with more success.

Not long after the night prowler incident, we rather foolishly allowed a burglar alarm salesman into the house. He went to great lengths to tell us how there had been a whole spate of burglaries in our area recently, and that we really should purchase one of his expensive alarms. Having heard about the break-ins from Tony, the salesman was doing a good job on me. I was on the verge of signing on the dotted line, but something wasn't quite right. The way he talked, it was if every house in the neighbourhood had been burgled, which seemed a tad exaggerated. The local papers weren't exactly full of reports of house break-ins and neither did I see police cars around that often. This chap was trying to scare us into buying an alarm.

'You must have read about all the break-ins around here in the local press,' he asked. I could tell he was getting desperate.

'Can't say that I have,' I said. Sure, we read about the odd one, but this sounded like there was a whole army of burglars prowling the streets of Congleton.

Once I came round to the fact that we were about to spend too much money, I lost all interest in his spiel, which seemed to be going on and on. I wanted him to leave. In an effort to get rid of him, we told him we couldn't afford his prices and we'd have to shop around. Surprisingly, it did the trick and he went on his merry way.

In the end, we decided that we already had the best alarm system there was: Beans. She'd proved highly effective in the field of burglar deterrent, and, best of all, she didn't require lots of wires, security codes and hire purchase agreements.

In The Limelight Again

Now that we were settled into our new home, I'd started to resume my efforts at getting my photographs published. I'd had a fair bit of success before we moved, but what with my health problems and then the house move; I'd lost interest. The odd publication kept the adrenaline going, but I seemed to lack motivation.

There was no excuse now though. I had space to organise all my files, photographs, books and stationery and my typewriter now had a permanent base. It was time to start taking some more saleable pictures. Even though it wasn't the more dramatic scenery of the Peak District, the Cheshire countryside surrounding our home had an awful lot to offer. I felt inspired again.

My stock of local photographs gradually started to build up. There was the beautiful maple tree in our front garden, that looked glorious in its autumn colours; the lovely view of Bosley Cloud from the canal; the little wood near the golf course, that came alive with bluebells in May; the heath at Brereton and the woodland walks at Biddulph Country Park. Walking through the woods on the golf course one sunny May afternoon, I stopped to photograph some bluebells, backlit by the low sun. Beans waited patiently as I composed the shot, sitting down once she realised I was going to be a while. Patience was something she had in abundance, never barking or whining for me to move on.

I remember taking her for a walk on one very cold, but sunny November afternoon to take some photographs of one of my favourite Peak District areas: Wildboarclough.

My plan was to photograph the Clough in all its autumn glory, with the hill of Shutlingsloe as the perfect backdrop; a shot I'd been planning for some time. I parked the car on the road that heads down to Wildboarclough, attached Beans to her lead and we followed the path up Birchenough Hill. It's only a short climb before arguably one of the best views in the Peak District opens up. Sometimes the views don't come without hard work and sweat, but this one was perfect for an afternoon outing.

Even though I was wrapped up well, the wind was still cutting through me. I could have done without it. Even with the camera on a tripod there was still the risk of an unsharp photograph. Beans was trotting alongside me, eyes half shut against the wind. Every now and then a sheep trail would distract her and take her mind off the cold. The sheep were nowhere to be seen, which was just as well. I didn't want Beans disappearing across the moors while I was distracted by shutter speeds and apertures.

Reaching the spot I'd selected on a previous visit, I dumped all my gear and found a secure place to tie Beans to on a nearby fence. The view was simply perfect. The low afternoon sun was bathing everything in a rich light, the sky was beautifully clear and sharp with just a few clouds and the autumn hues couldn't have been better. It was one of those days when it felt good to be alive. Just to stand and look at it was enough, but I had work to do if I wanted to commit this memory to film.

The cold made me work fast and before long I'd gone through a whole roll of film. I checked on Beans every now and then, but she just sat there patiently, shivering a little, probably wondering why we couldn't just go off looking for rabbits or sheep.

'Nearly finished,' I shouted to her, at which point her ears pricked up and she tilted her head to one side; something she only normally did if I mentioned some of the words in her vocabulary: cat, bunnies, squirrels, pheasants or funny birds. I think it was her way of indicating that she would like a bit of a walk now please.

I needed a walk myself now, just to warm up and get the blood flowing, so I packed everything away and we carried on a little further up the hill. The sun, which only a short while ago had lit the rocks providing my foreground interest, was sinking ever lower in the sky. The top of Shutlingsloe was soon in shadow, but over to the right, Shining Tor, Cheshire's highest point at 1,834 feet, was still a beautiful golden colour; the heather moors around it, a carpet of russet. It was time to head for home.

The photographs were everything I'd hoped for and I even managed to sell a few. The nicest surprise was when one shot was runner-up in a photography competition staged at The Outdoors Show held in Birmingham's NEC. The organisers had enlarged and displayed the photograph beautifully, together with a short caption I'd written to accompany it.

When the print was eventually returned, I had it professionally mounted and framed. It still hangs on our wall, a reminder of a beautiful autumn afternoon spent in one of my favourite places. When I look at it now, I can still picture Beans sitting there, just out of shot. I always wish I'd included her in one of the shots, perhaps looking over towards Shutlingsloe, her coat matching those autumn colours.

Now that I was back in photography mode, everything started to fall into place again. Jan and Beans started appearing in the walking magazines regularly and I found picture buyers in other areas too. My work appeared on postcards; calendars; the front of a walking book and even in a glossy brochure for a house builder.

This was all very exciting and it got even better when my two models appeared once more on the front of *Country Walking*. This time it was a winter scene, taken near Kinder Scout on one of those brilliantly clear days that are only found at that time of the year. There was a light covering of snow on the ground and the sky was a deep blue with cotton wool clouds. It was also very muddy. We'd walked over from a place called Brown Knoll, heading towards Kinder Low End where the path meets a stony track. Heading left would take you eventually to Hayfield, while taking the right would take you steeply down towards Edale; a track known as Jacob's Ladder. The latter was going to be our route, but first there were some photographs to take.

Having just walked through acres of some of the Peak District's finest mud, Beans was not exactly what you might call in pristine condition. Great clumps of matted fur, mud and peat hung from her and she looked like she was wearing black boots. But this was not studio, front cover of *Vogue* stuff, it was rugged outdoor material. This was Beans in her element – covered in mud in 'funny bird' country. I set up the shot with the plateau of Kinder Scout in the background, the path leading into the scene – and my models – with that beautiful blue sky crowning the whole thing. I was practically visualising it on the magazine's cover, the sky adorned with the masthead.

Jan was looking towards the plateau, but Beans was standing side on, looking straight at me. The low winter sun turned her coat almost gold in colour. It was perfect.

The magazine thought so too. The picture appeared on the front cover the following January, Beans looking resplendent in her golden, mud encrusted coat. It remains my favourite photograph from our hiking days, bringing to life memories of tramping through mud, enjoying flasks of hot coffee or chocolate and faces glowing with the cold.

Shortly after the photograph appeared on the front cover, another magazine used it on their editorial page. It seemed that where pictures containing Jan and Beans were concerned, I couldn't go wrong. They appeared numerous times inside magazines and even on promotional tourism leaflets and advertisements. The very first cover shot, taken on the Windgather Rocks, put in another appearance; this time on the front of a leaflet depicting the beautiful East Cheshire countryside. It felt good to see my own pictures being used to advertise an area of the country I loved. Things were definitely on a roll. Jan and Beans were appearing so often in various publications that people started asking if they'd started to demand modelling fees.

Beans decided that it was time to use her new-found fame and celebrity status for the benefit of her fellow canine friends. It was all well and good being the centre of attention, with your face gracing the pages of magazines, but Beans didn't want all this going to her head. Lots of less fortunate dogs out there needed her help.

We were enjoying a walk we'd done many times, following the path up William Clough to Kinder Scout. This walk never fails to delight with its blend of stunning views, wild moorland, clear streams and tumbling waterfalls. The route climbs to arguably one of the finest views in the Peak District where the Kinder plateau is arranged in a natural amphitheatre around the Kinder Reservoir. The calls of grouse and golden plover fill the air and it is hard to imagine that only 75 years ago such sights and sounds were only for a privileged few; the gamekeepers and grouse-shooters. Thanks to those 'trespassers' of 1932, who'd trodden this same path, Jan, Beans and I – plus countless others – were able to walk unhindered to enjoy such fine scenery.

Ours was a beautiful, hot sunny day and the climb up William Clough following the stream was punctuated by plenty of stops to top up on water. Jan and Beans had stopped just ahead of me, where the stream became a little waterfall. Beans was standing facing me, her pink tongue flopping out of her mouth as she panted. Jan was facing the other way, about to carry on climbing. With the plateau in the background and a deep blue sky overhead, it was a perfect shot.

'Can you stay there?' I shouted to Jan, 'I've got a cracking shot lined up.'

My willing models duly stayed where they were, I rattled off a few shots on my trusty little pocket camera and we carried on to enjoy a great day on Kinder Scout.

The photograph turned out well. There was plenty of colour and Beans looked like a dog who was enjoying herself. Even the bright red of her extending lead looked good in the photograph.

I sent it off expectantly to *Country Walking,* wondering whether it would grace their cover again. Some months later the postman dropped the by now familiar magazine-sized envelope through my letterbox. I eagerly opened it. There was nothing on the front cover. That was slightly disappointing, but never mind, what was inside the magazine? I flicked through the pages and had almost reached the end, thinking they'd sent me a copy by mistake, because I'd found nothing of mine. When I reached page 95 my fears were allayed – there they both were, on that sunny day in William Clough. The magazine had chosen the picture to illustrate a short piece advertising sponsored dog walks in aid of the PDSA – The People's Dispensary for Sick Animals. The charity provides free veterinary care for people who otherwise couldn't afford it, and was celebrating its 80th anniversary that year.

The PDSA is a charity I always try and support, because of the valuable work they do. Many pet owners are elderly or have limited means, so when their animals are sick or injured they are suddenly faced with bills for treatment that they simply cannot afford, which is where the charity steps in. I have always believed that pets enrich the lives of people in so many ways, so why should they be deprived of such valuable companionship for the sake of a vet's bill?

Many years ago my dog Benji was hit by a car as he chased a squirrel onto a main road. I wasn't there when it happened, but mum told me of the awful screams of pain as he lay there with a shattered leg. Luckily, the vet was able to save his leg after many weeks of treatment, although Benji was left with permanent stiffness and minus one of his toes. The eventual bill came to about £500. Although Benji wasn't insured, we were able to pay the bill and I remember thinking that even if finding the money had been a problem we would somehow have scraped it together. A pet deserves nothing less.

So when I saw my photograph on the page, I felt happy that Beans in her own small way had helped both people and animals. She hadn't made the front cover that time, but I'm sure her happy face and lolling tongue had inspired people to step out to help a worthwhile cause.

Memories

Long before I met Jan, the Peak District had been a feature in my life. Dad took us all off for long walks at the weekend, invariably to places that I would be re-acquainted with when I introduced Jan, and then Beans, to this beautiful area.

Dad had grown up on the fringes of the Peak, so knew many of the places intimately, long before the area became the country's first National Park. He knew the Goyt Valley long before it was flooded to make way for the Errwood and Fernilee reservoirs. Wildboarclough, Lathkill Dale, Millers Dale and the Roaches were soon added to my store of favourite Peak District places. Even before I got my first pair of boots, the Peak had always been in the background somewhere. Whether it was gazing at Shutlingsloe from granddad's kitchen window with his old binoculars, or passing the imposing-looking Ramshaw Rocks and Hen Cloud on the way to Sunday lunch at The Three Horseshoes Inn, I had a longing to explore these areas, but, perhaps because I had other interests, they remained strangely elusive until I stepped into my first pair of walking boots.

Back in the early 1970s, spending my days at granddad's homely bungalow in Gawsworth, during the long school summer holidays, Shutlingsloe, a distinctive and inviting-looking hill above Wildboarclough, didn't even have a legal public right-of-way up it; that had to wait until 1978. So the hill that had fascinated me for years was even more out of bounds than I could have imagined.

Granddad however, had a particular spot of his own to show me - and that did have a path up it: The Cloud, at Bosley, near Congleton. We drove out there one summer's day in his lovely big old *Wolseley,* and took the path the short distance to the summit. From there I was treated to my first view of the Cheshire Plain where it meets the foothills of the Pennines. Little did I realise back then how much the Cloud would come to feature in my life years later.

It would be nearly twelve years before I stood on its summit again, this time with Jan. Granddad, who had taken me there for the first time all those years before, died a year later.

People will always have their favourite places. For some, it is an entire country or just a part of it; others may have a special place on their doorstep – a park, or a favourite walk; while some have a special connection with a particular town or village.

Whatever that place is doesn't matter; what is important is that sense of belonging; a feeling that there is always somewhere familiar to come back to. For us, the Cloud became that place. The climb up it – although not long – provided exercise and it was always the first prominent landmark visible after we'd turned off the motorway returning from a holiday. I even made it the subject of a photo-essay I had published.

It seemed that Jan and I were somehow connected by it. During the war Rita went to stay at a nearby farm. She remembered standing on the Cloud in the evening and seeing an eerie glow towards the north. It was the city of Manchester, ablaze following a bombing attack. Years later, Jan and her mum would go up the Cloud to pick bilberries. Whether our paths ever crossed when I was up there with granddad, I'll never know.

From our early walks up the Cloud we spread our wings further out into the hills and dales of the Peak District. Before long it became difficult to pick a favourite place because we had a whole list of them. Some places, such as Gun Moor, we discovered for the first time and they became regular dog-walking spots. Gun Moor became a special photography location for me too. It wasn't far to get to and the views from it were good in every direction. Much to Beans' delight, it also had a resident population of grouse. Sadly, the grouse disappeared from the moor, though I never discovered why this was so. Perhaps they decided that it was time to head for somewhere bigger, now that

Beans had disturbed their peace. Mind you, she wasn't the only dog to be found on the moor, so there must have been a more scientific reason for their absence. Whatever the explanation, it seemed that one minute they were there, the next not.

We soon realised that the Cloud had something else to offer Beans, apart from lots of heather to run through and woods to play in. From the top there is an excellent view of the railway viaduct far below. Trains pass over it before coming into Congleton station, disappearing into a cutting just before the station approach. This fact did not evade Beans for very long and she was soon to be found standing on the summit rocks, with the wind in her face, watching the trains as they passed over the viaduct. It seemed she just liked to stand at this spot whether there were any trains passing or not, just surveying her surroundings. This reverie would, however, be occasionally broken if something more interesting warranted her attention. It was usually in the form of food and peoples' picnics.

On one occasion a family had set up camp on the rocks where she liked to stand and were happily enjoying a picnic. Never one to miss an opportunity, Beans took full advantage of the situation. Using her cutest 'pulling power' she casually – but systematically – moved from person to person, gratefully accepting whatever tasty morsels came her way. The fact that all the children were holding bags of crisps, made the entire operation even more enjoyable. Beans loved the odd crisp.

We made every effort to try and stop this intrusion by our dog, but in truth nobody seemed to mind. Children were attracted to Beans as if by a magnet. Her gentle nature coupled with the fact that she didn't take fingers along with the food being offered, was a winning combination. Each offering was gently removed and devoured, before she moved on to the next willing victim; all to the accompaniment of lots of head-stroking and nice comments – what more could a dog want?

If we thought Beans' need to chase trains was confined to the park when we lived in Macclesfield, we were very much mistaken.

Bosley Cloud was one of the few places where we could release Beans from her lead to let her run free, without the worry of sheep disturbance. One day, as we neared the top, her ears suddenly pricked up – she'd spotted a train through the trees, crossing the viaduct. It was heading in the Macclesfield direction.

She went from a sedate trot to a sprint before we even had time to grab her, hurtling down the side of the Cloud in a mad pursuit of the train. Thankfully, she'd never felt the need to do this when watching them from the top, which was just as well, because between her and the train was nothing but a steep drop of several hundred feet.

Quite what she was hoping to achieve, considering the train was at least half a mile away, was anybody's guess. She'd no chance of catching it, but that wasn't the point; the fun was in the chase.

I ran after her, shouting for her to come back. I didn't want her ending up at the road only to be side-tracked by sheep in the fields. Once a dog has its mind set on something, nothing will deter it until it decides to come back. The distant train was the very least of my worries. What was worrying me was the nightmare scenario of panicking sheep being scattered in all directions by Beans.

Then I realised I'd lost her to the heather and bracken.

But I needn't have panicked. After a few minutes (it seemed longer) she re-appeared on the path above, panting and breathless.

'Well that's another one seen off,' you could almost imagine her saying.

For as long as I can remember, castles have fascinated me. Family holidays to Wales – which is blessed with some fine examples – were not complete unless I'd pestered dad to take me to at least one during the holiday. So we would walk the towers and battlements of such places as *Beaumaris, Caernarfon* or *Criccieth.* Luckily, dad was as keen as me to see these magnificent 700-year old structures, so mum and my sister Pam just had to indulge us.

I could never have imagined, some twenty five years later, owning a dog who would share this interest with me. We knew already that Beans had a very inquisitive nature and a strong need to explore. Show her a cave and she had to enter it; pass a footbridge and she had to cross it – even if we weren't going in that direction. When she discovered the delights of rabbit burrows at nearby Brereton Heath, she was in her element. Every burrow had to be carefully and meticulously checked for signs of its occupants.

Our walks on the heath took ages as she inspected each one in the vain – but always hopeful – chance of spotting a rabbit. I'm sure word got round the local rabbit population pretty quickly that Beans was on the prowl, but it didn't stop her trying. It was as if she expected to find a bunny at each entrance, standing there, waiting to ask her in for a nice cup of tea.

Then there was the digging. This activity was only reserved for certain burrows where she felt there was a good chance of disturbing the occupants. Once she'd selected the most promising looking burrow she set to work, scooping out great clods of earth as if her life depended on it. It wasn't a very good idea to stand behind her – unless you didn't mind being showered with soil.

Beans' preoccupation with trying to find rabbits blinded her to the fact that she was not the size of a little Jack Russell terrier, and that dogs of her size were not meant to go down holes. The scent of the poor bunnies, cowering deep within their burrows, was simply irresistible, and she quite forgot about the small matter of getting wedged. It was bound to happen sooner or later. When it did, she had to suffer the indignity of being hauled out by her rear end. There was no way she'd ever reach the rabbits – and we weren't about to let her either – but she had a lot of fun trying.

Caves were a different matter altogether. It was impossible for us to pass one unless she'd thoroughly investigated it. If we tried to move on she would dig her claws in and refuse to move; a bit like a child when it can't get its own way. Quite what she expected to find in them who knows. Giant bunnies maybe? A strange species of cave-dwelling grouse, or perhaps even a train?

Several caves can be found along Dovedale or Lathkill Dale. Some are little more than fissures in the rocks, with dead ends; others are more elaborate affairs that a dog – or a human – could get lost in. We didn't want the embarrassment of calling out a team of pot-holers to rescue our cave-dwelling dog, so despite the fact that she probably would have loved to venture to the centre of the earth, she was firmly attached to her lead. The connection between Beans' subterranean interests and castles didn't become obvious until she was taken on her first visit to one.

Beeston, in Cheshire, is our nearest castle, standing in a superb position atop the Peckforton Hills, towering over the Cheshire Plain. It is real film location stuff, although the acting honours go to its neighbour, Peckforton, a replica twelfth-century castle, built by wealthy Victorians, which provided the location for a Robin Hood movie. Beeston was built in the thirteenth-century by the earl of Chester to protect the English border. Its almost impregnable position held out until the English Civil War, when the Parliamentarians captured it from the Royalists. Three hundred odd years later it was about to be besieged by Beans, although she had nothing more arduous to do than climb the steep path up to it, cross the elegant bridge, pass through the Inner Bailey and then she was within the castle walls – or rather, what was left of them.

Despite the castle's ruinous condition, the remains were well preserved, so there was still much to see and explore. Beans was going to make sure she covered every inch and we were certainly going to get our money's worth. First stop was the view from the wall as we made our way in. She perched her paws on the wall, surveying the splendid view over Cheshire. Satisfied with that, she headed over to the remains of the castle's well and peered down into the blackness – not much of interest there. We did the obligatory throwing a stone down to see how long it took to hit the bottom, and then it was off to check out one of the towers. Or rather it would have been, if Beans hadn't decided to stop at every nook and cranny on the way. Any hole in the battlements had to be inspected; every blocked up stairway and passageway; if it looked remotely like a cave it was duly given the Beans treatment. She was enjoying herself and then some.

The Beans storming party did eventually reach the tower, passing through the low entrance into the gloomy interior. Once satisfied that every hideout had been checked for the enemy, Beans and her men – well, man and a woman – moved on to clear the rest of the castle of enemy troops.

Along the way the party paused to admire the views towards Peckforton and the Shropshire Union Canal;

but this was no time for dawdling – there was more to investigate and Beans was determined to do a thorough job. Her orders were to ensure that none of the enemy should be allowed to escape. All possible hiding places should be checked, and checked again if necessary. Any fugitives discovered skulking in the shadows were to be barked at furiously, relieved of any food they might have secreted about their persons – and then to be taken out and given a damned good licking. They were then to be freed – providing, of course, that they threw the odd stick for her.

We had a happy day at Beeston, made all the more enjoyable by Beans' continuing fascination with the world around her. Another of her adventures that would remain forever in our memory.

CHAPTER SIX

Mad Dogs and Englishmen

Connections

1997 was memorable for three events: it was the year we tried our first camping holiday – failing miserably at it – and also (more importantly) the year in which the country lost Diana, Princess of Wales, on that tragic night in Paris.

It was also the year when the night sky was enhanced by Comet Hale-Bopp. I remember taking Beans out for her night-time walks and then standing for ages on the doorstep gazing up at this amazing sight in the sky. We often stood there together just listening to the sounds of foxes or owls in the distance; Beans' ears pricking up at the unearthly sounds, her head tilting from side to side as she recognised the foxes' cries. Now, as well as the sounds, there was this nightly show in the sky, which held me fascinated for weeks.

As long as there were no late-night revellers walking past or silly boy-racers in cars to disturb the peace and quiet; I loved those special moments I spent with Beans. It was somehow calming and relaxing – the perfect bedtime nightcap.

The superstitious believe that comets are harbingers of doom or tragic events, but I never had those feelings when looking at Hale-Bopp. It was just a fantastic cosmic event that I'd never seen before. It made me feel like a mere grain of sand in the vast universe; but that was it. Then again, nobody could have imagined what was to happen later in the year. Our thoughts, as the year progressed, turned towards holidays rather than worries about comets and catastrophes.

The year before, we'd gone north of the border to Scotland again, to the Isle of Mull. The two weeks we spent on that stunning island will join the ranks of our all time favourite holidays. We climbed the island's highest mountain, Ben More; we crossed the short stretch of water to Iona, the Holy Isle of Saint Columba, where it is said lie the remains of forty-eight Kings of Scotland; we gazed at Golden Eagles and Otters and we took the boat on a beautifully sunny day to the Treshnish Islands and Staffa, famous for the incredible basalt rock columns known as Fingal's Cave. The composer Mendelssohn was so inspired by Staffa that he wrote his famous overture, *The Hebrides*. We'll never forget the moment our little boat approached Staffa, and this stirring piece of music was played over the loudspeaker.

After a holiday like that it was hard to know how to follow it. Our finances could do with a little relief, so we decided on the cheaper option of camping – this time in Pembrokeshire, South Wales. My only previous experience of camping was during my schooldays of the early 1970s, when I joined the annual school camp to North Wales. Try as I might to only concentrate on the good bits of the trip – and there were some – it was the unpleasant bits that seemed to have glued themselves to my memory. Sharing a tent with too many other people in the middle of a muddy field, with the nearest toilet a wet traipse some 50 yards away, was not my idea of fun – and if I'm honest I don't think it ever will be.

The after-meals washing-up routine is my worst memory of school camp. I remember something that resembled a large oil drum that was used as a sort of communal washing-up bowl, positioned near the exit to the canteen. It also had a daily 'oil-drum' monitor to look after it and ensure it was regularly filled with lots of lovely hot water and plenty of washing-up liquid. I wish I'd been given that job – I pride myself on my pot washing – because I don't recall seeing much evidence of any suds. What I did see was a slurry of over-used, foul-coloured water with a scum of nasties floating on its surface.

In true school fashion we would form an orderly queue for washing-up. For some reason I always seemed to be near the end of the queue, so by the time I reached the dreaded 'oil-drum' it had become a *Witches Cauldron* of unidentifiable ingredients. I'm surprised there weren't frogs' legs and newts' eyes bobbing around on the surface, in amongst the bits of vegetables and pieces of gristle. I would hurriedly dip my plate and utensils into this revolting slop of left-overs and then scurry off to the toilets to run them under the taps. Jan has always criticised me for the amount of washing-up liquid I use, leaving the sink overflowing with an excess quantity of suds, but it just might have something to do with that oil drum.

Jan had no previous experience of camping and mine was sufficiently far back in the past that I was prepared to give it another try. We picked our location, bought the tent and all the other paraphernalia and booked Beans in at Wilmslow for her holiday.

In fairness, had the weather been fine and sunny, our first camping holiday *might* have been okay, but the weather gods were not with us that year. The site couldn't have been better positioned, right on the stunning Pembrokeshire coast. It was June but it was *cold*; cold and very windy. Even on the days when the sun did shine it was still chilly. Then, on the second night, it started to rain.

It hadn't taken us long to realise that we should have got a larger tent and that it is still a pain to have to walk across a field in the darkness to the toilets. And call me old-fashioned, but I don't like taking a shower next to someone answering a call of nature in an adjoining cubicle.

My six-foot frame felt entombed in our small tent. Then we had to contend with the noisy couple who rolled up in the middle of the night and spent what seemed like the rest of it constructing their large and well-equipped tent. As I lay there listening to them for what seemed like hours, I wondered whether it was a tent they were erecting or whether they were building a house. There was a full-scale military operation going on out there. Finally, just as the dawn chorus was getting underway, they stopped. Some time later, I gazed out of the tent flap, bleary-eyed and angry, to see what had killed my attempts at getting to sleep. These people had brought what looked like the entire contents of their house with them. Saucepans of every size hung from ropes stretched across the canopy attached to the huge tent. There were tables and chairs, sun loungers, a barbecue, and utensils of every kind hanging neatly alongside the pans. I wouldn't have been surprised if there'd been a sofa, television and a double bed inside the tent.

No, camping had not lost any of its charms in the last twenty-four years. Jan was definitely not a fan. Perhaps if we'd got one of those bigger walk-in tents and it had been hot, things might have been different. Being lovers of the great outdoors, camping was something we should have enjoyed, but I guess we just weren't used to it. Years of staying in cosy bed and breakfasts had spoilt us, but, paradoxically, we still liked the idea of pitching a tent somewhere out in the wilds, just like those people we'd seen years before, in the Lake District, encamped by the side of a beautiful pool near Scafell Pike. Next time perhaps.

We packed everything away, loaded the car up, and headed into St. David's in search of a nice bed and breakfast.

After a week, we came home. There was nothing wrong with the accommodation, but the rain hardly let up. We ran out of wet weather activities, the sea was too rough for any boat trips and coastal walks lost their appeal. It was time to cut our losses and head home to Beans.

Beans, naturally, was delighted to see us. She didn't care whether she spent the rest of her holiday with Bob and Rita or at home with us. All that mattered was that everyone was back where they belonged.

If we thought that the weather might have been better at home, we were sadly mistaken. At one point we even contemplated saving our leave and going back to work, but that would have been unfair to Beans. In any case, we still needed the break. Who needs work when there's a kitchen to re-decorate?

August 31st 1997 was like most Sundays in our house. We'd either head to the Peak District or take Beans out locally, spending the rest of the day doing those jobs that never get done, or pottering in the garden. This was going to be a pottering day.

Beans enjoyed her usual walk over the fields, stopping for a spot of energetic stick-throwing, and then it was back via the corner shop to pick up a Sunday paper. Normally I don't buy a newspaper on a Sunday because there's just too much to read, but today I decided to immerse myself in one for a change.

Entering the shop, I scanned all the papers to see which had the most interesting offerings on its cover. I stopped dead in my tracks. Only one appeared to be carrying the awful headline: *Diana dies in Paris car crash,* alongside a photograph of the beautiful Princess. I read a few words of the report, but I couldn't take it in, it seemed unreal; surely this was a mistake – no other paper as far as I could see was carrying this news.

Picking it up, I headed to the counter to pay.

'I can't believe this,' I said to Peter, the shop-owner.

'It's awful isn't it?' he replied, 'happened last night.'

Still shocked and disbelieving, I called out to Jan, who was standing at the shop entrance with Beans.

'Have you seen this?' I shouted to her, holding up the paper.

'Oh no,' was all she said as she stared at the newspaper.

I handed over the money and we walked the short distance home, the pair of us still in a state of disbelief and shock. What had started as a typical Sunday had now become somehow unreal, as if time had stopped. Princess Diana was too young and had so much more to do. We'd seen her on the news, in Africa, highlighting her landmines campaign. Ten years previously we were lucky enough to see her when she visited Chatsworth House in Derbyshire, as part of that year's Festival of National Parks. I still have the official souvenir programme from that day, plus a handful of not very good – but treasured – photographs of her as she passed, smiling, through the crowds – in a pair of green Wellington boots.

As I turned on the television, part of me was thinking this was still some horrible dream from which I'd soon wake up. Perhaps the papers were wrong and Diana was just injured – injured but alive. But this was no dream. The news reports, the ghastly site of the crumpled Mercedes in the tunnel, the news that the Princess's lover, Dodi Fayed, was also killed and then

171

Tony Blair's address to the nation said it all. The dreadful reality began to sink in.

We sat in front of the TV for what seemed like hours as the tragic events unfolded. It was wall-to-wall coverage on every channel. We heard the reports of the desperate attempts by the doctors to save Diana's life in the early ours of that Sunday morning, the fact that her bodyguard had survived and that Prince Charles was on his way to France. I remember feeling quite numb with disbelief, something I hadn't felt since that terrible day back in December 1980, when John Lennon was shot outside his New York apartment. This is how people must have felt at the news of John F Kennedy's assassination. I was only three at the time but even so I still have a vague recollection of that day; of Mum shouting out to Dad about a shooting in America. Something had stuck in my memory.

Over the next week, prior to her funeral, every paper carried stories and features about Diana, people talked about her at work and, unless you had a heart of stone – or were a fanatical republican – many tears were shed; some in public, at the huge shrine outside Kensington Palace, or in private. The Queen returned to London to be with her people and the announcement of a state funeral for the Princess was made.

The following Saturday, a week after her death, Jan and I, along with millions of others, sat down to watch the funeral. That day will remain in the memory forever. I'll never forget the cries from the crowd as the Princess's cortège appeared, or the dignity of her two sons, together with Prince Charles and The Duke of Edinburgh, as they walked behind the coffin.

Throughout all this, Beans sat quietly at Jan's side, as if she too could sense the sadness of the day. Outside, there was no-one about, and few cars passed by. There were no sounds of lawn-mowers or hedge-cutters to disturb the solemnity of the occasion.

I'd managed to keep it together until the moment when all the people – some in wheelchairs – from the many charities Diana supported, joined the procession. These people had lost their champion and Britain had lost someone who wasn't afraid to speak up for them.

As I sat there, my lips trembling, Beans got up, walked quietly over to me and rested her head on my knee. I stroked her head as the tears fell. My teeth left imprints in my lips as I tried to maintain the British *stiff upper lip* approach, but I couldn't hold back the emotion.

Beans stayed by me, sitting at my feet, throughout that service in Westminster Cathedral, until Elton John performed his moving version of *Candle in the Wind*. I looked over and could see that a few tears were now streaming down Jan's cheeks. Beans wandered over and took up her position at Jan's side again.

I wish people who think that animals don't feel anything could have seen our dog that day. This ability by animals to know when we are upset is, I believe, one of the things that connect us so strongly to our pets. People talk to their pets, even though the animals cannot respond in the same way. The animal's eyes or its actions often show what it might be thinking. If Beans was upset her ears would go back and a doleful look come over her. If she knew we were cross with her for some misdemeanour, she'd either roll over on to her back, paws in the air, in the typical submissive posture, or slink off to a quiet corner with her tail between her legs.

Stroking her – especially around her chest or tummy – elicited a fairly instant response. This was serious relaxation, dog-style. The first sign was her head slowly starting to droop, then her ears, which, rather than drooping, seemed to almost imperceptibly slide down her head towards her eyes.

Then her eyes started to shut. You could see that her eyes were the hardest to shut down, because the slightest sound would have them open again briefly, and then close again. She was fighting hard to stay alert, but the relaxation was winning.

Next it was the turn of her face. All the skin and muscles in her face started to sag, the jowls flopped and the skin above her eyes collapsed. This was the funniest bit, because she looked like she was morphing into one of those Chinese Shar Pei dogs with the distinctive wrinkled faces.

Beans was now at the point of no return; it was either come round or total collapse. When the collapse came it was sudden and complete. One minute my hand was stroking her, the next she was on the deck, legs in the air, head to one side – a picture of absolute relaxation.

By this time of course, I'd been induced into quite a sleepy, relaxed state myself and inevitably, my eyes would start to shut. It wasn't unusual for Jan to come home from a visit to Wilmslow to find us both asleep.

Many years ago, I remember my Granddad Peck, mum's father, on one of his regular visits, sitting in his armchair with Judy the beagle on his lap. As he rhythmically stroked Judy's distinctive long velvety ears, he would gradually fall asleep. Who needs relaxation tapes when all you have to do is stroke a dog.

I've always believed that looking after a pet – whether a gerbil or a dog – is good for us. Children hopefully learn the concept of compassion for another creature, as well as the responsibility that comes with looking after it. With any luck they'll grow up caring about the other creatures that share the planet with us; becoming better people as a result. It might be naïve of me to think that this will always be the case, but if you've grown up loving an animal in the home the likelihood is you aren't going to turn into one of those mindless thugs who deliberately harm animals for 'kicks.'

Apart from the obvious yelps if we accidentally stood on a paw or her tail, Beans had her own individual way of letting us know that she was in pain and needed help. One day, when we'd just taken her up the road for a short walk, she suddenly stopped in the middle of the path and sat down. She was holding up one of her front legs, with a mournful expression on her face. Careful examination of the paw revealed a nasty thorn sticking out of one of the pads. It must have been painful, but other than a slight curling of the lips, she didn't utter a sound as Jan carefully pulled the thorn out.

Having been around dogs for over thirty years, I'm sure it contributed towards my concerns over animal welfare and conservation issues. It's probably true to say that I would still be just as upset by TV and newspaper reports about animal cruelty if I hadn't had dogs, but I'm sure it helped. Trying to make sense of terrible abuses towards animals is even more difficult when you couldn't imagine inflicting such harm on your own pet.

Fun and Games

Beans' stamina and capacity for fun was undiminished, even though she was now in her twelfth year. She never ceased to amuse us with the things she got up to, or astonish us with her endurance when playing some of her favourite games. If she'd been a school pupil, her report would probably have read: *excels at swimming and athletics – Grade A+*. To this could be added: *competent at sheep-herding.*

Despite Beans' great interest in trying to get at them, sheep, bizarrely, seemed to be very interested in following her. This strange phenomenon happened many times as we crossed the fields and dales of the Peak District.

Sheep, despite their undeserved reputation as not being the sharpest knives in the drawer, are, to me, intelligent and very maternal creatures. To watch the ewes tenderly caring for their new-born lambs is one of the highlights of walking during the spring. The way the mother can find a lamb that has become separated from her, purely by scent, is surely one of the wonders of nature. Farmers routinely wrap the skin of a stillborn lamb around a rejected animal, so the ewe thinks it's hers. It's a simple and effective way of ensuring no lamb is without a mother.

Despite all this, we did wonder whether their ability to recognise their farmer was as good as their ability to pick out their own lambs. When we holidayed on Mull we'd purchased a couple of really good quality wooden walking poles. They proved invaluable for some of the terrain we crossed and although they've since been replaced by high-tech collapsible ones, we still have them. To sheep's eyes they probably looked like shepherds' crooks, which might have been the reason why they started to gather in large numbers behind us as we crossed their field.

Beans found this rather alarming. Surely she should be the one rounding them up, not them following her. Before we were even half way across the field an entire flock of the woolly animals had gathered behind, calmly following us in an orderly fashion. Beans had given up barking and pulling at the sheep and merely wanted to get away from them as quickly as possible. The tables had been turned and she felt rather threatened. The sheep, however, posed no threat whatsoever. As far as they were concerned, we were their shepherds and Beans our trusty sheepdog.

By the time we reached the gate we had a nicely grouped flock of sheep on our hands. They stood there in a semi-circle looking at us as if they expected something to happen next. Perhaps they thought we had some food for them, or that they were about to be sheared. Had a convenient sheep enclosure been available I would have been tempted to try my hand at a spot of sheep-herding, although I doubt Beans would have been up to the job. Undoubtedly, she'd have got them moving, but not in a way that would win prizes at the local sheepdog trials.

Before we left the sheep to their field, Beans had a surprise in store for them. She'd tolerated this situation long enough; it was time these stubborn beasts were taught a lesson. As they stood there looking at her quizzically, some stamping their feet at her, she gave a quick lunge on her lead and a sharp loud bark. In seconds, the sheep were dispersed. No doubt with a great sense of satisfaction, she turned away and carried on.

Apart from our regular walks in the Peak District, Beans enjoyed other forms of exercise to the full, pushing herself to the point of exhaustion. She was truly the athlete of the dog world. Our main local walk took us past a field which we nicknamed the 'ring field' because it became Beans' main training ground in the rubber ring throwing championships. We found a ring was safer than a stick – and could be thrown further. There were no nasty splinters to cause harm when she started chewing it either. It could also be rolled, making it much more fun to try and catch.

Rolling could only be done if the grass had been cut and the earth was dry. If conditions were favourable it was all systems go. Beans was on the starting block and I was poised, ready to throw. Of course, you had to pitch it just right; throw it down too hard and it simply bounced straight into Beans' waiting jaws. Get it right and it fairly motored along, with Beans in hot pursuit. Watching her catch it reminded me that this was the instinctive behaviour of an animal who was going through the motions of bringing down prey; the urge to chase, catch, rip apart and devour. Make no mistake; had the rubber ring been a rabbit or squirrel the outcome would be bloody. She would dive on that ring with a series of angry-sounding growls and then shake it furiously. This was Beans finishing off her prey.

Sometimes, I think we forget that our loveable, cuddly pets are, under that affectionate exterior, hunters and killers. Thankfully, we never had to witness what Beans might have done to a squirrel or a rabbit, but of her ability to hunt and kill, we were in no doubt whatsoever. Her enthusiasm for watching every wildlife film on the TV, including scenes of foxes, wolves or coyotes dispatching their prey, had perhaps awakened the killer instinct in her. These animals were going about their business slaughtering everything in sight; leaping on prey, chasing it and ripping it to pieces, and Beans fancied a piece of the action.

The pieces of the puzzle were all in place: the instincts that she already possessed, the scenes of bloody slaughter on the TV and the innocent little rubber ring that was – in her imagination – the prey. The trouble was; Beans' choice of prey was hardly what you would call Big Game. Her victims were field voles or mice.

So as I played tug-of-war with Beans, trying to wrestle the rubber ring from her vice-like grip, I realised she was merely playing out a version of those scenes I'd seen on the wildlife films, where pairs of wolves tugged on pieces of flesh from a kill. This was a test of endurance between man and dog. Who would let go first? The outcome was never in doubt; I could swing her around on that tooth-marked piece of rubber and still she wouldn't let go. In the end dizziness got the better of me and I had to give in. Beans had won again.

Beans was not the only one who benefited from physical activity in the ring field. I found that launching the ring as if I was an Olympic discus thrower was wonderful exercise. Quite what passers by thought, seeing this lunatic spinning around before launching a dog's rubber ring into orbit, is anyone's guess. We didn't care; this was all part of the fun of dog-ownership.

Very often, she was already half way down the field before I'd even thrown her ring, trying to get a head start on it, so inevitably it would come to earth in a totally different part of the field from where she ended up. This was the interesting bit, because not having followed its trajectory; she had to rely on the sound of it landing.

Tracking it down was no problem if the grass had been cut – I'd even try and beat her to it with a quick sprint – but if it was knee-high then she'd have to work a little harder. Despite this, she never failed to find it, although it took her some time to home in on its scent. But find it she did. This ability that dogs possess never ceases to amaze me. It made me giddy just watching Beans going round and round, backwards and forwards, tail wagging enthusiastically with her nose to the ground.

Suddenly, there she was, with the ring in her mouth, running back towards us triumphantly. Then we would have to reluctantly pick up the slobber-covered piece of rubber and hurl it off into the air again for her. Dogs are so easy to please.

Our Peak District walks took us over a variety of terrain, but a lot of the paths we followed took us over fields with crops growing in them, or pastures, where the grass was so tall a variety of small animals could hide there, undisturbed – at least until Beans came along. Sometimes we would see these creatures before she did; a stoat or a weasel bobbing across the path in front of us; a lizard, darting quickly back into the undergrowth, or a vole, scurrying away to its burrow. When we saw them, evasive action could be taken, and Beans quickly pulled away, much to her annoyance.

Despite our best efforts at protecting the flora and fauna, it was impossible to prevent some successful 'kills.' Beans proved, on a number of occasions, that when it came to hunting she was the supreme predator, even if her unfortunate victims were only a couple of inches long. Her ears were constantly on alert for the slightest scuffle in the undergrowth, her eyes scanning the ground in front of her as she walked along. When she pounced it was lightning fast and executed with devastating precision.

Without warning, her entire body sprang into the air, her back arched, eyes fixed on whatever had caught her attention. Then she'd dive into the ground like a dart and whatever creature was at the receiving end was usually doomed. Once we'd finished laughing at her acrobatics, a tell-tale squeak from somewhere in the grass brought us swiftly back to reality. Something had been caught. If she ever ate those voles or mice, we never knew, because they would probably have been downed in one; a mere snack. Sometimes she'd emerge with one unfortunate victim in her mouth which we would persuade her to drop. The tiny creatures were usually dead, but I'll not forget in a hurry the sight of one that she hadn't finished off, trying to crawl back to its burrow with a series of pitiful squeaks. It made it, but I really wish that I'd let Beans finish it off.

It wasn't the most pleasant experience watching Beans catch something, but, at the same time, it was fascinating – and also very funny – to see her leap into the air in exactly the same way as those foxes and coyotes in the wild. Our dogs are closer to their wild friends than we realise.

Sometimes, if she was feeling particularly lazy, she went for even smaller prey – flies. The best part of this hunting technique was that the prey came to her. All she had to do was sit there and snatch the insects out of the air. If she was feeling a little more energetic, they could be chased around the house until eventually caught. It wasn't exactly a feast, but if enough flies were stupid enough to buzz around her, together they would form a decent meal.

Flies, unfortunately, are the bane of walkers and animals. Walk through Peak District fields during the summer and there can be an entire swarm joining you on the walk; a cloud of irritating insects buzzing around your head. Whether they are attracted to sweat, or just fancy a change from cow dung, who knows. We can at least try to swat them away with our hands; animals such as cows or horses just have to grin and bear it, the flies tormenting them mercilessly. Beans addressed the problem by eating them. In this, she had considerable success.

We'd stopped for lunch on the hillside overlooking Eyam, just before the path enters woods on its descent to the village. It was a good place to stop, with fine views over the village. We settled down to enjoy our sandwiches and then maybe catch a few rays afterwards.

Beans was anything but settled. She too wanted to relax and enjoy her own lunch, but a swarm of the local fly population had decided to target her and were pressing home a determined attack. This was more than she could tolerate. It was time to go on the offensive.

As we sat and watched her, she set about grabbing every fly she could. Her head was everywhere as she devoured the annoying insects. Every second, her teeth chomped down and another fly was on its way to her stomach. The more they buzzed around her, the faster she got. Her teeth were banging together so fast, it was impossible to count how many she'd swallowed. Her picnic lay on the ground, untouched. While there were still insects to pluck from the air, her lunch could wait. This was much more fun.

Gradually, the flies diminished. A few individuals hung around, but the thought that most of their comrades were slowly being digested by Beans' gastric juices must have persuaded them to give up the assault. Beans gave up the fly-catching and started on her snacks, but she was still on alert in case a few diehard flies returned to try and push their luck.

Every now and then she'd suddenly whip round with dazzling speed and another fly that had dared to disturb her was no more.

We already knew from her sticks and stones activities that Beans was a definite water-baby, but she also loved to swim purely for the pleasure of it.

A little encouragement was sometimes required to get her in the water – usually in the form of a stick – but once in there was no getting her out. If it was hot she was in there with no prompting whatsoever.

It was great to watch Beans swimming. She cut through the water effortlessly, her nostrils flaring noisily as she breathed. If the water was clear enough you could see her legs doing their work, propelling her along almost like an otter, using her tail as a very effective rudder.

Apart from the Peak District rivers, she had two favourite swimming locations: a small lake, not far from Bob and Rita, and the lake at Brereton, near Congleton. Swimming in the Wilmslow lake was not without its problems. Although we took care not to disturb the local fishermen and kept to the paths, Beans could not always be relied upon to keep out of the water during the fishing season. Fortunately, there was usually a part that was fisherman-free, but it didn't always help matters.

One sunny day Jan and her mother were relaxing at the side of the lake, watching Beans cruising lazily up and down through the water. They hadn't realised that it was the local fishing bailiff who was walking purposefully towards them.

'Didn't you see the No Swimming signs?' he said gruffly. 'You're disturbing the fish.'

'Oh yes,' Rita replied. 'But I'm afraid our dog can't read.'

No doubt surprised at this cheeky reply and following further assurances that Beans wasn't doing any harm, he wandered off, muttering to himself. Beans was nowhere near the fishermen and, in any case, if she was disturbing the fish, they'd probably all headed away from her in the direction of the fishermen's rods. Beans was doing them a favour.

Mad Dogs

Rita's life had changed considerably now that she had a disability, so various aids and adaptations were acquired to make life easier for her. Although she could walk, it was only slowly and with support, so an electric buggy was purchased which proved very useful on local trips. Despite the seriousness of her situation it was also rather fun to use. Beans thought it was fun too; not for riding on, but for chasing. No sooner had Rita set off up a quiet cul-de-sac on her test drive, than Beans was chasing after her in hot pursuit, barking. Thankfully, she hadn't developed this habit to include cars and motorbikes, but quite what was so interesting about the buggy only Beans knew.

This was yet another trait to our dog's character; chasing, barking at, or even – and this was the dangerous part – trying to attack various household gadgets or implements.

One of the first things we bought after moving was a lawnmower. It was that or allowing the back garden to become a 'conservation' wildflower meadow-cum-wildlife area. This was a very tempting proposition, given the fact I find mowing the lawn a tedious chore, something that takes up valuable time that could be better spent doing something more exciting. Nevertheless, so as not to let the neighbourhood down plus the fact that, despite my non-interest in gardening for its own sake I don't like an untidy garden, a mower was duly purchased and I reluctantly joined the ranks of the Sunday morning lawn cutters.

Despite my dislike of lawn-mowing, it was made more interesting by Beans' reaction to the mower. She was relaxing on the lawn unaware that her peace was about to be disturbed. That fact was probably the reason why her reaction to the machine was so extreme. The moment I turned it on a sudden and violent change came over her.

As if the mower was a living thing about to attack her – which to her it probably was – she charged at it barking madly. I shouted at her to keep away, but she persisted with her assault on this terrifying object that had disturbed her world of sunshine and relaxation. How dare it.

The last thing you need is a crazed dog trying to attack a lawnmower – especially when it's an electric one. I managed to shoo her away, but she soon pressed home another attack, this time trying to bite the damned thing. The cable, luckily, escaped her attentions, but the rest of the machine was fair game. She was intent on destroying it.

There was nothing else for it; she would have to go inside. Stupidly, I'd already managed to nick the cable with the spinning blades, which was now wrapped in strong electrical tape. I didn't want an electrocuted dog on my conscience.

So with her tail between her legs, looking decidedly unhappy, Beans was ushered indoors until mowing was finished. The lawnmower assault became a regular event every few weeks throughout the summer.

It was strange the variety of ordinary household objects that Beans took exception to. There was the wooden clothes-maiden that Jan used when helping Rita with the ironing that was singled out for a dose of Beans treatment. Normally, this onslaught on the defenceless wooden object took place on a Friday night, when Jan visited her parents after work, but every few weeks we'd go for tea on Saturday, which was when I witnessed Beans' onslaught on the clothes-maiden.

It was one of those collapsible contraptions that had probably been in Jan's family for years, but still in good working order, despite the nerve-jarring noise it made when erected. Somewhere within its simple mechanism it needed just a few drops of oil, but nobody had ever bothered to discover which part, so it carried on screaming every time it was opened out. The noise was akin to someone dragging their fingernails down a blackboard, like the famous scene in *Jaws* where Robert Shaw's character uses this technique very effectively to attract the attention of a roomful of people.

It set *my* nerves on edge, so the effect it had on Beans was perhaps not surprising. Even before it was half unfolded she'd pounced on it, like a lion bringing down a wildebeest on the Serengeti. Further attempts to raise the maiden to its full height were impossible. Every creak and rattle from it provoked another frenzied attack. If the clothes-maiden wasn't going to be reduced to matchwood by Beans' teeth, some

185

decisive action was required. Despite Jan shouting at her to move, Beans was determined to kill the maiden, so I stepped in.

'Beans, come here!' I bellowed, above the din of creaking clothes-maiden and barking dog.

'Beans, stop it!' I'd shout for a second time, only louder.

The second reprimand usually did the trick and she'd trot over to me in the way she usually did when she knew she'd done something wrong; head down, tail between her legs.

Then, as if she expected the maiden to come to life again, she would sit there staring at it, just to make sure it didn't.

To Beans, these ordinary household devices were noisy, frightening and threatening living objects that she had to destroy. Over time, she'd added the vacuum cleaner, the grill pan being pulled out of the oven and, strangely, tin foil to her list of hated objects.

My nightly routine of making sandwiches for us to take to work was always accompanied by Beans, sitting quietly by the kitchen door patiently waiting for the odd piece of cheese or ham to 'accidentally' drop into her mouth.

However, the moment she saw me take the roll of tin foil out of the drawer to wrap the sandwiches, she was off, to hide in a corner of the room somewhere. Sometimes I'd catch her out and pull the foil out of the container before she'd realised what it was, but the moment that foil rattled, she was gone – titbits or not.

Dogs are strange creatures at times.

Walking is probably the least risky of activities compared to other outdoor pursuits, such as climbing or mountain-biking, but that isn't to say that accidents never happen. They can and do.

Ankles can be turned walking over a seemingly innocent field, especially if that field is pitted with ruts where tractors have driven, or holes where cattle have walked. After a few weeks of summer sun a previously muddy field can dry up to form a hard, rutted, ankle-turning assault course.

Climbing the Peak District wall stiles is not without risk either. One wrong step trying to cross a wall, or a slip, and you could be in trouble. On one occasion, I tried to be clever when crossing a simple step stile and hurt my back in the process. It was a move I'd done many times before – and still do – but this time the stile caught me out – *literally*. Once on the first step (or the second, if it was a high stile) I would use the wooden posts on either side to vault over the stile, landing neatly on the other side. I did this for no other reason than I enjoyed it and – if I'm honest – to show off my athletic prowess to Jan.

There was no prowess this time though. As I launched myself over the stile, my foot caught the crossing post and I was sent flying, twisting myself as I went, to land spreadeagled in the field. Picking myself up, I realised that some muscle in my back had been pulled and I spent the remainder of the walk in considerable pain.

Beans was no stranger to walking injuries herself. In fact, she once hurt herself in a similar way to me, although the effects of her injury went beyond pain and a few tablets from the vet. She'd climbed a wall using the stone steps and was in the process of coming down the other side, but, instead of letting Jan help her down the steps she decided to jump. She landed awkwardly and as she did so there was a rather sickening grunt, as if the wind had been knocked out of her. We carried on with the walk but it was obvious something was wrong. She was walking very stiffly, but not limping and when we cleaned her up back at the car, she winced if her back was touched. It was time to visit the vet.

Even though we weren't on holiday, Bob and Rita had said they would have Beans to stay for the week. The weather was fine and we thought that Beans deserved to spend some time with them, so Jan took the Monday morning off and made an emergency appointment with the vet there. Beans seemed to be cheerful enough, but she still winced and yelped a little when her back was touched.

'It's nothing to worry about,' the vet assured Jan, after giving Beans a thorough examination. 'She's just pulled a muscle in her back.'

Relieved, Jan asked him when it would be safe to take Beans hiking again.

'No big walks or stiles for a couple of weeks,' he replied, 'but she'll be okay with short gentle walks.' I'll give her a short course of anti-inflammatories and that should sort her out.'

'Are there any side effects?' Jan asked.

'Not usually,' he paused, 'but she may lose a bit of bladder control.'

With those cautionary words in her head, Jan left the vet's and headed to her parents to drop Beans off for the rest of the week. She gave Beans her first tablet, left instructions with Rita on the dosage and went off to work.

Despite the vet's reassurances, we couldn't help worrying about Beans, so we decided to take some last-minute leave on the Wednesday to go and see how she was. Her usual enthusiastic greeting instantly allayed our fears. However, it seemed that the vet's warning about loss of bladder control was not unfounded. Rita told us what had happened.

After Jan had left on the Monday, Beans had decided to spend the rest of the day asleep upstairs, curled up on Bob's side of the bed. As she slept, warmed by the afternoon sun streaming in, she was totally unaware that at some point during her siesta her bladder had decided to release its contents all over the bed. The hours passed and so gradually did the urine, making its way inexorably through the duvet, then the sheets, finally reaching the mattress. Later on, she wandered downstairs for her tea and before long it was time for her evening walk and then bed.

Not long after they'd turned the lights out, Rita was suddenly jolted out of semi-consciousness by a stream of expletives and commotion from the other side of the bed.

'I'm wet through,' Bob shouted. 'The whole bed's soaked,' he carried on ranting.

At this point, Rita was probably wondering whether he had suddenly become incontinent.

'It's piss,' he bellowed, as the strong smell reached his nostrils.

Stumbling out of bed, he turned on the light. Pulling back the covers revealed a large wet patch extending from just below the pillow to almost half way down the bed. His pyjamas were wet, his hands smelt of pee and now, to add insult to injury, he would have to spend the early hours of the morning changing the bed. He was not happy.

'Has Beans been on here today?' he asked angrily.

Realisation suddenly dawned on Rita. She'd seen Beans creep upstairs after Jan had left and later on had spotted her curled up on the bed – but she'd forgotten Jan's warning about the unfortunate side effects of the pills.

'All afternoon,' she replied.

Then she told Bob about the tablets the vet had given Beans and the fact that there *might* be some side effects – such as peeing everywhere.

Despite the mess, it was unfair to be angry with Beans; after all, she didn't know what she was doing. Unfortunately, where peeing was concerned she didn't know what she was doing several more times over the next few days. The tablets had to go. Jan returned to the vet and told him about Beans' bed-wetting and her parents' pee-soaked house. The prescription was duly changed to a milder dose.

Before long, Beans' back was better and she was soon clambering over walls again, only this time we took extra care with her when she got into difficulties. Whether she could do it or not, jumping off without using the steps was not going to happen. That incident had proved that dogs, despite their climbing and jumping abilities, are not built of steel. Besides, seeing the effects of the tablets on her was enough to make us even more careful.

Despite her tumble from the wall, Beans still seemed to have the knack of making a fool of herself, sometimes in the most innocent of situations. Thankfully, these didn't result in injury. The only injury she suffered was to her dignity.

When we wanted a good walk but didn't necessarily want to travel miles, we'd often head to Lyme Park, a beautiful old stately home with magnificent parkland, just on the fringes of the Peak District. Lyme Park recently featured in the BBC's adaptation of *Pride and Prejudice* and many people now come to see the places where Elizabeth Bennett and Mr Darcy walked and talked. Despite always being busy with visitors, it is still possible to enjoy some peace and quiet in the surrounding countryside.

We could walk up to the 'Cage,' an Elizabethan hunting tower, which has a commanding position on a hill beyond the main house. From here there are splendid views over Lyme Park and towards the distant plateau of Kinder Scout.

People walk their dogs, fly kites, have picnics or just simply enjoy a magnificent piece of Cheshire countryside.

Another route took us behind the hall through tree-lined avenues out onto moorland where it was possible to see some of the Park's herds of fallow and red deer. Autumn was always a good time, especially during the 'rut' when the bellowing of the red deer stags echoes around the park and the woods become a joy to walk through, resplendent in their autumn colours. It's always been my favourite time of the year, even though winter is just around the corner. We both look forward to spring because the countryside re-awakens after the long winter months, but there's something special about autumn. Kicking through piles of fallen leaves, early morning mists, the trees dropping their seeds – and watching Beans listening to the rutting stags.

It was obvious that Beans was going to be captivated by the awesome roaring of the stags and we always made sure we took her on an autumn visit to Lyme. Given her interest in wildlife on the TV, this was as near to reality as she could get. She'd sit and watch the distant deer on the moors intently, tilting her head to one side like she did when anything made a noise. As the magnificent stags postured and bellowed she'd follow their every move. If two decided to lock antlers she'd bark, but they were too far away to be bothered.

Once Beans' wildlife watching had been indulged we'd head down to a small lake near the café, where Beans could have a paddle and a drink. It was the drinking that got her into trouble.

The fact that she decided to wait until we were crossing the embankment at the end of the lake, instead of having a drink at the water's edge was the deciding factor. The path here was raised up and as she leaned down she lost her balance and that was it. There was no proper dog dive into the water; she slid in head first as if she was pushed. She floundered a few seconds and then tried to clamber out, but her paws couldn't get a purchase on the slippery bank. The more she tried, the more she slid back. I had her on her lead, but I could hardly strangle the poor dog as I tried to pull her out. After a couple of attempts and with some help from me, she managed to haul herself out. She stood there forlornly, dripping, perhaps hoping that other dogs hadn't seen her plight. This was just too embarrassing.

For some reason probably best known to her, Beans had developed a strange way of having a pee. To be sure, she squatted the way lady dogs are supposed to do, but with one back leg always raised, which affected her balance. It was as if she wasn't quite sure which way was correct.

Perhaps the first dog she'd seen peeing was a male one so she thought that was the right way to do it; or maybe she just preferred it that way. She stopped short of cocking her leg up against every lamppost she met, so I didn't have any worries that perhaps I had a transsexual dog on my hands. I did worry, however, that this somewhat unbalanced way of having a pee would someday land her in trouble. Sure enough, it did.

When we moved to our new home our dog-walking route took us along the canal towpath, a route well used by locals and their dogs. Although canals are cleaner than they used to be, you still wouldn't want to take a dip in one. Despite the water not being exactly drinking quality, the canals are fine for use by the many narrow boats that cruise up and down them.

Many dog owners let their pooches swim in the murky water, but we'd seen too many unsavoury objects bobbing along on the surface, to let Beans anywhere near it. The odd dead duck or pigeon, mouldering bits of bread thrown in for the ducks or swans, the odd slick of diesel from a narrow boat and other detritus, combined to form a soup containing some very unpleasant ingredients. Beans managed to fall into it.

We'd only just joined the towpath when she squatted right next to the canal bank for a pee. She'd been busy sniffing where umpteen other dogs had sniffed and peed and this was obviously the ideal spot, even though it was precariously near the canal. This was the right spot and she was going to pee on it – no matter what.

Putting her raised right leg down, she realised to her horror that it had nowhere to go, other than straight into the water. As we watched the inevitable about to happen, she almost seemed to topple into the canal in slow motion, just like that classic sequence in the BBC comedy series, *Only Fools and Horses,* where the character, *Del Boy,* leans against a non-existent bar and crashes to the floor with a silly grin on his face. At least Beans had a softer landing.

As she floundered in the brown murky water, all Beans wanted to do was get out as quickly as possible. She wasn't hanging around for a pleasant swim in this stuff. After a couple of unsuccessful attempts to haul herself out of the bilge, she staggered, dripping, onto the towpath – and promptly shook herself all over us. Well I suppose it served us right for laughing at her.

Heaven knows whether she'd swallowed any water. I know dogs' guts are lead-lined (they have to be, considering the things they eat) but I didn't fancy her chances with this stuff. If either of us had fallen in and ingested any of it, we'd have been straight down the hospital for tetanus and any other jabs they could give us. A good stomach-pumping would not have been out of the question either.

By the time we'd finished the walk Beans was nearly dry, but if she thought that was the end of her water adventures that day, she was wrong. As I sniffed her I realised why it was I kept her out of the canal. A rank odour emanated from her that worsened when she moved. It wasn't the breathtaking stench you got if she'd rolled in something, but it was still unpleasant.

Trying to clean Beans up was never the easiest of tasks. If proper cleaning was required – a full valet – it was upstairs to the bath for a shower and plenty of dog shampoo. This was not easy due to her determined attempts to leap from the bath, but it beat the outdoors method, which was the dog-washing equivalent of one step forward, two steps back. Let her escape the water and shampoo and she'd promptly run to the lawn and roll on it. At least in the bath, the warm water from the shower seemed to soothe her. As long as you didn't mind a frequent soaking every few minutes when she shook herself violently, it was pretty straightforward.

It's a good job that most dogs seem to positively relish a good rub down with a towel. When we attempted to dry Beans with a hairdryer, she ran a mile. We might as well have pulled a gun on her. Switch one on to dry your own hair when she was in the room, and the effect was the same. Later on you'd find her hiding in some dark corner, safe from the fearsome hairdryer.

Christmas in our house revolved mainly around Beans; or to be more specific: Beans and her Christmas presents. Forget over-eating, credit card debt, yet another pair of socks and the eternal 'who shall we spend Christmas with' nightmares – just enjoy Christmas with a dog.

The nicest thing about Christmas with Beans was that she was so easy to please. There was no badgering, day after day, for the latest computer game or designer trainers; no tantrums or tears when such expensive items were denied. Instead, all we had to do was head to the pet shop and choose a suitable squeaky toy for her.

Of course, the toy had to be selected with some care. The squeak had to be a good one and preferably located where her teeth wouldn't destroy it too easily. On several occasions she'd managed to wreck the squeaking capabilities of her new present within days of receiving it, so the larger the toy, the longer it lasted. If she couldn't wrap her mouth around it completely, she'd enjoy many more days of happy squeaking.

Over the years she built up an entire collection of toys. Squeaky newspapers, snowmen, dumbbells, a poodle, a banana and a rugby ball to name but a few. And it wasn't just Christmas that produced another to add to the collection; her birthdays were usually marked with the addition of another offering from the pet shop. We could have given her different presents I suppose, chewy bones or jumbo biscuits, but the trouble was; Beans loved her squeaky toys. Trying to choose one that she hadn't had was becoming more of a challenge, but we usually found something.

The toys had to be wrapped as well. That was all part of the fun. Watching Beans unwrap her presents was one of the highlights of the year. The moment she saw her gift, you could see her excitement. She'd carefully take the wrapped toy from you, settle down in the middle of the room and start to unwrap it. Holding it with one paw, she'd methodically tear small pieces of wrapper away with her teeth until, eventually, the entire paper was removed. Sometimes the toy would squeak as she held it down, which only made her more determined to rip that paper off. At that point, she'd start to squeak with excitement herself.

Once unwrapped, the new toy would be given all the attention it deserved. She'd squash it with her paws, throw it in the air, roll on it or just sit there with it in her mouth. Until the next toy came along, or she managed to break the squeak, this would now be the favourite. We wondered if the squeaky noise had some connection to those 'phantom pregnancies' you hear about dogs. Strangely, if she broke the squeak, she lost all interest in the toy, as if it had 'died.' Was this why she took such great care not to break it?

Strangely, Beans adopted a rather odd routine with her squeaky toys after her meals. Once finished, she'd trot into the living room, find one of her toys and then madly roll on it for several minutes. A favourite move was to roll on the toy on her back; legs everywhere, and then try to make it squeak. Finally, she'd let out a loud satisfied belch.

Beans wasn't content with just opening her own gifts. If there were any others around she'd have a go at them as well. Parcels at the bottom of the Christmas tree were particularly vulnerable. Chewed up corners of parcels usually gave the game away. It seemed she couldn't separate the fact in her brain that not all gifts were hers. They were all fair game. Christmas visits to relatives had to be accompanied by warnings to watch those unopened gifts left lying around.

She even tried to muscle in on our birthdays. No sooner had gifts appeared from their hiding places than she was there, eager as always. Much as we tried our best to convince her it wasn't her birthday, she still lived in hope. You could almost see her disappointment when the last gift was produced and it didn't come in her direction. It would have been taking things too far to include a small gift for her at every celebration, but that's what we felt like doing. A dog can have too much of a good thing. She'd have to wait until her birthday in July.

I'm sure there are people out there who wouldn't dream of indulging their dog like we did, a sentiment I could quite go along with if the animal didn't appreciate its gift. The trouble was; Beans did. Her reaction to those modest, inexpensive squeaky toys was always a treat. There was never any disappointment once she'd opened them. No half-hearted thanks at yet another pair of socks or a bottle of aftershave to join all the others in the bathroom.

She couldn't give us a gift in return, but she made up for it with sheer, unconditional, no-strings-attached delight. Another lesson for us perhaps?

The Windgather Rocks, on the western fringe of the Peak District, lie neatly along the county borderline which separates Cheshire from Derbyshire. Compared to some of the other great edges of the Peak, such as Stanage or Froggatt, they are more of a short rocky outcrop, but what they lack in length they more than make up for with their dramatic setting, rising out of the east Cheshire landscape.

They provide a fitting finale to the end of a magnificent walk through some of the area's finest scenery. Starting from the Cat & Fiddle inn – the second highest in England at 1690ft – you head up to Shining Tor, Cheshire's highest point, and then follow a wonderful path across miles of moor and heather over Cat's Tor and Pym Chair to arrive eventually at the Windgather Rocks. The area is steeped in history and legend. Wild cats are supposed to have roamed around Cat's Tor in the distant past and Pym Chair may be the sight where the 17th Century Puritan John Pym preached. Trains of packhorses used to cross the ridge, bearing loads of salt dug from the Cheshire salt mines.

It's an area that we walked many times with Beans over the years, sometimes deviating from the ridge to head down to the Goyt valley on the Derbyshire side, or the Todd Brook valley on the Cheshire side. Our footprints – and Beans' paw prints – have covered almost every inch of this place.

Climbers, as well as walkers, like to use the Windgather Rocks. They aren't the highest climb in the Peak District, but nevertheless provide a great training ground for some of the bigger climbs. Many have cut their 'climbing teeth' at the Windgather Rocks.

Beans loved these high places. She didn't, as far as we could see, have any fear of heights and we constantly had to shout at her to come away from the edge. Her natural curiosity seemed to draw her there like a magnet. This desire to get as close as possible to some precipitous drop very nearly got her – and a climber – into trouble.

We were almost at the end of a walk that had taken in the Goyt valley and were heading back to the car at Pym Chair, via the Windgathers. Climbers were busy along most of the length of the edge, so we kept well out of the way of ropes and all the other paraphernalia. Those who had made their climb were busy guiding their companions up the rock face. I get mixed feelings when I watch climbers. Much as I'd love to have the guts to climb, my fear of heights and exposure would no doubt get the better of me, although I have no fear of being on high mountains; in fact I love those places, providing the getting there only involves physical effort rather than personal risk. There's still a part of me that wants to get out and climb or scramble and feel the adrenaline rush.

Beans needed a little adrenaline too. She wanted to peer over the edge. We'd passed most of the climbers on the highest stretch of the ridge so decided to venture a little nearer to the edge to indulge our adrenaline-junkie dog. Beans peered over the side into the void. At the same moment a climber's face appeared over the edge. Like opposite sides of magnets, both dog and climber jumped back in shock. The poor climber – who thankfully was roped up – was only inches away from Beans' cold wet nose. When you've just hauled yourself up a sheer rock face the last thing you expect to see at the top is a dog's tongue flopping in your face.

Whatever the climber was thinking, he kept to himself. Was that a grin I noticed on his face as we made our apologies and hurriedly scuttled off?

Pet shops are great places. Where else can you find evidence of peoples' love of pets? There's food to cater for all tastes and diets, toys of every shape and description, various devices to stop your dog pulling, beds, coats, poop bags, tempting treats, books on every breed under the sun, animal calendars, animal mugs, animal greetings cards, animals, shampoos, conditioners and grooming implements. When we moved to our new home we were delighted to discover two pet shops nearby. In the interests of supporting our local traders, we did our best to patronise both stores regularly. Beans couldn't have cared less which one we shopped in. As long as the food – and the treats – kept coming, she was happy.

Pet shops are great for another reason – you can take your pet inside them. I've yet to see any pet shop with a *Sorry, No Dogs* sign in the window. How else would you be able to find out which treat your dog preferred? It would be a bit like saying *Sorry, No Children* in a toy shop.

Beans of course, was delighted that she could stroll freely around the pet shop. The self serve section was her favourite. People would fill bags with their choice of dog biscuit, mixer meal or kibble and then pay at the counter. Naturally, a good deal of the produce ended up on the floor – and was promptly and very efficiently removed by Beans.

Very little of this detritus was missed as she vacuumed the floor. This was terrific fun. She wasn't doing any harm either. In fact she was doing the shop a favour by cleaning the floor for them. The stuff wouldn't be put back in the containers, but thrown away. Waste not, want not, thought Beans as she shovelled down another biscuit bone. This would all have been fine had she not decided to start stealing food that hadn't ended up on the floor. Beans became a shoplifter.

By necessity our favourite pet shop was laid out with all sorts of goodies that were too tempting for a dog to pass by. Some of these delights were out of reach, but many were laid out on the bottom shelves, where they could be swiftly grabbed by any dog walking past.

There were boxes of dried pigs' ears and trotters, dried liver, dried sausages, tasty hide chews, large bones, small bones and other unidentifiable bits of animals. To be honest, I found the whole lot rather revolting, but to Beans this was the *Pick N' Mix* counter in *Woolworths*.

Beans was always greeted and petted by the shop assistants. After all, she was a regular customer. If other people had brought their dogs as well, the whole shopping experience was very convivial. People chatted; dogs sniffed each other and, while all this was going on, other, more enterprising dogs would pilfer the odd pig's ear or sausage from the goodies shelf.

Beans became adept at the *snatch and grab* method of shop-lifting. As we passed the treats shelf en route to the stacks of cans and bags of kibble, she'd carefully weigh up the offerings in each box. On the way back to the counter she'd then grab whichever treat had taken her fancy. Despite pulling her away she was far too quick for us. By the time I'd yanked the lead, a pig's ear or piece of liver was already half eaten. She'd refined her technique to perfection.

Perhaps not surprisingly, the staff turned a blind eye to their canine thieves. After all, you can hardly prosecute a dog. The signs saying *CCTV Cameras in Operation* were merely there to warn any human customers who fancied running off without paying. The dogs could hardly understand their warning message, so the four-legged customers carried on with their illicit activities safe in the knowledge that they weren't going to end up in the dock.

We did our best to apologise for Beans' behaviour but no-one seemed to mind. In fact I think they secretly enjoyed their mischievous customers. Chatting to an assistant one day, we were told about the escapades of one particular villain. This dog lived nearby in one of the houses behind the shop. He was obviously an opportunist and had figured out a way into the shop through the rear entrance, which was usually open for deliveries.

Most days would see him sneak in through the back, head straight to the box of dried sausages, and then off he'd run – with a link of sausages grasped firmly between his teeth.

CHAPTER SEVEN

The Twilight Years

At The Vets

As the last year of the twentieth century marched inexorably on towards the new millennium, several landmarks of our own loomed over the horizon. The year 2000 would mark our tenth wedding anniversary and also my fortieth year.

How we would mark such a momentous year could wait for the time being. Beans was approaching her eleventh birthday and, although she was still perky and very active, those little signs were starting to appear to remind us that she would not be around forever.

Throughout our years of walking around the hills and dales of the Peak District we thought nothing of covering anything from ten to twelve miles. Beans was more than up for these hikes. Only on the hottest days of summer would she decide that she'd had enough. We once did a twelve miler around the Staffordshire Moorlands, linking the villages of Warslow, Wetton, Butterton and Grindon.

This area is one of the delights of the Peak District and perfect for a lazy, unhurried walk. The tall church spires of Butterton and Grindon can be seen for miles around, whilst Warslow and Wetton are more tantalisingly hidden between valleys and hills. A myriad of paths and bridleways link the villages, following rivers, streams and old hedgerows. Heart-pumping hill climbs are rewarded by stunning views and exhilarating descents to the next village with the possibility of a tea stop at a welcoming café. The whole area was made for summer walking. Wildflowers fill meadows and fields full of buttercups stretch away into the distance.

The evocative sound of skylarks fills the air on the moor tops, reminding me of the composer, Ralph Vaughan Williams, and his inspirational *The Lark Ascending*. We loved to just lie in a field and listen to them. Actually spotting a skylark was harder though, but a careful scan of the sky would usually be rewarded by the sight of one of them, way up high, a tiny bird, but with a clear and beautiful song. Sometimes we'd see them lift off the ground, flutter gracefully upwards, sing for a little while and then quickly drop down, disappearing from view in the long grass.

It was just such a day when we started our walk from Butterton; a day for being out in the countryside and nowhere else. After walking for some miles Beans had cooled off in the River Manifold at Wetton Mill, but by the time we were walking up the hill towards Wetton village she let us know in no uncertain terms that she'd had enough. As I walked up the field through the buttercups, I felt her extending lead stop abruptly. I turned round to see her sitting there among the yellow flowers with a look that quite clearly said: *you carry on; I'll just stay here and catch up with you later.*

Beans had bucketfuls of stamina; of that there was no doubt, but we certainly couldn't take it for granted. We had to rest every so often and so did Beans, but the only way she could tell us was by steadfastly refusing to move another inch. Never forcing her to move on, we just took it as our queue for a rest. Beans dictated the pace of the walk, not us.

Gradually, it became obvious that her rest stops were becoming frequent, so we started doing shorter walks on those really hot days. It was fairer to her and, if we were honest, better for us. Although we were perfectly capable of doing much longer routes, we found we could relax more and enjoy the scenery, without the pressure of another six miles looming when we'd already done six.

Beautiful scenery deserves better than a mad headlong dash through it. To stop and look – or listen – at what there is around you is part of the enjoyment of walking. We'd see kestrels hovering almost motionless, eyes glued to the ground, looking for prey, buzzards soaring on the thermals and swallows expertly grabbing insects from the air.

Beans loved to look and listen. Her nose twitched and her ears moved at every smell or sound she picked up. I often watched her, when we stopped for our breaks, trying to imagine what she could smell, what she could hear. What must it be like to have a dog's senses? I wanted to know what was going on in that dog world of hers – but I could only imagine it.

Despite our differences, we all had one thing in common: falling asleep on top of hills. When the sun is shining and it's quiet and peaceful, there's nothing more relaxing. Pick the right spot and the only sounds are natural. The skylarks of course, singing their sweet songs; the sound of bees moving from flower to flower or the distant tunes of a song-thrush, high up in a distant tree. This is nature's own relaxation tape – completely free of charge – no strings attached.

It didn't even matter if we weren't high up somewhere. Anywhere away from man-made noise would do. Quite what other passing walkers thought, seeing us lying there, using our rucksacks as convenient pillows and Beans using one of us as a pillow, is anyone's guess.

There's a photograph in my collection, taken at one of our favourite places on a hill overlooking Cressbrook Dale, on one of those barmy summer days. It's a sneaky picture I took of Jan, lying there asleep on the rucksack pillow, dead to the world. Beans, also asleep, has her head resting on Jan's chest and her leg on Jan's arm. It's a picture of total relaxation.

The route-march walkers would no doubt think us a lazy lot, but we didn't care. We felt we'd earned our lunchtime snoozes. It was a reward for climbing the hill. If we'd chosen a flat location for our moment of relaxation we could always use the excuse of not wanting to walk after eating. That's not very good for the digestion is it?

Beans never cared where it was we settled down for our 'siesta.' She was the queen of sunbathing. It didn't matter to her whether it was inside or out. Inside, she'd just follow the sun around the house, moving from floor to armchair, from armchair to sofa and then from the sofa to our bed. You could almost see her on some sun-kissed Caribbean beach, relaxing under a palm tree in her sunglasses, enjoying a cocktail.

We'd often come home to find her asleep on one of the chairs, nicely warmed by the sun shining through the window. More often than not she was off the chair as soon as she heard the key in the lock, but we often caught her out as she slid off it, stretching and yawning as she went. It was often easy to trace her sunbathing progress through the house, simply by feeling the warm patches on the chairs, or where she'd made a 'nest' by moving cushions or piles of ironing to one side. How I wish we'd set up a webcam to watch her activities while we were out.

In the afternoon, the sun moves around to the front of our house, very conveniently shining directly on to our bed; an opportunity for another sunbathing session never missed by Beans. Close inspection of the duvet revealed disturbance right in the centre of the bed, where she'd made herself very comfortable thank you very much.

Where sleeping on our bed was concerned, we'd totally spoilt her. A case of we'd made our bed and now she was going to lie on it. Weekend lie-ins were usually accompanied by Beans, fast asleep at the side of one of us – or even in the middle, if she wanted to be really awkward. A mere tap of the hand on the side of the bed and she was up. Sometimes she never waited for the signal, getting on before we were even fully awake. She was too far-gone for any disciplinary measures; besides, we liked those morning cuddles. It became a cosy weekend ritual. Who cared about dog-training and dominant behaviour?

Naturally, as far as Beans saw it, we had given her *carte blanche* to jump on the bed whenever the fancy took her – whether it had been made or not. We had given her the freedom of the house – could we blame her for taking advantage of it?

Now that most of her walks had been shortened, Beans was quite happy. As long as we were out in the countryside, among the funny birds and rivers full of stones, that was fine by her.

Much of the Peak District is out of bounds to us during the winter. Roads can be blocked by snow or made treacherous with black ice, so the car spends a lot of time snug in the garage. If anyone needed a 4X4 vehicle it was us. Forget the people just using them for the school run. Just think of all those places we could have reached. Despite this, the expense couldn't be justified. On snowy days we just contented ourselves with walking from home. We'd get the boots on and head off in whatever direction we fancied. The Cloud was an easy seven mile round trip, or we could head up to Congleton Edge or Mow Cop. It didn't matter; there was plenty of choice without even waking the car up.

There's something more liberating and satisfying about walking from home and exploring those local paths. Apart from the obvious worry about the car ending up in a ditch, there was the satisfaction of starting and finishing a walk from our front door. No wasted travelling time, no muddy paw prints in the car and being able to wash Beans down in the back garden instead of coming home with a bagful of filthy towels.

After her day's adventures, Beans wanted nothing more than her evening meal followed by a good long sleep. You could call it the dog equivalent of our 'get the kettle on' routine. A big steaming mug of tea or coffee always tastes better after a long walk. Beans was happy with a bowlful of tripe mix, a roll on one of her squeaky toys, a satisfied belch and then a nap.

Hours later she'd wake up, yawn, stretch and head to the kitchen for a drink. She looked like someone who has just got out of bed in the morning as she staggered into the kitchen, only half awake. Refreshed, she'd wobble back into the living room and settle down again.

One evening, we noticed a change in her gait as she walked to the kitchen. The drunken stagger was there, with one alarming addition: she was limping markedly and her limbs were stiff. After a particularly strenuous walk we sometimes felt the same after sitting for a while, so perhaps Beans had overdone things a little. Once she'd been up and about for a while she seemed to loosen up and the limp disappeared.

Although the limping carried on, we tried not to worry about it too much, putting it down to just general stiffness after walking. What worried us more were some strange lumps that had started to appear on her belly. The lumps were soft, of varying sizes and seemed to move around under the skin. With an awful sense of dread, we made an appointment with the vet.

Taking Beans to the vet had always been something of an occasion. She always seemed to know where she was going, pulling and barking all the way from the car to the surgery. Then there was the grand entrance. She'd march in as if she owned the place, pulling like mad on her lead, whether from fear or excitement we could only guess. The Wilmslow surgery we used to take her to was of particular interest to her. You walked into a small waiting room off which there was an examination room and, on the right, a high counter, behind which the receptionists worked. Fascinated by the sounds of tapping keyboards and the noises of office equipment from behind the reception, she'd promptly head straight for it, jump up and peer over the counter to see what was going on. She looked like she was about to order a beer.

Sometimes the receptionist hadn't spotted her gawping over the counter, a situation Beans used to her advantage. A small bark was just enough to surprise the poor woman. Then she'd see Beans' inquisitive face looking at her.

'Oh hello,' she'd smile at Beans, 'and what can we do for you today?'

Beans' celebrity status carried on when we moved to our new home. We usually parked just around the corner from the surgery, but the staff were never in any doubt that Beans' arrival was imminent. They could hear her. The barking would be a faint sound in the distance at first, but by the time we reached the front door, the receptionists were well prepared for Beans' barnstorming entrance.

Still barking frantically, she'd storm in – dragging me in the process – and plonk her front paws on the reception desk. No one complained about her rather boisterous behaviour. Staff and customers alike loved her. Whatever the purpose for her visits, she always greeted the staff the same way. Quite what the other trembling pooches waiting patiently thought of all this I don't know, but Beans' confident arrival was always tempered by the fact that she too ended up sitting there trembling with all the other dogs, awaiting whatever treatment the vet had in store for them. Underneath the bravado, she was as scared as the big shaking German shepherd sitting in the corner.

The occasional miaow from a cat-carrier would temporarily distract the dogs from their impending consultations. Some would take their minds off their fears by investigating the myriad of smells on the floor, probably mainly pee, released by unfortunate animals whose fear of the vet's booster jab or probing thermometer was simply too much.

Beans' behaviour changed completely once she was on the examination table. Fear took over. As long as the vet didn't take an overly-enthusiastic interest in her rear end, or her mouth, everything was fine. For Richard, our vet, however, that spelt trouble. If he examined her at the back end he was likely to be bitten. If he examined her mouth – or, indeed, any part of her head – the outcome was likely to be the same. Beans was not a very good patient. She could whip round in an instant with that mouthful of teeth, and she wasn't playing. She meant business. If this guy thought he could shove something up her backside, he was very much mistaken and would pay dearly for it. Richard was left with no choice: out came the muzzle.

'It's the same when we try to groom her,' we'd say pathetically.

'Yes, she's got quite a bite there,' Richard replied, looking rather nervous as he fastened the plastic muzzle on Beans.

This time though, there would be no need for a muzzle. Beans was tolerant of any prodding around her tummy. Even so, you could never be complacent and as Richard gently examined the strange lumps I'm sure the thought was in his mind that Beans could unleash one of her fearsome attacks at any moment.

As he carefully felt the mystery lumps around Beans' abdomen, we were both thinking the worse. What if they were cancerous or she needed an operation? One of the lumps was particularly large and it was hard not to be pessimistic.

'I'm certain they're benign fatty growths,' Richard said, 'you tend to find them a lot on Labradors or Golden Retrievers.'

We were certain Beans had at least some Labrador or retriever in her make-up so this seemed a pretty fair diagnosis. Even so, we were still worried. The lumps had increased over the months, but Richard didn't seem unduly concerned.

'Is there any way we can be certain?' I asked him.

'Well, we could do a biopsy and take some blood tests, but that would mean she'd need to be sedated,' he replied.

He went on to explain what the lumps were in an effort to allay our fears, but we needed to be sure.

'So it's not a general anaesthetic job?' Jan asked.

'Oh no. We'd just give her a mild sedative to relax her and then a local anaesthetic while the samples are taken.'

'Would she need to stay in overnight?' Jan continued.

'No, but she might be pretty dopey afterwards,' Richard cautioned.

We booked Beans in for her biopsy the following week. All that remained was the blood test. It was muzzle time. True to form, as the needle went in, Beans tried to take a piece out of our friendly vet, but a combination of the muzzle and my firm grip on her, prevented any damage. With a sense of relief, I relaxed as he withdrew the syringe full of blood. Beans was so strong when she wanted to be, that I had visions of the needle ending up in me, if Richard missed his aim.

The day of Beans' biopsy arrived. I couldn't get the day off, so Jan decided to walk down to the surgery with her. It was a sunny day and Jan decided that Beans wouldn't be as stressed if she thought she was just going on a nice walk.

Of course, by the time Beans reached the place where we normally parked the car, she knew exactly where she was heading. There was no fooling her. *Think you can get me to the vets without me realising? Think again. Time for some serious barking!* By the time the two of them reached the front door of the surgery, Beans was in full swing. Jan barely had time to close the door behind her as Beans pulled her through the entrance hall into the waiting room.

'Hello Beans!' said Linda, the receptionist, as Beans announced herself in the usual way, paws on the counter, ears pricking up at the sounds of computer printers and credit card machines.

The usual line-up of suspects were all sitting there: a couple of dogs, cats, safely hidden away from the dogs in their carriers, and the odd rabbit or hamster. Beans couldn't resist a little cat-taunting to brighten up her visit. At least there wasn't much chance of a scratched nose when she stuck it up against their carriers. All they could do was whine at her, but little else.

Richard appeared from the examination room.

'Right Beans, let's have a look at you!' He was holding a syringe-full of sedative.

He crouched down to stroke Beans, who'd probably realised something unpleasant was about to happen. Whether it involved a cold thermometer inserted where the sun never shone, or the *thwack* of disposable gloves preceding a rear-end check, she'd no idea. *If he tries to stick one of those needles in me I'll have him this time. I'll have sunk my teeth in him before he's even thought of the word 'muzzle.'*

Jan held onto Beans while Richard prepared to inject her. Her lips were starting to curl almost imperceptibly, even before he'd touched her.

'This is just a mild sedative to get her nice and relaxed,' he said reassuringly. Just for once, Beans didn't flinch as the needle went in. But those lips were still curling.

With the sedative safely administered, all Jan could do now was sit and wait with her while it took effect.

'It'll be several minutes before she starts to feel drowsy,' Richard said, 'so I'll see some of my other patients while you're waiting.'

Beans sat upright at Jan's side while a succession of animals came and went. She was probably wondering what she was doing there. Without so much as a *by your leave* this man had stuck a needle in her and then walked off. Was that it? If so, why wasn't Jan walking her home? It was all very odd. Then she started to feel drowsy.

Jan noticed Beans' eyelids were slowly starting to droop, then open again, as if she was fighting the drowsiness starting to overcome her. Then, slowly – oh so slowly – her front paws began to slide forward. For a moment, they'd stop; she'd sway a little from side to side, and then start moving forward again.

Beans' head was starting to droop now. The skin around her face was starting to relax and sag. A small amount of drool escaped from a corner of her mouth. Her battle with the sedative was almost over.

Now, instead of sliding forward, her legs started to splay out to the sides. As they did so, she tried to stop them, but it was futile – they merely carried on sliding forward. Her eyes were now completely shut and her head hung down limply. Finally, sleep overcame her and she collapsed to the floor.

'Okay Mrs Johnson,' Richard said, looking at Beans' relaxed body, 'you can bring her in now.'

Bearing in mind Beans weighed about 20kg and was sedated, Jan wondered how she was going to carry her to the examination room.

'I think I'll need some help,' she said, attempting to lift Beans' floppy body.

'Yes of course,' Richard replied, seeing Jan struggling with the limp Beans.

He took hold of her front end, while Jan brought up the rear, and the two of them carried Beans into the room, her tongue lolling out of her mouth. She was away somewhere else, a land where grouse and squirrels could be found in abundance, there for the chasing.

In no time at all Richard had taken the samples from Beans' lumps and it was time to transport her back to the waiting room. It was going to be a while now before Jan could walk her home, so she just had to sit and wait for the sedative to wear off enough.

Richard had warned her that the sedative might relax all Beans' bodily functions, but luckily her bladder decided not to release itself all over the floor. It's rare to go into a vets' surgery and not see a tell-tale wet patch on the floor and a recently used mop. Some dogs routinely manifest their fear of a vet visit by evacuating their bladders – or worse – on the floor. That was one problem we never had with Beans, but then again, she didn't get sedated every time she visited.

After about half an hour Beans started to come round. Her eyes opened and she started to lick her dry lips. Stretching, she tried to get up, but it was too soon and she flopped down again. Another few minutes and she was on her feet, but looking decidedly unsteady and bewildered.

With no car to transport her, Jan would have to wait until Beans was capable of walking back under her own steam. As she wobbled over to a bowl of water to quench her thirst it was obvious she wasn't going to get very far.

Another half hour or so passed by and Jan decided Beans was awake enough to make her way home.

'Give us a ring in a few days and we should have all the results back,' Richard said, as Jan led the dopey dog out of the surgery. The blood test results were not back yet either, so those few days would be torment until we new whether Beans was in the clear or not.

It was still a beautifully sunny afternoon as Jan and Beans began their walk home. Well, Jan at least was walking. Beans was attempting to assume something that resembled a walk, but not doing very well at all.

Later on, when I asked Jan how things had gone at the vet's she told me all about the afternoon's events – and the long walk home.

'She was walking like one of Billy Connolly's Glaswegian drunks,' Jan said.

At first I couldn't quite see the analogy, but then I remembered one of Billy's achingly funny descriptions of drunks in his home town, making their slow, laborious way home, staggering from side to side, stumbling and carrying fish suppers that he said looked like they weighed several pounds.

'It must have taken you ages to get home,' I replied, with that vision of Beans' drunken-like gait in my mind.

'Just a bit,' she said, 'but we made it didn't we Beanie?'

Beans, now back in the land of the fully awake, looked none the worse for her experience. As she greeted me in her usual enthusiastic way, I knelt down to cuddle her.

'Where's her bean bag?' I asked Jan, noticing the empty plastic bed.

'Hanging on the washing line,' she replied, in a matter of fact tone.

As soon as they'd got home, the first thing Beans did was make for her bed. Some time later, with the last effects of the sedative gone, she'd woken up and headed outside.

It was then that Jan noticed the wet patch on Beans' bed, where she'd peed away to her heart's content during her sleep. What was it about Beans and peeing on beds?

Several days later we rang the vet for the results of Beans' tests. The seconds seemed like minutes as we waited for him to come to the phone.

'All clear,' Richard said cheerfully, 'the blood tests showed nothing up and the biopsy was clear. They were just benign lumps as I thought.'

We both breathed a huge sigh of relief.

Landmarks

Although we now knew that Beans' mystery lumps were harmless, her limping was still cause for concern. We couldn't help worrying that she was perhaps doing too much, even though her enthusiasm was still very much there. She still hobbled around for a while after her hikes, but it seemed to be taking her longer to recover, even though we'd reduced the mileage drastically.

The problem now was that the limp was starting to appear before the walk had finished. The stiffness when she woke up later on we expected; this was a new development. We started to worry again.

Despite our concerns about Beans, she was otherwise in good health, so our thoughts turned towards holidays again. We decided to mark the final year of the twentieth century with our first trip to Ireland. Beans booked in for her usual two weeks bed and breakfast in Wilmslow, while we headed off for the delights of County Kerry.

It was a memorable – if not totally enjoyable – holiday, marred by the fact that our ferry crossing back was cancelled. Technical problems was the reason given, another way of saying the ship had broken down. After much messing about and downright incompetence by the ferry company, we were told there was a ferry we could catch: from Rosslare in County Wicklow. Great! We were in Dublin, a hundred miles away.

Then they told us what time the ferry left Rosslare: midnight. A quick look at my watch and I figured we could just about make it, providing there were no hold-ups. I would also have to drive like an idiot.

Someone must have been looking after us that night, because the entire journey down the east coast of Ireland was hold-up free. It also seemed to be police-free, which was just as well because my speedometer rarely dipped below 80 mph on the main roads. I crawled through the towns and villages and then it was full speed ahead to Rosslare. It was not the sort of driving I ever want to repeat.

To add insult to injury, we arrived in Rosslare in plenty of time for the ferry, only to be told it had been delayed an hour. The end of our holiday was becoming a farce. We were tired, hungry and all we wanted now was to get home to Beans.

We eventually arrived back on the British mainland about 2am, sailing into the little port of Fishguard in south west Wales, 163 miles from where we should have ended up – Holyhead in north Wales. All we wanted to do now was sleep, but there was nowhere open at that time of the night. It was going to be a long drive home through the night.

Some good did come out of the entire adventure: the ferry company kindly gave us handfuls of duty free vouchers as compensation, which were promptly spent in the well-stocked shop, and we saw the sunrise over Aberystwyth Bay as we awoke from a fitful sleep in the car. I was too tired even to get my camera out.

Compared to our adventures, Beans had an uneventful two weeks' rest. Evening walks with Bob, searching for foxes, and sun worshipping in the garden was all she needed. Having a rest from her usual activities had done her good. The limp had become more of a hobble when she got up, that soon lessened once she got moving.

She had even put on a bit of weight, which was hardly surprising when we discovered that she'd developed a sneaky habit of pinching biscuits from Bob's table after he dozed off in the evening. How many she managed to consume during her stay was anybody's guess, but given that he liked a couple every evening with his milky coffee, then the maths wasn't too difficult. No wonder she was looking a little rounder than usual.

Despite leading the life of Reilly for two weeks, she'd not lost any of her enthusiasm for going out on her Sunday hikes. The walks had been slimmed down, but it was now time for Beans to slim down.

It was good to get back on our familiar Peak District paths – or even our local ones for that matter. Despite enjoying some great walks in Ireland – and some tremendous views – there is nowhere to beat the path network and right of access Great Britain enjoys. There's something very satisfying about walking a path that has probably been a right of way for hundreds of years, following in the same steps as thousands of people before you. It's a direct link with the past.

We've always enjoyed finding out about the old paths and trackways that criss-cross the country. Our bookcase is full of books on history, archaeology and geology. When we moved to Congleton we discovered that many of the local paths connected the town with outlying villages and churches. Despite the local golf course altering the lie of the land, you can still see the dip in the ground where a sunken lane once ran.

Beans wasted no time in sniffing out all her local routes. This was her 'patch', full of interesting smells and alive with squirrels. Following the scent trails of squirrels and other creatures through the woods was what Beans lived for, but as we'd already discovered, it did sometimes get her into trouble. Once on the trail of something she was in her own little world, oblivious to everything else, including us.

Whether disappearing into the woods on the Cloud, or following the many trails of rabbits or foxes at Brereton, one thing was obvious: she panicked if she lost sight of us. We put this theory to the test by playing a rather unkind game of hide and seek with her. When we followed the path from the Cloud summit into the woods, we usually let her off her lead to go off on her adventures. Before long, she'd picked up an interesting trail and was soon in front of us, nose to the ground, lost to the scent. We picked the biggest tree to sneak behind – and waited.

I carefully peeped around the trunk; she hadn't noticed we weren't following her. This must have been a good trail. Then I looked again. She couldn't see us, but she'd stopped, turned round and had a distinct look of panic on her face. She turned this way and that, wondering where the heck we were. Then she started trotting back in our direction. Everything about her demeanour suggested she didn't want to be lost. She seemed to have forgotten about following scents and was now using her eyes, desperately trying to find us.

Sometimes she would sniff us out, but on other occasions she trotted past, totally oblivious. At that point it was time to put her out of her misery and call her over. Her reaction when she found us was as if we'd just returned from six months holiday, not a few minutes hiding behind a tree. After barking and running around excitedly, she'd then daub a nice set of mucky paw prints on us. Served us right I suppose.

Having a bit of fun was one thing, but something still needed to be done about Beans' occasional disappearing acts. It would have been cruel to just keep her on her lead and deny her all those wonderful dog adventures, but how could we keep tabs on her? The answer was really very simple – a bell attached to her collar. Okay, it wasn't the most innovative, earth-shattering answer to our problem, but it worked. Now, when she did her vanishing act into the undergrowth all we needed to do was make sure we kept that tinkling bell within earshot. If she'd been gone too long, all we did was home in on the direction of the sound and sooner or later we'd all be reunited.

Beans seemed to like her new collar bell, or 'activity bell' as we liked to call it. It was as if she felt more secure with it on. We certainly felt happier, hearing that familiar ringing sound as it echoed through the woods.

Autumn was soon upon us again and those last few weeks of the twentieth century were passing fast. Newspapers were full of 'Millennium Bug' scare stories and all manner of doomsday predictions.

The end-of-the-world people were hard at work putting the fear of god into everyone and we all wondered whether the end of the world was indeed 'nigh.' The prophecies of Nostradamus were being even more twisted to suit those who wanted us all to believe that an apocalypse was imminent. According to one doom merchant a gigantic asteroid should have hit the mid Atlantic in 1999, causing far-reaching catastrophe. And so it went on. Internet sites were awash with such tripe for the gullible to absorb. People seemed to be forgetting that doomsday prophets down the ages have been predicting the end of the world on various dates. None have come true.

So I wasn't too worried about all the end of the world nonsense doing the rounds. Nevertheless, I did share some of the unease about what *might* happen when the clocks ushered in the new millennium. I read my Millennium Bug pamphlet, secretly worrying about computers the world over crashing, aircraft dropping from the sky when their on-board computers failed and banking systems going into meltdown.

If you believed all this stuff, people were going to wake up on January 1st 2000 to worldwide anarchy and social breakdown. There would be no need for an asteroid – our global dependence on technology would be our nemesis. I found the best policy was to ignore it all and hope it would go away. It did. New Year's Eve 1999 arrived and the world held its breath.

We woke to a beautifully sunny January 1st 2000. Instead of doom and gloom, the newspapers were full of colourful photographs of the worldwide Millennium celebrations and stunning images of dawn as it broke in the different time zones. There were no news reports of computer bugs or major catastrophes. It was just another New Year's Day, with one difference – we were now in a new century and a new Millennium.

A walk up the Cloud seemed the best way to celebrate the day. Many people had the same idea; some no doubt arriving earlier to see the dawn break over the neighbouring Peak District hills. It was a stunning start to the year 2000. We were treated to one of those amazing temperature inversions, where fog had formed around the Cloud and the Dane Valley, but above a certain level there was nothing but a clear blue sky as far as the eye could see. It was also the first time we saw a 'Brocken Spectre;' a ghostly, shadowy figure of you that appears in the mist when you look at it from a height with a low sun behind you. With a multi-coloured halo or 'glory' above the figure, it looked amazing – Biblical even.

January 2000 came and went and we looked forward to the spring. There had been no worldwide calamities or computers deciding to do strange things with their dates. The doom-mongers went back to finding something else to frighten us with, while we all got on with the job of living.

Spring arrived as only spring could. Daffodils lined the lanes and paths of the Peak District, their bright yellows cheering up the still bare winter landscape. Soon, the first hints of fresh foliage started to appear in the hedgerows and on the trees. Nature was starting to wake up. Before long, bluebells would start to appear in the woods and blossom on the trees. It was time to get my camera out of hibernation.

Although we enjoyed our walks in all our familiar Peak District places, we felt we were neglecting other, equally beautiful, parts of the country. The Yorkshire Dales were a longer drive away, but we felt like a change of scene. We decided on a trip to Wharfedale. It would have to be a short walk to suit Beans, but that wasn't difficult, given the stunning scenery. She would even have a good long stretch of the River Wharfe to paddle in. Off we went, to the pretty little village of Buckden, in Upper Wharfedale.

It was a perfect May walk. The sun shone all day and the scenery was glorious. Primroses grew among the limestone pavements above the dale, lambs played in the fields and everything shouted 'spring.' Beans was delighted to discover the River Wharfe on the final stage of the walk, wasting no time in splashing into the water to cool off. She even relieved the river of some of its stones – her first Yorkshire Dales collection. The day was rounded off nicely with afternoon tea in the sunshine, outside Buckden's tea room. This was what walking in England was all about.

Despite a lovely day in Yorkshire, a shadow loomed on the horizon. Although she seemed to have enjoyed the walk, Beans appeared more tired than usual. This wasn't so surprising. It had been a hot day and we were pretty tired too, but despite shortening Beans' walks, her limp refused to go away. If anything, it seemed to be getting worse. By the time we got home that evening, after a good sleep in the car, she seemed to have recovered, but the pay-off for an enjoyable day was an evening of limping and hobbling.

Even a modest five or six mile walk like this took her a day to recover from. But as long as her enthusiasm and enjoyment remained, we didn't want to have to curtail her activities any more than was necessary. Nevertheless, I couldn't help feeling that she might have just preferred a nice slow ramble along the river, paddling and fishing out stones.

Our worries were compounded by the fact that she was becoming a little slower even when walking around the block on her early morning or evening walks. Instead of trotting along by my side, she was starting to lag behind. Sometimes it felt like she didn't want to be out at all. My morning walks were timed to give her a decent walk before breakfast and getting ready for work, so I had to adjust things to accommodate her slower pace.

I felt awful, one morning, when I'd got impatient with her for lagging behind. It wasn't her fault; it was mine, for not allowing enough time, but I was in denial.

I couldn't face the fact that Beans, like all of us, was getting old. She had plenty more years left in her. Why was she walking so slowly? Why couldn't she trot alongside me as she'd always done? To my shame, I was frustrated with her for not keeping up. Later, at home, I became overcome with guilt at my selfishness and would apologise to her with a cuddle. I meant it, and I think she knew that. Dogs always love you, despite your human failings. I don't care what anyone says – it's a love that is total and unconditional.

There was no escaping the truth: this affliction was something that wasn't going to go away. An injury would have healed itself by now, but this had been going on for months. We read the ailment chapters in all our dog books and reached the inevitable conclusion that she had arthritis, although we would need to have it confirmed.

With heavy hearts we made another appointment to see Richard. We described the symptoms to him and then he confirmed what we really knew already.

'I'm almost certain it's arthritis,' he said, gently examining Beans' limbs.

He went on to tell us there were several effective drugs available for animals with arthritis, which was certainly encouraging, but what worried us was how much longer she'd be able to go hiking with us. We'd drawn a line under the stick and rubber ring chasing when Beans' symptoms had started to appear, but what about everything else?

'She can certainly carry on with her walks,' Richard advised, 'because the exercise is good for her legs, but don't overdo it.'

'What about long hikes and swimming?' Jan asked.

'Swimming is the best thing for her, as long as she wants to keep doing it, because there's less pressure on her legs,' he said.

'And the hikes?'

'I think it would be best to give them a miss from now on, but there's no problem at all with short walks.'

It was the answer we knew we'd have to expect, but were hoping we wouldn't. Beans would have to retire from long walks. It was time for her to enjoy her life at a more sedate pace. We see plenty of elderly people still out walking in the country; the only difference being they're probably doing a more relaxed six miles as opposed to the fifteen they used to do. It's no different for a dog.

Beans' treatment involved trying to inject a small syringe of the drug into her mouth at mealtimes. It wasn't easy, but then again trying to give Beans any form of medication was fraught with problems. It should have been an easy process: just pour the liquid drug onto her food, which she would then eat. Trouble was, she didn't. Anything alien appearing on her food and that was it – game over. The entire bowlful would have to be thrown away, unless we could successfully remove any uncontaminated bits. Even then there was no guarantee she'd finish it. Unless the entire meal was replaced, she'd eye up anything else with suspicion. When it came to medicine, I don't think she trusted us.

Over the years, on the few occasions when we'd had to administer any tablets to her, we had to come up with many ingenious – or devious – methods of getting her to swallow the tablet. The simplest method was to mix it with her meals and hope it would pass down her throat with everything else. That was way too easy. Inspection of her bowl once she'd finished her meal revealed a small white tablet, carefully sifted from the food. She was far too clever for us. Her pill-detector senses worked extremely well. Another method would have to be found.

Putting the tablet on the back of her tongue was as ineffective as it was dangerous. She never swallowed it, regurgitating the partly-dissolved tablet on to the floor. There was also the risk of her teeth taking a piece out of us as she fought and gagged against this intrusion into her mouth. It was infuriating. We even resorted to taking a piece of her food and inserting the tablet in it, in the vain hope the whole lot would vanish down her gullet without her even noticing. Beans was quite a voracious eater (what dog isn't) and we hoped we'd cracked it this time. Sure enough, when we looked at her bowl, there it was: one tablet, lying in a bowl licked clean.

Crushing the tablet, in the hope that even Beans wouldn't be able to dissect her food that meticulously, didn't work. She just refused to eat the entire meal, until we'd replaced it with a non tablet-tainted one. Beans was winning this battle; what else could we try? The answer came in the form of one of Beans' favourite treats: cheese.

Beans loved the occasional piece of cheese. We didn't feed her vast quantities of the stuff, but if I was making the next days' sandwiches and they happened to contain cheese, I'd usually give her a morsel. I swear it never touched the sides as it went down. I wondered whether this might be the answer to our tablet problems.

The next time she was due a tablet, I cut a small cube of cheese – usually Cheddar which doesn't crumble too much – and carefully pushed the tablet into it. I gave her the cheese and down it went. A few seconds passed and I was convinced she'd spit the tablet out. Nothing happened. I opened her mouth and checked around her teeth and gums. No tablet. At last, a result. The tablet was on its way.

Unfortunately, her arthritis treatment wasn't as straightforward. Once the syringe was filled with the correct dosage, the liquid had to be injected into her mouth, to be promptly swallowed. That was the theory.

In practice, it proved to be a mess. Opening her mouth was no problem, but aiming the syringe in such a way that its contents were swallowed was tricky. Too near the front of her mouth and she'd spit everything out, too near the side and it just fell from her mouth with a load of drool. We couldn't stick it right down the back of her throat or she'd throw up everywhere. The trick was to squirt the liquid quickly into her mouth and then hold her jaws together. After a few seconds the reflex swallowing action would ensure the drug was safely on its way.

We felt cruel; having to resort to this method, but it was the only way to get Beans' medication down her. She never was a very good patient, but then again I remember clearly those vile tasting cough medicines from my childhood, which went down like a lump of lead, making you gag and retch as the pink goo slid down your throat. You held it in your mouth, trying to summon up the courage to swallow. When you were ready, down it went. Nobody was clamping your jaws shut to stop you spitting it out. Poor Beans; she must have hated it. We had to keep telling ourselves it was for her own good.

It took a few weeks before the treatment started to take effect, but gradually we started to notice a difference. The limp lessened and she didn't appear to be as stiff as before. Things were looking hopeful. We carried on with our usual local walks, with a few short hikes thrown in now and again. Everything seemed fine. She wasn't as energetic as before, but there was definitely more of a spring in her step. Unfortunately, it wasn't enough of a spring to enable her to jump on the bed in the morning anymore. That was perhaps the saddest part. Beans loved those morning cuddles, even though it was just pure indulgence. She contented herself with lying at the side of the bed on Jan's thick home-made rug.

Now that Beans seemed to be much better, we felt more able to start thinking about how we were going to celebrate the two milestones of our own that year: my fortieth and our tenth wedding anniversary. I'd always fancied going back to Austria to do some real mountain walking. My last visit had been in 1975 on a family holiday, so I was long overdue a return visit. Jan had never been there and she too liked the idea of those Sound of Music mountains. The decision was made for us; we would celebrate among the magnificent scenery of the Austrian Tyrol.

Although we'd enjoyed holidays in our own country for years, it was good to start looking forward to a bit more of an adventure. I'd not flown for more than fifteen years, Jan even longer than that, so we were both nervous at the prospect of boarding an aircraft again.

Strictly speaking, we wouldn't be away for either my birthday or the wedding anniversary. The anniversary had already passed, back in May, my birthday wasn't until July and we were going in June, but at least it fell in the middle of it all. Three months sabbatical in Austria would have been better, but not on our bank balances. In any case, we'd miss Beans too much.

They say time flies by quicker as you get older because it didn't seem that long since I'd celebrated my thirtieth, the same year we got married. I wasn't that bothered about reaching forty; to be honest, I was more bothered about boarding an aircraft again. The nearer it got to the day of our departure, the more anxious I became. Take off is the worst part for me. You've only got two chances: either you get airborne or you don't. There's no middle ground. By the time the aircraft has reached take off speed you've also reached the point of no return.

As I watched the Cheshire landscape pass below me, just after we'd taken off from Manchester Airport, I tried to block all thoughts of engine failure out of my mind. Statistically, you're much safer flying than driving, I kept telling myself as I squeezed the circulation out of Jan's leg. Then I realised she was squeezing mine as well.

Once at cruising height I started to relax more and enjoy the flight. To see the Stubaital Mountains below, as we started the descent to Innsbruck, was worth all that initial fear.

Austria was everything we hoped it would be: tremendous scenery, exhilarating walks and as much Apple Strudel as we could eat. It was a good job we supplemented the sightseeing with plenty of walking to burn off all that Austrian food. My camera was eating film at a fair rate too. I took so many photographs that it took me weeks to label all the slides when I got home.

Whilst we enjoyed our holiday, we couldn't help thinking how Beans was getting on. Detailed instructions on administering her treatment had been left with Bob and Rita, but how were they coping with Beans' stubborn nature? We had visions of pools of wasted medication soaking into the carpet, as they tried vainly to get it into her mouth, the air turning blue as she spat out another syringe-full.

We needn't have worried. Beans had co-operated fully during her two-week sojourn. She'd obviously got used to her routine of daily treatment. Perhaps the prospect of some illicit biscuit theft later on was enough incentive for her.

My fortieth came and went and those two weeks in Austria were soon a distant memory, but for country-lovers like us there was still something nature had left for us to look forward to. August soon arrived in the Peak District and the moors burst into colour as the heather came into bloom again. It was time to get out and enjoy it.

Beans was in her element on those purple carpets of heather. She loved to roll on it until she'd practically covered herself from head to tail in its heady fragrance. Watching her adorn herself in the heathery perfume made us wish that was all she rolled in. This was Beans' aromatherapy session. It was certainly far more entertaining than trying to remove all traces of fox dung from her. At times, all you could see of her were her paws waving in the air as she rolled on her back. Sometimes she vanished altogether, swallowed up by the heather. You knew she was there somewhere, because you could see the heather moving in all directions as she went this way and that. Just as we were wondering where she was going to re-appear, up popped her head from the heather; a look of sheer delight on her face.

The drug treatment for her arthritis, which up until now had been a success, didn't appear to be working quite as effectively on her ageing bones than the heather was on her wellbeing. She'd started limping again.

Although she'd more or less retired from long hikes, we just hadn't felt able to completely deny her the odd longer walk. We couldn't face that moment when we would have to draw a line under so many years of happy walking in the Peak District. We were a threesome; to lose one member of that team was unthinkable.

In the end, Beans decided things for us. In the autumn, we made another visit to the vet for a review of her treatment. Richard told us there was another drug he could try that had proved very effective with horses. This time, the drug could be given on a regular basis by injection. No spat out tablets or liquid slopping out everywhere.

It was now time to make a decision on the walks. We would take her back to the place where she'd enjoyed her very first hike with us and that would be it; Beans would then officially 'retire.'

So on a bright clear December morning we went back to the spot where we'd taken Beans for her first 'proper' hike and her first sight of the 'funny birds:' Middle Moor.

We took our usual route out of Hayfield, following the path as it climbed up to Lantern Pike. The view from the top was especially good that day, with Kinder Scout laid out in its entirety before us. Below Kinder, and across the valley from us, lay Middle Moor, our next destination. The landscape looked almost autumnal, despite the fact we were well into December. The heather was a rich russet colour and our lunch stop, the little white shooting cabin, was clearly visible, alone on the moor, the sun reflecting off its bright white paintwork.

From Lantern Pike we dropped down to the hamlet of Little Hayfield, passing a small herd of docile Highland Cattle. Beans gave them a wide berth as we passed, though they appeared totally uninterested in her, unlike their Friesian cousins, who took regular delight in following us menacingly across fields. We soon reached the main road, cursing the fact that we had to walk a short stretch of it, before picking up the path again. With the noise of traffic lessening in the distance, we paused to let Beans paddle in a stream before crossing the footbridge and so on to Middle Moor.

A clear, well-used path led us through the heather, rising until the entire moor came into view, dominated by the vast bulk of Kinder Scout. Beans' radar ears had already picked up the grouse calls and I half expected to be launched into the heather at any moment. That was the problem: you never knew when she was going to surprise one, or even a whole group of them. I braced myself for take off.

The day was perfect for photography, clear and sharp, the blue winter sky filled with perfect photogenic 'cotton wool' clouds. I took some general shots, but I felt the landscape needed some human interest. The path led into the distance across my perfectly composed frame, but it needed someone walking on it to bring it to life. Jan and Beans obligingly posed for me, Jan's red hat and gaiters standing out nicely against the brown heather. It was a good saleable shot, but, at the same time, a perfect record of Beans' last big hike. Although I couldn't persuade Beans to look at me, it's still a treasured photograph, because she's busy looking at – or listening to – something far more interesting: grouse.

Our lunch at the old shooting cabin took on a certain poignancy. Beans listened to the grouse calling and we remembered the first time we sat there, twelve years before, totally ignorant of what the birds were, watching Beans' unexpected reaction to their cackling and flapping. I looked at Jan. Tears were rolling down her cheeks. I hugged her close.

'Beans loved her long walks,' she said.

'I know,' I replied. I didn't know what else to say.

We left the cabin and Middle Moor, stopping for a while to enjoy the low winter sun of the afternoon, as it warmed the Kinder plateau. The reservoir below was calm and still, clouds and hills reflected on its surface. As the sun began to dip even lower in the sky, we dropped back down into Hayfield. There couldn't have been a better finale to Beans' last hike.

Compromises and Disasters

Now Beans wasn't going on long walks anymore, we had a dilemma on our hands. We didn't want to stop our Sunday hikes altogether because the exercise and fresh air was so vital to our wellbeing, but it was unfair to leave Beans at home and head off to all her favourite places without her.

The mere sight of a rucksack carried downstairs was enough to send her into a whirl of excitement, so how could we get her wound up and raring to go – then drive off and leave her? We needed a plan of action.

In the end, we decided we'd have to trick Beans into thinking we weren't going hiking. To do that we had to make sure all our hiking gear was already in the car without her seeing any of it. Once breakfast was out of the way, Jan would take Beans for 'her' walk, leaving me free to load up the car.

We felt awful doing this to her, but it was better than raising her hopes, only to cruelly dash them. She couldn't do those longer walks and this was all for her benefit, but that didn't make it any easier. We took no pleasure in it; in fact, it didn't take us long to realise that going hiking without Beans was just not the same. All those places we'd always gone to together were not as enjoyable without her. It was almost as if we no longer had her at all, even though we knew she was, in all probability, curled up on an armchair enjoying the warm sun shining through the living room window.

For several weeks we carried on like this, but we were not enjoying our walks. We felt selfish and cruel, despite giving her the exercise she needed. Something had to give, so we decided to compromise. Long walks would be taken every two or three weeks, interspersed with Beans-length walks. That way, everyone was happy. Besides, for a few years now we'd been going out cycling, which could easily be fitted into an afternoon, leaving the morning free for Beans. Once she'd had her morning fun, she didn't care what we did. An afternoon of armchair relaxing was plenty to look forward to.

Things were made easier knowing that Beans' new treatment was working wonders. She went from limping badly and being barely able to keep up with me, to happily trotting along at my side. Her arthritis seemed to be gone. It was truly remarkable. We wondered why a similar treatment couldn't be used on humans. Beans was happy again – and we were too. Those marathon walks were a thing of the past, but she could at least enjoy the ones we did take her on. One of her favourite 'retired' walks – and one of ours – became the lovely circular route from Alstonefield down to Milldale (and that nice café) and back via upper Hall Dale and Stanshope. We called it our 'Snowdrops and Daffodils' walk, because in February the narrow track from Stanshope comes alive with the beautiful white flowers of the snowdrops. As soon as March arrives, the snowdrops are replaced by masses of bright yellow daffodils lining the track.

Just as Lathkill Dale became our May pilgrimage walk for the Early Purple Orchids, this delightful little corner was our spring pilgrimage. As long as Beans could still do it, we were happy. She could no longer do the long Lathkill Dale walk, but what this little walk lacked in length, it more than made up for in quality.

In February 2001, disaster hit the country: Foot-and-mouth disease broke out on a farm in Northumberland. Within weeks the disease had spread. Television screens showed harrowing images of slaughtered farm animals being incinerated on huge pyres, the carcasses of sheep, pigs and cattle being hoisted into the flames. Not even people's pet farm animals were spared. Newspapers carried similarly graphic images of the culling and tragic pictures of new-born lambs starving in muddy fields because they could not be moved. For the farmers, it was practically Armageddon.

Soon, footpaths, bridleways and tracks were closed off to walkers and horse riders. The countryside was shut down. The effects on the leisure and tourism industries were almost as catastrophic, as people cancelled holidays, weekends away and pony-trekking trips. Cafés, hotels, guesthouses, shops and country pubs were all affected.

For walkers, the closure of all public footpaths was like taking barbells away from a bodybuilder and telling him to take up cross stitching. Every local path was shut: the canal towpath, the Cloud, the entire Peak District, and even a local country park we used regularly, which was nowhere near farmland or livestock. Most of the closures we could understand, but not that one. Beans was confined to permanent walks around the block.

There was some good news though. To their credit, one local council decided to keep an area open to the public; Biddulph Country Park, one of Beans' favourite walking spots. Every dog and dog owner we knew from the surrounding area was there, every weekend. The place was packed. Everyone was grateful that this small but pleasant piece of the country had been kept open.

Despite the frustration of the path closures, the need for it all was brought home to us all too clearly when a local farm was hit by the disease. Foot-and-mouth was an appalling nightmare. Farmers were given no choice than to have entire herds of animals slaughtered, in a horribly misguided attempt to stop the disease spreading. I was only seven when foot-and-mouth last struck the country in 1967, but I still remember those black and white news films of burning carcasses. Why hadn't the government learnt anything from the report following that disaster? The advice not to burn carcasses was ignored and so the wind spread the disease far and wide. Experts from abroad, where the disease had been successfully checked by a policy of isolating and vaccinating animals, were stupidly ignored.

For those small farmers, already struggling to make a decent living, such a cruel and abhorrent policy meant ruin. Our hearts went out to those hill farmers in the Lake District who lost thousands of the distinctive and unique Herdwick breed of sheep, who grace the Lakeland Fells. I don't pretend to understand the reasoning of the powers that be at times like this, but the slaughtering of thousands of healthy animals – even new born lambs – was surely not the answer. I hope I never have to see such ghastly sights again.

Another casualty of the disaster – although not as important – was our holiday that year. We'd already booked two weeks in Cornwall and Exmoor before foot-and-mouth struck. When the news broke, it became clear that virtually every footpath in the country was going to be shut. It just wasn't worth going on what was predominately a walking holiday. Reluctantly, we telephoned the bed and breakfast owners to tell them we would have to cancel. How many other people were doing exactly the same thing?

Great Britain, to all intents and purposes, was now out of bounds to walkers. Thank heavens we could go cycling. Country lanes were open, although all farm entrances were protected by disinfectant. Cycling past all those public footpath signs with closed notices on them was sad, but at least we could still get some exercise and fresh air. Beans didn't care, as long as she had her little park to visit where she could meet all her canine chums, she was happy.

There was still the small problem of where to go for our holiday. We'd enjoyed our two weeks in Austria the year before, and there was still so much of that beautiful country to see. It was down to the travel agents for some brochures. We didn't take long to make our minds up; it was back to Austria again, this time to a place called Rauris, near the Hohe Tauern National Park.

Coming from a country that was riddled with foot-and-mouth, we imagined that we would be sprayed from head to toe with disinfectant as soon as we set foot on Austrian soil, but apart from a disinfectant mat at the entrance to the arrivals hall at Salzburg airport, that was it.

I still felt distinctly uneasy stepping foot on Austrian soil in my hiking boots. They'd not been anywhere near infected land, but it still felt like we should not be there. All these worries were unfounded of course. If the Austrian authorities were at all worried, they'd have stopped anyone from Great Britain entering the country.

Two weeks later, after another fabulous holiday, we were on the plane heading home. After a fortnight of fresh mountain air, clear tumbling streams, flower-filled meadows and exhilarating mountain paths, coming back was a bit of a shock. Foot-and-mouth was still doing its worst, but there was some good news on the horizon. Because many areas had not been struck by the virus, the Peak District National Park Authority decided to open a small section of the Park.

Access was allowed to a small section of Stanage Edge, in the north of the Park. Although there were strict controls, it was much, much better than nothing. Boots had to be dipped in disinfectant at various access points and fields with livestock avoided, but at least one of the most magnificent parts of the Park was open.

Better still; the section we were allowed to walk was only a few short miles, so we could take Beans.

We savoured the walk on Stanage Edge; not just because we were able to walk in the countryside again after months of closures, but because Beans was with us. It was nice to see her enjoying herself, back in 'funny bird' territory.

There were smiles on all the faces that day. You couldn't exactly be alone in your own piece of wild country, but no-one cared; we'd all been like coiled springs. Because it had been denied to us all those months, it made us all appreciate the superb walking country we had even more.

Soon, the foot-and-mouth crisis was over. It had been a disaster for the country – farmers and businesses alike. If one good thing did come out of the disaster it was that the countryside could no longer be viewed as unimportant. Too many livelihoods had been destroyed or badly affected for anyone to think the countryside didn't matter. Millions of pounds of revenue from visitors had been lost. Many farmers had lost everything. For some, already struggling to eke out a living in farming, it was simply the last straw and tragically, they took their own lives. It would be a long time before the country recovered. Some people would never recover.

In September, we took a much-needed week's leave while we had the house exterior painted. Beans was always suspicious if there was a stranger on the scene, barking madly when the decorator kept appearing at the windows with his ladders and pots of paint. After some introductions and the realisation that he posed no threat to her, she calmed down, but still eyed him up nervously as he went about his business.

Beans loved it when we were off work. There was no early morning wake up call for a trudge around the roads, but instead a nice leisurely walk over the fields with the promise of an odd squirrel or two. She wasn't as fast at the chase as she used to be, but those squirrels still got a good run for their money.

During late morning on the eleventh we were busy clearing up after breakfast and looking forward to taking Beans out for her walk. Andrew, the decorator, had arrived early that day to take advantage of the fine sunny weather. A few wet days had put him behind schedule, so this was the ideal day to play catch up. He'd already been hard at work for three hours and had just started on the living room window.

We always have the radio on when we're off work and as the news bulletin came on I stopped my pot-washing abruptly when the announcer said something about an aircraft hitting a building in New York City. I'd not heard the start of the report, so thinking it was probably a light aircraft that had crashed, I turned on the TV to find out more. As the screen came to life, I couldn't believe what I was seeing. An announcer or reporter was saying something, but I wasn't hearing; all I could see was one of the Twin Towers of the World Trade Centre with a huge pall of black smoke billowing out near the top. Something inside me told me this was no accident.

'Jan,' I yelled out, 'come and look at this on the TV.'

She hurried downstairs to see what had stopped me in my tracks.

'What's happened?' she asked.

'An aircraft's hit one of the World Trade Centre towers.'

As we sat there, transfixed by that black smoke billowing out over the New York skyline darkening the clear blue sky, an airliner suddenly came into view, heading straight for the other tower.

'Bloody hell,' I exclaimed, 'it's aiming straight for it.'

The words had barely left my mouth when the Boeing 767 slammed into the South Tower. The aircraft vanished in a gigantic fireball as its fuel tanks exploded. Any doubts I might have had that this was some dreadful accident vanished in an instant. That airliner had been deliberately crashed into the building.

'Oh my god,' was all Jan could say. My reply was unprintable.

Film crews on the streets of New York, already stunned by the first impact on the North Tower, captured the moment the aircraft slammed into the South Tower. People at ground level screamed and shouted in total disbelief as the Boeing roared over the city. Cameras quickly panned upwards to film the terrifying impact as the aircraft tore through the upper floors of the building.

Andrew was totally unaware of what was happening as he sanded down the old paintwork outside our living room, although he must have been wondering why we were sitting glued to the television in the middle of the day, with our jaws dropping. I opened one of the windows to tell him what was happening. He stopped his sanding and peered in through the window at the TV screen.

'God,' was all he could say.

Time seemed to stand still as the three of us watched those shocking events unfolding in real-time. Even Beans' walk was forgotten as we sat there transfixed by the nightmare scenes across the Atlantic. After a while, Andrew had to get back to his work, but all we could do was stare at the TV. We watched as the emergency services went about their business. We stared in absolute horror as the cameras picked out tiny images of terrified people clinging to the burning shell of the building, waiting for a rescue that would never come. We saw some of those tiny images that were human beings jump to their deaths 1000 feet below, rather than burn to death in that inferno of acrid smoke and flames.

Then the South Tower collapsed.

At first it was almost unnoticeable. The smoke seemed to billow out a little more either side of the tower, but then the uppermost section suddenly dropped, disappearing into the smoke. Within seconds the entire structure collapsed on itself like a line of dominoes. It was terrifying to watch. A massive cloud of thick, choking smoke and dust billowed out over the surrounding area of Lower Manhattan. Buildings adjacent to the vast amount of crashing debris and rubble were either obliterated or severely damaged. At ground level, the smoke blocked out the sun and that beautiful blue September sky. People who only moments before had been standing watching the burning twin towers, now ran for their lives as the dust and rubble enveloped the streets in a choking cloud, like some terrible volcano that had just erupted in the middle of the city.

As the appalling events unfolded in New York City, news broke that it wasn't just New York that had been hit. An airliner – Flight 77 – had crashed into the Pentagon in Arlington County Virginia, and another – Flight 93 – had come down in fields in Pennsylvania. It was only later we learned about the brave passengers on Flight 93 who had stormed the cockpit in an attempt to overpower the hijackers. Some of the passengers had already heard about the New York attacks and made the decision to try and prevent another tragedy. Through their heroic action they stopped the aircraft from being crashed into possibly the White House or The US Capitol Building.

With all the dreadful events being played out on our TV we'd quite forgotten that our patient dog had not had her walk yet. It was hard to tear ourselves away from the constant news reports, but Beans was lying there with a look on her face that suggested she'd given up on getting a walk that day. We couldn't ignore her any longer. I left the TV on while we got our coats and boots together. Beans' tail started wagging as she realised she hadn't been totally forgotten. Oblivious to worldly events, all she wanted was the promise of a good walk with maybe the odd squirrel to chase.

Just as we were ready to go, the running commentary was suddenly interrupted. We turned to the set again. The North Tower was collapsing. We already knew that many brave fire-fighters, policemen and other rescue workers were still inside, attempting to get people to safety. Now they too were dying, trapped and crushed by tons of collapsing masonry. The magnitude of what was happening was overwhelming. We had to get out into the countryside to take stock and gather our thoughts together.

In the days and weeks following 9/11 many images imprinted themselves on my mind: the look on President Bush's face when he was first told of the attacks, during his school visit; the iconic image of the three New York firefighters raising the US flag at Ground Zero, an image reminiscent of the Marines raising the flag on Iwo Jima during World War Two; the photographs that started to appear in the newspapers of some of the thousands of victims, including all the New York fire-fighters who lost their lives, and of course those terrible fireballs from the exploding aircraft. Then there was the benefit concert, America: A Tribute to Heroes, with performances from New York, London and Los Angeles. Three of my favourite artists, Bruce Springsteen, Billy Joel and Paul Simon, amongst others, sang at the concert. Billy Joel performed his classic New York State of Mind with a firefighter's helmet poignantly placed on his piano.

But there was one more image that stood out for me as I scanned all the newspapers I bought in the days following the attacks. It was a photograph of one of the many search and rescue dogs – a beautiful Golden Retriever – being transported out of the ruins at Ground Zero after searching for any survivors. With his special red coat and golden fur highlighted against the dark and sombre background of the World Trade Centre ruins, it was a wonderful image of what these selfless dogs do to help us. We rescue them from abuse or neglect and in return they rescue us when disaster strikes.

A few days after the attacks, Britain, along with the rest of Europe, came to a virtual standstill at noon to remember in silence almost three thousand people who'd lost their lives.

That day, we took Beans for a walk at one of our favourite local spots, Greenway Bank Country Park. There's a mysterious little grove of ancient yew trees and well at the park, just off the main path through the woods, which we always seem to have to ourselves whenever we visit. It's known as Gawton's Well, after a hermit who apparently lived there in the seventeenth century.

The well bubbles up from the ground into a very old stone trough, before cascading down through a stone-lined channel to join a stream further down. Gawton is said to have been cured of the plague after bathing in the waters, an event whether it is true or not, only serves to add to the mystery of the place. The yew trees have been deliberately planted in a circle around the well. No-one knows how old they are, but they've probably been there for many hundreds of years before old Gawton.

It might be an ancient, mysterious place, but there's never a creepy or eerie feel to it. It's a peaceful place; almost other-worldly. A place to make a wish and hope it comes true, something we always did whenever we were there.

But this was no day for selfish personal wishes or desires. It was a day to think about all those people – including little children and babies – whose lives had been so cruelly ended. Whatever Jan was wishing for she kept to herself; for me, I wished that all those people were now at peace in a better place. I've never believed that death is the end of things, especially when lives have been so abruptly and violently cut short. At that moment I was even more sure of that belief.

Some years after 9/11 I remembered that photograph of the Golden Retriever at Ground Zero. I wanted to find out more about the other dogs who'd helped in the rescue effort.

I typed in the words: *rescue dogs ground zero 9/11* on Google. Within seconds, the wonders of modern technology had brought up a whole list of sites devoted to the canine heroes of that day. I've always wondered at the amazing abilities of dogs to locate trapped people in earthquake ruins or those lost or injured in mountainous terrain. Many people owe their lives to these brilliant dogs.

I clicked on one website. Sure enough, there was that famous photograph of the retriever being carried from the ruins, but there was so much more that I'd never seen before. Dogs of all shapes, sizes and breeds involved in the enormous rescue effort. Even humble mongrels were doing their bit. Some dogs were there to look for survivors; others only task was to seek out the dead.

I learned about 'Jake', the Black Labrador, who not only worked at Ground Zero, but also later helped in the rescue effort in New Orleans in the wake of Hurricane Katrina.

Then there was 'Worf', the German Shepherd who, on the very first day of the rescue effort found the bodies of two missing firefighters. So traumatised was he by this that he had to be retired. I discovered that the dogs felt stress and depression because they couldn't find the living.

There was the sad story of 'Sirius', the K-9 partner of New York Port Authority Police Department Officer David Lim. Sirius and his master spent their days in and around the World Trade Centre on security duty, searching vehicles for bombs. On the day of the attacks Officer Lim left his devoted Labrador in his kennel beneath the Twin Towers while he went to help rescue people. Lim was buried when the tower collapsed, but was miraculously pulled out alive. Sadly, Sirius was found dead in his kennel some time later. His feeding bowl, which was also recovered, was later presented to Officer Lim at a memorial ceremony, plated and engraved with the words: *'I gave my life so that you may save others.'*

I read about a special unit of dogs brought in to provide comfort and support to the weary and traumatised rescue workers. Just like Beans did with Jan when Rita was taken ill, they recognised distress and helped in the only way they could – just by being there.

In the face of such death and destruction there would have been few smiles among the rescue workers in those harrowing weeks after the attacks, but the sight of one Golden Retriever walking around Ground Zero carrying his handler's helmet in his mouth was all it took to get people smiling.

Only the hardest heart could not fail to be moved by the two guide dogs, 'Roselle' and 'Salty (Dorado)', who led their owners, Michael Hingson and Omar Rivera to safety, only minutes before the towers fell. Despite the noise, commotion and sheer terror that must have been going on around them, those dogs did what they'd been trained to do, and saved their owners' lives. At a special ceremony on March 5th 2002, the PDSA awarded both dogs the PDSA Dickin Medal. It's the highest honour that Britain can give to an animal in war or danger. If those two dogs were people, they'd be walking around with Victoria Crosses hanging from their collars.

Looking at all those words and images, I realised that there is a special bond between people and dogs – not that I really needed it confirming – and that they bring so much into our lives, either as devoted pets or helping us when we most need help. When they give us so much and do so much for us, dogs just don't deserve the often cruel treatment meted out to them.

After the ravages of foot-and-mouth, the autumn that year was especially beautiful, as if nature was trying her best to cheer us all up with a kaleidoscope of colours. In many parts of the country, it would take more than a stunning autumn to redress things, when the fields and hills were devoid of livestock. With no-one walking the countryside, nature had gone about her business undisturbed by human presence. In fact, in many places, wildlife had flourished because there was nobody to disturb it. Interestingly, we weren't overrun with foxes because no-one was hunting them. It was as if nature had managed perfectly well without human interference.

I was lucky enough to have some time off from work during those few sunny weeks of November, enabling me to enjoy it to the full. Armed with my camera, I took Beans out every day on local walks, over the fields, along the canal, or through the woods. If Jan was off too, we'd head up to Gun Moor to enjoy a walk through the heather, which was by now a rich reddish brown, set off beautifully by the silver birch trees that looked resplendent with their golden yellow leaves. This was autumn at its best. Despite those terrible events of the last few months, there was still so much beauty in the world to enjoy. I just wished that the human race would stop its madness and look at the wonderful planet we all inhabit. I've always felt the natural world could lead us away from hatred and suffering – if only we'd let it.

Showing that she was still game for getting as filthy as possible, Beans was delighted to discover that a favourite small pool, just off the main path, was now filled with the blackest, foulest water that a dog could wallow in. By the time she emerged from the swamp her bottom half was black with the peaty ooze. Apparently, it was also nice to drink.

After her day of adventure she was normally hungry, but we'd started to notice that she was becoming very fussy over what she ate, despite the fact that she asked me for her tea in the way she always had, by sitting at the kitchen door, waiting expectantly. We'd never fed her junk, always giving her the best food we could, but she no longer seemed to like her tripe mix or her favourite meals. What she used to chomp down in a matter of minutes was now either left completely or only half eaten. She loved her tripe so much that we used to time her to see how long it took her to devour it. There had to be something wrong for her to suddenly start turning her nose up at favourite foods.

Rather than worrying unduly we put her finicky eating down to the fact that at fourteen, she was now quite an elderly dog. Just like elderly people, dogs' tastes change and foods they used to enjoy become intolerable. Beans was telling us, in the only way she could, that she wanted a change of diet. After experimenting with various other foods, we finally hit on some that she could tolerate. For a while all was well, but just when we thought we'd cracked it, she'd start leaving her food again. It was disheartening – and upsetting – to see her walk away from a bowl full of food. We'd have no choice but to throw it away and see if there was anything else in the cupboard she'd eat.

We could have persevered with her diet until we found something that she would eat regularly, but something else came along to persuade us that all was not well.

Apart from the memorable broad beans episode all those years ago, Beans rarely woke us up in the middle of the night, unless she'd heard something outside to worry her.

One night, in the early hours of the morning, I became aware of Beans sitting quietly beside my side of the bed. I don't how she woke me or what made me become aware of her presence, because, apart from an almost inaudible whimper, she made no noise. Just like she'd done when needing to tell me that the broad beans were about to explode out of her, she managed to gently rouse me from my sleep.

Barely awake, I stumbled out of bed, flicked on the landing light and followed her downstairs. When I'd switched on the downstairs light, I noticed the time; it was about three in the morning. When the alarm was due to go off in another three hours, I wasn't too happy, but Beans obviously needed to go out. I wondered whether she'd snatched something from the pavement that had disagreed with her.

I grabbed a torch and opened the back door. Out she went into the night. I followed her movements with the torch and watched as she peed against one of the shrubs. I thought she'd come straight back in but no, she fancied a bit of a sniff around the garden. I was desperate to get back to bed.

'Beans,' I whispered loudly; well, as loudly as it was possible to whisper. Nothing.

'Beans!' I tried again. Still no sign of her.

I was getting exasperated. As I was about to call her again, in she trotted.

'Thank you,' I said. *Some of us have to get up in a few hours.*

Beans went back to bed in the room next to ours, and I sank back into the pillow and was soon fast asleep again, despite having stood at the back door for what had seemed like half an hour but had probably only been a few minutes.

I thought that Beans' urgent need to pee at some unearthly hour of the night was just a one-off. I was wrong. The next night the same thing happened. Then the night after that. Beans' waterworks had obviously gone into 'elderly dog mode.' This was now the nightly pattern. Rarely did I go a night without Beans' gentle presence at my side, telling me – almost telepathically – that she needed to pee. Gradually I got used to – and came to expect – Beans' nocturnal toilet visits, but it wasn't doing much for the quality of my sleep.

Beans' diet, coupled with her nightly visits to the back garden, was now becoming a cause for concern. We'd been trying all sorts of diets for her: boiling up rice or mince; giving her pieces of cooked chicken or fish. For a while she ate whatever new recipe was put in front of her, but then lost interest. It was time for another visit to our friendly vet.

Once we'd explained to Richard what was going on, his diagnosis was not long in coming.

'It's her kidneys,' he said confidently, 'she's an elderly lady now and like elderly people, the kidneys don't function as well.'

'What can we do for her?' Jan asked.

'We'll need a urine sample to check the kidney function, and we'll give her some special food for dogs with kidney problems,' he said assuringly. 'Oh and we'll also take some bloods to make sure there's nothing else going on.'

We left the surgery armed with tins of low-salt, low-protein food, wondering how the heck we were going to get a urine sample from Beans.

Had she been a he then trying to get a sample would have been a little easier, though still somewhat tricky. At least with a male dog you can see the stream of pee as he cocks his leg up, and then try and catch as much as possible in a container. Not that I'd ever had cause to attempt such a procedure. Lady dogs like to squat, although in Beans' case it was her own three-legged method of squatting. That could be our salvation.

'Perhaps if we take her out for a walk and bring a flattish container with us, we could quickly slide it under the raised leg just as she squats,' Jan said.

Try as I might, I couldn't think of a better way to get the sample. In fact, there was no better way. I couldn't really see Beans peeing to order in to the receptacle. That would be far too easy. It was going to take quick reactions, a bit of embarrassment – and strange looks from passers-by.

It would be a while before the blood test results came back, so we decided to make another appointment once we'd crossed the urine sample bridge. We wondered what would be the ideal container to collect the sample: too small and most of the pee would miss its destination; too tall or too wide and we wouldn't be able to slide it under Beans' rear end at the opportune moment. After a look at several potential containers, we chose a bright yellow – but suitably flat – margarine tub. *Reusable container*, it said on the side of the tub; *I wonder if they'd thought that it would end up being used for collecting a dog's urine sample,* I thought to myself.

The obvious place to try and get the sample would be in the relative privacy of our back garden, but Beans had other ideas. She was going to make this as difficult as possible for us. We let her out in the garden and waited.

And waited.

And waited.

Nothing. Not a single drop of pee.

It was time to face the embarrassment and public humiliation.

Working on the assumption that dogs will generally 'perform' within minutes of starting their walk – usually where some other dog has peed – we had no choice but to walk up the road, armed with our bright yellow margarine tub. Would we make it to the fields where there was less chance of being spotted, or not?

No.

We crossed the road from our house and aimed for the grass verge opposite; a popular pee-stop for the local canine population. Within seconds of reaching the grass Beans began the pre-pee sniffing and circling.

'I think she's going to do it,' I said to Jan, who was holding the tub, 'get ready.'

Jan got down behind Beans. She was going to have to be quick.

Just when we thought it was a false alarm Beans began squatting.

'Now,' I shouted.

At the precise moment Beans started to squat, Jan shoved the margarine tub under her back end. Slightly surprised by this intrusion into her bodily functions, Beans turned around to see what was going on, but thankfully it didn't put her off doing what she had to do. A nice steady stream of urine released itself into the tub. Success!

'Oh thank heavens for that,' I exclaimed. I'd imagined we'd be chasing Beans with the tub, desperately trying to catch just a trickle of urine. Although we weren't exactly jumping up and down with glee, we did feel quite pleased with ourselves. In all the excitement we hadn't even bothered about the passing cars or pedestrians, wondering what the hell we were doing.

Within a couple of weeks all the various tests were done and Richard confirmed that Beans' kidneys weren't functioning as they should. Despite the bad news, there was no further cause for concern, now that her diet had been adjusted. As long as she stayed on the special food and the tablets he prescribed, there was no need to worry.

The problem was; Beans didn't like the tins of special food. She'd had a go with it, but it didn't last and she started leaving most of it. It was back to finding something she would eat, but was okay for her kidneys.

We sought more advice from Richard.

'She needs to eat,' he advised, 'so try and get something down her, as long as it's bland. Chicken and rice or fish are best.'

We knew we'd been down that road before, but now Beans was on drug treatment for her kidneys, we wondered if her appetite would improve. To a certain extent it did, but we still had to be prepared for those moments when she'd suddenly decide that one particular food was no longer flavour of the month. At times it was maddening when she'd reject something she'd been eating for a while, but we had no option than to just keep giving her whatever her body felt it needed. I almost broke down with the sheer frustration of it one evening, when I'd specially prepared something for her – which she then promptly left.

'For pity's sake Beans, please eat something,' I'd shout, then immediately regret losing my cool.

Then she'd look at me in the way she did when she knew I was cross. Only I wasn't cross; my frustration had got the better of me, but she didn't know that.

Please don't shout. I'm not hungry, that's all.

'I'm sorry Beanie,' I'd say to her.

I wanted so much to see her eating like she used to, but that wasn't going to happen. If she ate in the morning but not in the evening, then that was fine; it was all she wanted, or needed, for that matter.

Despite Beans' new health worries, it was good to see her walking more easily, even if she couldn't manage those long hikes any more. There were still plenty of places to take her and she loved her car trips, if we were going somewhere further away. She sat in the back quietly, looking out of the window, or asleep, depending on whether it was before or after her walk.

She surely put her 'stamp' on that car. It wasn't the one we'd had when we first got her – that had long gone – but the back of it left you in no doubt that it was dog territory.

Our early experiences of car travel with a dog had taught us that it was sensible to cover the back seats, but that still didn't prevent a gradual build up of detritus in the back of the car. Closer inspection revealed an interesting collection of material: bits of broken half-eaten dog biscuits, fragments of dog chews, dried up pieces of mud, gravel and enough dog hair to stuff a small cushion. It wasn't a pretty sight. The car was a mobile kennel. There were also streaks from her nose and mouth on the side windows, where her face had rested against them.

Of course, all this mess did get cleaned up every so often, but not as regularly as it should have been perhaps. When I did find the time – or the inclination –

to get out the car vac and the dog saliva removal rag, the hairs had multiplied to such an extent that they now formed a thick carpet over the floor. The window streaks had built up to form an unpleasant – though removable – thin crust on the windows. Frankly, it was a disgrace.

Such a collection of filth must have given off its own distinctive scent, which was perhaps the reason Beans nearly always managed to pick out our car in the car park. As with most things in life it wasn't that simple.

They say that dogs don't see in colour; I beg to differ. We initially thought that Beans was able to know our car by the familiar scent that she could pick up from its interior, and that might have been the case, but for one thing. Every now and then she chose the wrong car in the car park. It may have been the wrong model – but it was always the right colour.

CHAPTER 8

Time, Precious Time

Life in the Old Dog

Sometimes, it seems that a year flicks by quicker than others. It doesn't of course, but that's the way it feels. No sooner had the dramatic events of 2001 been in the news than 2002 was almost half way through.

The two weeks holiday we'd planned – and cancelled – the year before had already come and gone and Beans had reached the grand old age of fifteen. She marked this special occasion with a new addition to her extensive collection of squeaky toys – this time a rugby ball. Like all its predecessors, it was very carefully unwrapped, until it lay on the carpet surrounded by small strips of torn, wet wrapping paper.

It hadn't been the best of weather while we were away in Cornwall and Exmoor, and, as is always the case, the weather improved once we'd gone back to work. But it was a holiday and a break from routine; a time to relax. It would also be the last long holiday we'd take for a while.

Beans had spent her usual two weeks in Wilmslow with Bob and Rita, but the news when we returned was not too good. As soon as our car drove up Beans was normally at the gate, wagging and barking; but not this time. We already knew she was going a bit deaf, which would account for her not hearing the car, but when she did appear at the side gate she didn't seem to know who we were straight away. Perhaps her vision was going a little, but we hadn't noticed any signs of it. This seemed to be more confusion than anything else. Once she recognised us then it was all guns blazing with her usual welcome, but nevertheless it was a little worrying. She was also much thinner.

We'd left Beans' dietary requirements with Bob and Rita, but they'd had problems getting anything down her at all, finally resorting to giving her the leftovers of their meals in an effort to get nourishment into her. Feeding the leftovers, although not ideal, had done the trick eventually, but it had been a battle.

Jan's parents had always been happy to look after Beans for us while we were away, but it was unfair to leave them with the responsibility of trying to get food down her and give her the drugs she needed. We decided there would be no two weeks away next year. Instead, we'd either have two weeks at home with Beans, or split the weeks up over the year. Apart from the odd weekend away, that would be it. It was fairer to Bob and Rita and much better for Beans.

Beans spent as much time as she could in the sunshine for the remainder of the summer. I think the warmth on her elderly body did her good, and it certainly looked like she was enjoying herself. It didn't matter whether she was outside in the garden with her toys or snacks, or inside, lying in a patch of sunlight.

Her thin frame was still a worry. She ate as well as could be expected, but it was just to keep her going; she didn't seem as if she was really enjoying her food, neither was she putting any weight on. How would she cope during the impending winter?

We bought her a new blue coat with a warm fleece lining, and Jan made her a cosy bed to lie on if she was floor-sunbathing in the house. She bought a large oblong piece of foam from the hardware store and

255

some fleecy fake fur tiger skin to cover it with. Beans was delighted with her new 'Tiger Bed,' as it came to be known, spending as much time as possible curled up on it. As a special treat we'd put it on my armchair and she'd quite happily spend the day there.

Pandering to a dog is probably not something that dog trainers would condone, but since she would probably jump on it anyway as soon as our backs were turned, it made sense to keep all the dog hairs and doggie aromas off it.

Dogs don't lose any of their sense of naughtiness or fun just because they are elderly. Beans had slowed up and was losing some of her faculties, but the mischief was still there. If she wanted to find even a small piece of sofa to sleep on, she would manage it somehow. If we had to go out for a while, we'd block the sofa off with books, cushions or even a chair. The sofa – when no one was sitting on it – made a convenient place to put piles of ironing. Piles of ironing were just what Beans needed to fashion an extremely comfortable bed.

Beans' increasing deafness meant that she was often unaware of our return until we'd opened the front door, in which case she was either still curled up on the sofa, gazing up at us half-asleep, or just in the process of clambering off guiltily when she'd suddenly heard the door handle turning. Either way, it was too late; her misdemeanour had been discovered.

The ironing piles were the easiest to make into a comfortable bed. Some could be nudged up a touch to create a space to lie in, with the adjacent pile providing a convenient pillow. Fleece jumpers and fluffy towels were the best, making a soft and luxurious bed. It was all so easy.

More of a challenge were the other items we used to block the sofa off. Cushions were easily pushed off or moved aside, as were books or piles of newspapers. A chair – thankfully – was too much for her, but since it couldn't stretch the length of the sofa, she made her 'nest' on the bit it didn't cover.

Despite her age Beans proved that she was not beyond creating mischief, and we loved her even more for it. Seeing the lengths she'd go to when creating her 'sofa-bed' was testament to her problem-solving skills. She must have loved looking for something naughty to do once we'd gone. If only we'd had a web cam to capture it all.

Although she delighted us with her antics, Beans was also capable of making us sick with worry and panic. Her health problems were something that had to be taken in their stride, although we couldn't help worrying that something else was round the corner. On New Year's Eve 2002 – just to frighten us – she decided to do a vanishing act on us.

December 31st 2002 was grey and dull in a way only the gloomiest of winters' days can be. It was also freezing cold with flurries of snow sweeping over throughout the day. The leaden sky hung over the bare landscape like a shroud. It was miserable.

The roads were clear for now, but I didn't fancy venturing far on them. We'd planned to go to some New Year's Eve celebrations in Wilmslow with Bob and Rita, but it was looking increasingly likely we wouldn't be going.

In the afternoon we took Beans for her usual afternoon walk along the track towards the stables. We planned to cross the golf course and then return along the canal, hopefully before the light – what there was of it – faded into night.

It was one of those days when all you really want to do is get back to the warmth of the house, and let the weather do what it wants outside. But we wrapped up and took Beans out for her constitutional.

Once away from the road, we let her off her lead and she trotted along, sniffing and investigating where every other dog had been. Because her sight and hearing were no longer as sharp, she didn't like to stray too far from us. Besides, she was wearing her activity bell, so we could hear her tinkling along behind us.

Halfway to the stables something made us stop in our tracks. There was no sound of her collar bell. We'd been so wrapped up talking about what to do that night that we'd forgotten to make sure she was still with us. We turned round. She wasn't there. We backtracked down the bridleway, half expecting to see her trotting towards us, but the track was deserted. I looked in the adjacent field, thinking perhaps she'd got carried away with some interesting smells, but there was no sign of her.

Why weren't we listening to the bell? I cursed inwardly. *Why hadn't we noticed it had stopped tinkling?* I cursed out loud, annoyed that we'd let her out of our sight. Memories of Rita's panic on the Common all those years before flooded back. We tried to stay calm but the light was fading, it was one of the coldest days of the year so far and Beans was nowhere to be seen. A younger dog would most likely survive the night, but Beans was practically deaf, her sight was going and she'd lost a lot of her body fat lately. Dogs are more resilient than we think, but nevertheless, the odds were against her. A night spent out in freezing temperatures could worsen her kidney condition.

We started calling her. Would she hear us? What direction had she gone in? All we knew was that she hadn't followed us. We didn't know what to do or which direction to walk in to try and find her. My stomach was turning over and Jan was visibly panicking. I tried to appear calm and collected and in charge of the situation, but on the inside I was worried as hell.

Just when we thought no one else was about, a jogger came running towards us. Perhaps he'd seen her. At least he could tell us what direction she was heading in. We didn't want to interrupt his run, but we had no choice.

'Have you seen a dog on its own?' I asked, describing Beans' appearance to him.

'No I'm afraid I haven't,' he replied breathlessly, 'but I'll keep my eyes open for you.'

We thanked him and he carried on with his run. Beans always wore an ID tag on her collar, so if anyone did find her they'd know who to contact. That was the only comfort we had at that moment.

There was little point heading over the fields or towards the golf course. We clung to the hope that Beans had lost sight of us and made her own way home, thinking that we'd gone back without her. Besides, if she'd gone in the direction of the fields we would have surely spotted her. We turned for home.

As that thought came to us, so did another, but it was one we prayed wouldn't have happened. To get home, Beans would have to cross a busy main road. No problem with that, except Beans had no road sense – at least not as far as we knew, because she was always on her lead near a road. Did she have the sense to wait until the cars had passed? Now I really was panicking.

A group of dog walkers met us as we neared the canal bridge. Had they seen Beans? Our spirits sank again when they said no, but they promised to help us if they spotted her. Not having children, I can't compare losing Beans to losing a child, but I'm sure the emotions must be the same: a horrible sick feeling in the stomach, a fear of the unknown and panic so strong that you feel unable to think straight.

Just as we'd crossed the bridge, we passed another dog walker heading in the same direction as us. We asked him if he'd seen Beans. Expecting the same negative reply, we couldn't believe it when he told us that a dog matching Beans description had passed him, walking down the canal towpath towards the road.

Oh no, she's crossed the road! A frightening image of blaring horns and screeching brakes came in to my mind, as I thought of Beans trying to cross that road.

'How long ago did you see her?' Jan asked the man.

'It must have been about half an hour ago,' he replied.

I couldn't believe so much time had elapsed. She could have covered a fair distance in that time. No wonder we couldn't see her anywhere. Rather than both of us going home, I decided to carry on up the towpath in case she'd gone that way rather than the road.

'I'll go home and see if she's there,' Jan said.

It wasn't long before I followed her. As I walked up the path it was clear there was no sign of her. I prayed that Jan had found her.

There were few cars about as I crossed the road. The snow looked like it meant business now and a thin layer was starting to stick. At least the absence of cars would have given Beans a better chance of crossing. All I wanted now was for the three of us to be reunited, safe at home.

Just as I'd passed under the canal bridge I saw Jan walking towards me. She was smiling. There, at her side, was Beans, safely on her lead. With a tremendous sense of relief, I ran to greet them.

'Where did you find her?' I asked, bending down to hug Beans.

'She was sitting at the front of the house, waiting for us,' Jan replied.

'You clever girl,' I said, still hugging Beans. She jumped up at me excitedly.

Despite all our worries she'd done the very thing we hoped she would, and made her own way home. After all, it wasn't as if she hadn't done the same route a hundred times. No doubt sidetracked by something along the track, by the time she realised she'd lost us we were too far ahead for her to see, so she had turned for home, thinking that was where we'd gone, which was probably the most sensible thing to do. She would have panicked, but thank heavens she had made it across the road and stayed where she was. As for us, we'd been so absorbed in our own thoughts we hadn't even noticed she wasn't with us. We'd never let her out of our sight again.

The winter months dragged on as only winter months do, but before long spring came around again and everyone – including Beans – looked forward to the promise of sunshine. I don't mind winter if there are at least some bright sunny days to lift the gloom, but they always seem to be so few in number.

When spring arrived, nature made sure it was a good one. The days of March and April were sunny and warm, new-born lambs played clumsily in the fields – or slept in the sun if they'd tired themselves out – and, once again, we looked forward to longer days in the Peak District.

Beans still enjoyed those shorter walks with us, but she did seem to be slower than usual. After a long winter, that wasn't surprising. Like Superman, she needed the heat and power of the sun to recharge herself. After I'd spent the best part of a day wandering around the picturesque villages of Alstonefield and Tissington, taking some seasonal photographs, I thought Beans would appreciate a relaxed day out with us around that area, wandering along by rivers and gathering the odd stone or two.

The day had already warmed up nicely when we parked up at Milldale, heading down through the village to the River Dove. Compared to what it would have been like at the weekend, it was blissfully quiet. The only walkers about were mainly retired folk or people on holiday like us. Beans had a date with the river and she wasted no time in making for it. She was soon hard at work doing what she did best, and before long a few stones were drying in the sun.

Passing the remains of the old mill and the cheery daffodils that always appear by it every year, we crossed the old packhorse bridge and wandered up Dovedale, walking beneath hawthorns laden with blossom. Beans would have been happy just to paddle her way up the dale via the river if we'd let her. It was hot for April, and she was clearly looking tired, but the frequent river stops perked her up no end. This was what she liked to do and we were quite happy following her lead.

After our picnic by the river it was time to head back to Milldale. We'd got used to gauging when Beans had had enough and although it was tempting to go a little further, we knew it would be too much for her. A few paddles in the river on the way back though, and she was fully recharged. After driving to Tissington for a tea stop we made for home. Beans slept the entire journey.

Although we worried about overtaxing her, Beans still surprised us with her sudden bursts of stamina. Later that week she showed us just what she could do. We'd bought a new self-assembly shed to house all those garden bits and pieces, spending most of the morning trying to figure out how it went together. It was algebra with parts.

Fix Part A to Part A1 and Part B to Part B1

Fix both these to Part C and ensure Part D is attached to the top

Don't forget Part E; that needs to be screwed to Part B

Curse loudly, look at instructions again, pull apart what you've just put together, curse again and throw screwdriver down in a temper.

By lunchtime it was up and ready to be filled. But not before we'd had something to eat and drink.

While we sat relaxing in the sun, I noticed that one of the local cats had wandered into the garden and was making itself comfortable by some plant pots. Beans hadn't seen it; she was well away, asleep in the sun. At least we *thought* she was asleep. Her eyes were shut, but that didn't mean she wasn't hearing anything. Whatever her state of consciousness, she still managed to pick up on the whispered word cat when I told Jan we had company.

It was one of those cartoon moments again. Just like Spike, the dog from *Tom and Jerry*, asleep outside his kennel, her eyes opened and she was ready for action. In an instant, she was up and scanning the garden. The cat, who hadn't spotted Beans when he walked into the garden, suddenly realised that he was in serious trouble and decided to make a run for it. His chances of making it to the safety of the fence were pretty good, but he hadn't reckoned on Beans.

Beans' eyesight may not have been what it once was, but it was good enough to see the cat, even though it wasn't moving. I hadn't seen Beans move so fast in ages. The cat didn't know what was about to hit it. Beans shot in the cat's direction like a missile. The cat sprang into action, but, instead of making for the safety of the fence – which it could have climbed easily – it charged straight into our newly erected shed. Heaven knows why it decided to do that, but Beans must have thought her luck was in.

Fearful of the awful scrap about to happen, I screamed at Beans to come back, but it was a pointless exercise. There was no way she was giving up this chase. She hurtled into the shed. I braced myself for what was about to happen.

There was a brief bark, a scuffle of paws on the plastic floor, a piercing scream from the cat and then Beans shot out as rapidly as she'd gone in. After swiping Beans with its claws, the cat saw its chance, bolted out of the shed and literally vaulted over the fence into next door's garden. Beans, considering she'd been soundly thrashed by the cat, trotted over to me looking like she was the victor. I checked her over for any injuries. Apart from a slight nick on her nose where the cat's claws had found their mark, she was fine.

As far as Beans was concerned her work was done. The cat had been ejected from her territory and that was a result. She was too old for all that fighting business anyway. The chase was the best part.

A Ride on a Train

Spring became summer, and it turned out to be a good one, much to Beans' delight. She was going to take full advantage of those warm lazy days relaxing in the back garden.

I'd been asked to provide some photographs for a Peak District calendar and, being short on images of the famous Well Dressing ceremonies that take place in the Park throughout the summer, I planned a relaxing day out for us while I took the pictures.

Well Dressing is a colourful tradition that harks back to a time when people gave thanks for the wells that provided their water. Nowadays, the tradition carries on in villages up and down the Peak District. Villagers spend weeks creating elaborate, beautifully crafted floral pictures to decorate the village wells. They are intricately constructed from many different coloured flower petals, featuring biblical or historical scenes.

Each one is a work of art that would put some of the offerings in the Tate Gallery to shame.

Youlgreave, situated above beautiful Bradford Dale, is one of the best places to see the decorated wells. Bradford Dale also happened to be one of Beans' prime swimming and stone-gathering spots. It would be a day of indulgence: my hobby and Beans' hobby.

You could never tire of Bradford Dale. The River Bradford makes its way along a lovely wooded dale crammed with wildlife. Spring and summer are the best times to wander down the dale, when the coots and moorhens have had their young and the crystal clear water is alive with trout. Ducks glide along with their young desperately trying to keep up, their tiny webbed feet paddling like crazy. Every now and then one duckling gets left behind and then has to catch up with his siblings. Ducklings seem to be born with an 'on demand' turbo boost that propels them through the water like a speedboat, so they soon catch up.

I needed a good day for the photography. Luckily the gods were with me that Sunday. It was perfect. After wandering around the village photographing the colourfully decorated wells, it was time to take Beans down to her watering hole. Bradford Dale is always busy, but we managed to pick our spot, right next to the river.

Beans loved the river here. Because the water is so clear, anything lying underneath it is clearly visible, making the serious business of stone gathering that much easier. When she wasn't relaxing in the sun or eating her picnic snacks, she spent most of the time in the river, bringing back stone after stone. Age had made the effort of carrying some of them harder, but she was as determined as ever. The day she stopped enjoying this strange activity would be a day to start worrying.

I took a great sequence of photographs of her as she played in the water. In every one there's a different stone in her mouth. Happy days.

In July, Beans marked her sixteenth year with a trip to one of her favourite grouse-spotting places on The Roaches. It wasn't a long walk; just up to the summit marker and back. In days gone by we'd have carried on to Doxey Pool, at the far end of the ridge, to let Beans cool off, but she seemed more tired than usual that day. But appearances – as they say – can be deceptive.

For some reason, the grouse seemed much fewer in number. We could remember days when they were all over the place; Beans going wild as bird after bird flew up in front of her. Something had made them pack their bags and go elsewhere, but that didn't stop Beans having a good look for them. Her slower progress up to the summit was an excellent chance to spend more time than usual hunting them out. We didn't mind – this was her day.

Somewhere far off in the heather a few grouse cackled, and Beans' ears sprang to life. Once, she would have heard them from even further away, but not now. It didn't matter; she was in her element and enjoying it.

Suddenly, my arm was wrenched violently to the side and I almost fell over. From the heather came that familiar cackle and then a grouse shot up only feet away from Beans. It carried on with its chattering go back, go back calls as it flew off, as if expressing its annoyance at being disturbed. Beans was beside herself with excitement. No longer was she sixteen. Now she was that two-year-old youngster on her first hike near Kinder Scout, coming across the grouse for the very first time. She might not have had the stamina she used to possess, when I was dragged this way and that for practically the entire walk, but she was going to have a damned good crack at it. Beans was still there, inside that elderly frame. It was good to see.

With Beans' birthday wish fulfilled, we found a cosy place hidden behind some rocks for our lunch. Beans ate some of hers and then lost interest. She was somewhere else, looking and listening, hoping that another grouse would perhaps pop its head up in front of her.

She'd been going grey around her eyes and muzzle for some years now, but as I watched her that day I realised how tired she looked and I felt sad. Her ears were alert, and she'd proved she could still take us by surprise, but there was still weariness – maybe even sadness – in those once bright eyes.

The three of us lay there for a while, enjoying the sunshine, and then it was time to get the cameras out. Still on grouse alert, with those ears ready to pick up the slightest hint of a grouse, Beans posed for her birthday photographs. They were good pictures, just Beans in her element; surrounded by all her favourite sights, smells and sounds.

Summer was over for another year and a distinct chill in the air accompanied those early morning walks with Beans. Autumn was on its way. Before long, the first frosts would arrive and Beans and I would pick our way along pavements made treacherous by black ice.

For years we'd been putting paper down in the kitchen for her to use when we went to work, or had to go out. Despite the fact she hardly ever used it, we'd made it a part of our going out ritual. There was always the risk that the cold weather would weaken her bladder as she got older, so she didn't have to worry about waiting until we got home.

There were those odd occasions when we were glad we'd spread the kitchen liberally with newspapers. One day, I came home to the most appalling smell, which hit my nostrils as soon as I opened the front door. Had she tried to use the toilet again I wondered?

My nose took me to the kitchen. It looked like the local farmer had sprayed it with slurry. Poor Beans had obviously eaten something that had disagreed with her. She'd tried desperately to contain everything on the paper, but it had been hopeless. This was an explosion of spray-like proportions that she'd been unable to control. Floor and cupboard doors were sprayed and splattered. Memories of the infamous scout hut incident flooded back, as I remembered Beans' ill-fated visit to the dog trainer.

I'd got used to Beans' nocturnal visits to the garden, adjusting my sleep pattern to get out of bed, go downstairs, let her out, wait for what seemed like ages, let her in and then go back to bed, without really waking up fully. Her bladder was obviously getting weaker though, because for the first time, she was starting to use the paper in the kitchen. At least it proved she knew what it was there for, even if she was starting to have more 'accidents' around the house.

Beans was a very proud dog when it came to her bodily functions, so it was heartbreaking to see her gradually losing control. One night, I awoke to a soft slurping noise coming from outside our bedroom. For a moment, I wondered what it was, then realised she was probably licking her paws. So far that night she hadn't woken me up to go outside, so I flicked on the bedside light and stepped on to the landing, thinking I'd let her out now I was awake.

She was standing on the landing, licking the carpet. I'd never seen her do that before, so what was she up to? Then I noticed the wet patch around the spot where she was licking. Perhaps unable to wake me, she'd peed on the carpet and was now desperately trying to remove it in the only way she knew. And people think dogs are dirty creatures?

In all the years Beans had been an avid train-spotter, she'd never actually ridden on one. We wondered whether her reaction to one close up had put her off, but we still thought she deserved a trip on one of the machines that had fascinated her for so long.

One of our local walks took us to nearby Rudyard Lake, where enthusiasts operate a splendid little narrow-gauge steam railway. Most often, we'd do the complete circuit of the lake on foot, but that September afternoon Beans was looking tired as we rounded the head of the lake. This was the ideal opportunity to give her the train ride we'd always promised her.

A train was already waiting at the stop as we approached it. How would Beans react to the hiss of steam, the shrill whistle and the clank of machinery? As she'd got older, her fear of fireworks had got steadily worse, so we prepared ourselves for the worst – and the long walk back.

The less imposing size of the train must have been of little threat to her, because she clambered into the miniature carriage with no hesitation. As the driver prepared the train for departure, she sat there, eagerly waiting for us to start moving. This was what she had been waiting for.

With a slight jerk from the carriage, we were off. Beans sat there calmly watching the passing scenery. People walking the lakeside path smiled and pointed to her. Other dogs looked enviously at her, probably wishing they could have a ride too.

It was a sedate, relaxed little ride to the other end of the lake. This was no *Flying Scotsman*, but it wasn't meant to be; just a pleasant ride for families, steam train enthusiasts, weary walkers – and train-spotting dogs.

The rest from walking had perked her up, and as we climbed down from the carriage, she looked like one very happy dog. At last, she'd got to ride on a train and she'd enjoyed it.

After that happy day at Rudyard, it came as a blow to realise that Beans' health was deteriorating more than we realised, or were prepared to accept. It was time to face facts and come out of the denial that we found ourselves in.

Because she'd led such an active healthy life I thought Beans would be one of those dogs who are lucky to reach the twenty mark. Anything else just seemed unthinkable.

In October, we were again at the vets. It wasn't good news. For several days Beans had woken me in the usual way, but before I could let her out she'd soiled the carpet. This was a worrying new development. Whatever was wrong with her, she was unable to hold it until she was outside. Perhaps it was something she'd eaten, I wondered. Sadly, it carried on for several days, despite the bland diet she was on. I hated not being able to get her outside quickly enough. She just couldn't get her stiff ailing body downstairs in time.

Richard wasn't on duty that afternoon when we took Beans to see him. Instead, we saw Jane, a kind and caring girl who loved Beans. She listened to our concerns and checked Beans' tummy.

'It's her liver,' she told us quietly.

'Is it cancer?' I asked. I needed to know the worst, whatever it was.

'No, it's just an old liver,' Jane replied reassuringly. 'It's just not doing its job as well as it used to. We'll give her something to control the diarrhoea and put her on a light diet. Chicken and rice is best.'

We felt a little better than when we arrived, but despite Jane's reassurances, one thing remained: Beans was ill and there was only so much the vets could do for her.

It was a beautifully sunny autumn afternoon and, although the circumstances could have been better, I was so glad I wasn't at work that afternoon.

'Do you want to come for a short walk up to the stables?' I asked Jan. 'Seems a shame to waste such a lovely afternoon.'

'No, you go. I'll stay here and potter around the garden,' she replied.

So I left her to the garden and Beans and I set off for the stables. I think we both wanted to be alone with our thoughts.

The autumn colours were at their best that afternoon along the path. A combination of colour and clear blue sky raised my spirits, and I felt better, despite my worries about Beans. At least she hadn't got cancer. That would have been like a punch to the stomach that no amount of beautiful afternoon could have helped.

As we walked along the track, passing the solitary house, I heard a familiar sound from above. An evocative – almost haunting – whee-eur, whee-eur. I knew instantly what the sounds were.

Looking upwards, I saw two buzzards, gliding and wheeling around each other, rising on the thermals. Against the blue sky, they looked magnificent, the sun highlighting their plumage beautifully. Buzzards had become more common around here, but I'd never seen them this far away from the open fields. These were birds of prey: truly wild and free. They always lift my spirits when I see them.

'Everything's going to be okay,' I said to Beans as I gazed up at the buzzards. 'Everything's going to be okay.'

Autumn was soon over, but again it had been a good one. I'd been able to get out and take some good photographs, and best of all, Beans was about to become a celebrity again.

I'd written an illustrated article for 'Dogs Monthly' magazine about Beans' hiking adventures and the problems we faced when she semi-retired from walking. When the acceptance letter arrived, I was delighted. They were using the article – plus photographs – in the January 2004 issue. They even liked the title: *A Dog's (Hiking) Life.* I couldn't wait to see the published article.

Throughout October and November we took Beans to some of her favourite places, enjoying the last few sunny days of autumn. We went up to Gun Moor, where Beans' coat almost matched the autumnal colours, making it easy to lose her in the heather. We took her to Brereton Heath, where she loved to investigate the rabbit burrows and paddle in the lake. I took photos: Jan and Beans on Gun Moor, sitting on a collapsed wall, surrounded by heather; Jan and Beans at Brereton, sitting at a picnic table, Beans in her best fleecy blue coat, Jan in her red fleece. They both stood out well in a photograph.

There was a change in Beans that day. She loved the place normally, checking out the rabbit burrows and getting lost in the woods, but it was as if she'd lost interest. She walked slowly along with us and made a few attempts to see if any bunnies were at home, but that spark of enthusiasm was gone. After one circuit of the park, she was tired. We sat in the sunshine for a while at one of the picnic tables, and then made our way back to the car.

Before long, November had slipped by, the leaves had all fallen and winter's grip beckoned. Beans was glad of her Tiger Bed and even wore her coat indoors when it got really cold. The bed was placed in front of the radiator, so she was as cosy as we could make it. She spent a lot of her time asleep now, so it was important to keep her warm.

I don't know whether dogs can get coughs and colds, but Beans seemed to be developing one. The cough irritated her more at night and, worryingly, it seemed to be worsening.

Beans usually slept upstairs in the room next to ours. Most nights, after we'd heard her make her way upstairs and settle down on her beanbag, the coughing would start. It was a gagging, unusual, distressing sound, as if she was trying to bring something up. Just as we'd heard the familiar 'rustling' noise as she made herself comfortable on her bed, we'd hear her get up and go to the landing, still coughing. She just couldn't settle.

I'd get up to help her and try and get her to go back to bed, but she was obviously in discomfort. Eventually she'd settle down and get off to sleep – until I got the early morning call to let her out. All she wanted to do was sleep, but her body was denying it.

Reluctantly, we made another appointment with the vet. This time, Richard was on duty. He didn't seem too concerned, thinking, like us, that it was just a cough.

'It could just be something on her chest that's irritating her more at night when she lies down,' he said, 'so I'll give her something to try and ease it, but do come back if it gets worse.'

Christmas was fast approaching, but thoughts of festivities were even further from our minds. Beans' cough was no better; in fact it was worse. She was waking up from her sleep, almost choking from phlegm. Although on a light diet she was again losing control of her bowels – yet she was barely eating anything. Most nights were spent cleaning up after her. It broke my heart to hear her having to 'go' on the carpet, because she simply couldn't make it downstairs, let alone outside. I did my best to try and get her out as

273

soon as I awoke, but inevitably, I was too late. We tried to make her sleep downstairs, but she'd always slept upstairs near to us and she wasn't about to change that now. As long as she could drag herself upstairs, she'd do it.

There was one happy event during this black time. One morning, a large brown envelope dropped through the letterbox. It felt quite thick, like a magazine. I'd not had one of those for a while. I knew what it was before I even opened it. I eagerly opened the envelope. Inside was the January 2004 issue of Dogs Monthly magazine.

I turned the cover to the contents page. Greeting me was a photograph of Jan, standing by a squeezer stile, that Beans was firmly wedged in. A warm smile spread over my face as I thought of all those times we'd had to un-wedge her. I searched for the article itself. There, over two pages were ten photographs of Beans; all the ones I'd sent in. As well as the stile picture, there was Beans wallowing in a muddy pool; Beans looking for stones; Beans befriending a donkey; asleep in the sun and on her last big walk on Middle Moor, looking for those grouse. I was overjoyed. As if she would understand what she was looking at, I showed Beans the magazine.

'Look, Beans,' I said, 'you're a celebrity again!'

I think she could sense my excitement, because she started to wag her tail. She loved being in the limelight.

Beans was due for a check-up again at the vets, so I took the magazine to show everyone. They were all delighted to see photographs of their favourite patient adorning the magazine. Beans enjoyed the attention, but she wasn't about to let fame go to her head.

In all the excitement, we'd temporarily laid aside her health problems. The mystery cough was no better and her appetite had dwindled to just a few mouthfuls of food. Eating was starting to lose its appeal. When an animal starts to do this, you know they are giving up. Nightly clean-ups were becoming the norm, but you could never be cross with her. She did her best to get downstairs to go out, but she simply couldn't make it.

One Saturday morning, a couple of weeks before Christmas, she went to the back door, asking to go out. She made her way to the lawn, did what she had to do and turned to come back in. At that moment she seemed to stagger and sway, her legs buckling beneath her. Then she collapsed. I called out to Jan and ran out to the garden. By the time I got to her, she'd sat up, but there was something wrong. She looked confused and frightened, as if she didn't know where she was. My first thought was that she'd had some sort of stroke or seizure.

Jan joined me and we both knelt down to comfort her. The cough that had been troubling Beans was there too. I felt sure the two things were connected. After a few minutes she seemed to recover and join the world again, so we got her inside to the warmth.

'I'm getting her to the vets now,' I said to Jan. They were only open until lunchtime and I wasn't going to hang around worrying until Monday.

'Bring her straight down,' the receptionist said without hesitation.

Neither Richard nor Jane was on duty that morning, so we saw Anna, a friendly young vet we'd only seen a few times before. She listened to Beans' chest. I could tell from the look on her face that something was worrying her. She moved the stethoscope over Beans' chest again.

'There's fluid on her lungs,' she said, 'that's probably what's been causing the cough.'

'What's the prognosis?' I asked her. I could feel the colour draining from my face.

'Not very good,' she replied. 'The fact that her liver and kidneys are not functioning properly is only making things worse. I'll put her on something to ease the congestion, but we'll just have to wait and see.'

Driving home, I felt as though I had a lump of lead in my stomach. I couldn't think straight and I tried to push the thought out of my mind that my beloved dog had not got long to live.

We'd already bought Beans her Christmas present; a squeaky Christmas garland from her favourite pet shop. In my heart, I really didn't think she was going to make it. We'd give her the present early.

So she wouldn't see me, I went into the kitchen, shut the door and took the squeaky toy from the cupboard where it had been hidden. I started to wrap it. There was a little *From* and *To* label attached to it. As I started to write Beans' name, I broke down in tears. The thought that this might be the last time we'd see her carefully unwrap her present was too much to bear.

The worst thing would be to let Beans see that I was crying, so I composed myself and finished wrapping the toy. As I handed it to her I wondered if there would be any interest. She looked at the gift and started to sniff it. She made a half-hearted attempt to open it, and then lost interest. I unwrapped it for her and squeezed the toy to attract her attention. That got her interested. She played a while with the toy, but I could tell that her heart just wasn't in it. In years gone by she'd have spent the rest of the day rolling on it, trying to make it squeak, but not now.

In the few days before Christmas we took some leave to be with Beans. Neither of us wanted to be at work. It was an annoying irritant that got in the way of life.

Beans was now leaving any food we put in front of her, only managing the smallest morsels of chicken. We even tried soup, thinking that it would be a good way of getting nourishment into her. It was reasonably successful, but not for very long. Just when we thought we'd found something we could give her regularly our hopes were dashed.

On one of my days off I'd walked down to the town to try and pick up a few extra copies of Dogs Monthly. When I returned, Beans was still lying in her bed where I'd left her, nice and snug in her fleece coat. Once the delayed reaction to my coming through the front door had passed, she was pleased to see me, her tail wagging a little as she realised I was back.

It was getting dark outside and somehow I'd lost interest in whatever else I'd planned for that day. Beans looked so vulnerable lying there and I wished I'd not gone out and left her. I suddenly felt tired. After drawing the curtains and switching the heating on, I lay down beside Beans, put my arm around her and fell asleep.

At the weekend there was a glimmer of hope. For a moment, the Beans of old returned. She was lying in her bed facing the television, after making an attempt to lick some chicken soup from my fingers, which was the only way I could get anything down her.

As I thumbed through the TV guide I noticed that one of her favourite shows, *One Man and His Dog*, was on. I felt sure the sheep and sheepdogs running around the screen would perk her up.

'Look Beans,' I said, pointing to the set, 'your favourite show's on.'

She looked up at the moment the dogs were rounding up the sheep, so there was plenty of activity for her to enjoy. Up went the ears, her head twitched and there was the briefest of barks. It was heartening. As long as she still had that spark of interest in the world around her, there was hope.

On Christmas Eve we came home at lunchtime to a more enthusiastic greeting than usual from Beans. What cheered us up even more was that she went and grabbed one of the treats we always left her if we went out – and promptly devoured it. We hadn't seen her eat like that in weeks.

Christmas Day arrived and we headed over to Jan's parents feeling a little better than we had for the last few days. Beans was not well, and how long she had left we couldn't know; it was a case of taking each day as it came.

The usual 'which parents shall we spend Christmas Day with' dilemma had been won by Bob and Rita that year. They were treating to us a meal out and we'd spend New Years' Day with my mum and dad. Christmas is always a compromise.

'We've not got much longer with her have we?' Jan suddenly asked me, as we waited in the bar before the meal.

'I don't know,' I replied, 'I think we'll know when it's time, but she did eat those treats yesterday, which was a good sign.'

I don't think she felt as optimistic as I was trying to be.

The meal was excellent, and to a certain extent we enjoyed ourselves, but Beans was never far from our thoughts. As she'd done all those years before with the unfortunate brandy sauce episode, Rita managed to lift our spirits as only she could.

Restaurants always over face you with large platefuls of food that could quite easily feed two people, never mind one. No matter how good the meal – or your appetite – you can never finish everything. *Mr Creosote,* that gargantuan over-fed character in Monty Python's famous '*The Meaning of Life*' film, may have cleared all his various plates and then been defeated by a '*Wafer Thin Mint,*' but most of us are reluctantly forced to leave perfectly good food on the plate. Of course, it helps if you have a dog at home, willing to finish off what's left. It leaves one very happy dog and assuages the guilt of all that food going to waste.

Rita had come well-prepared for such an eventuality. Before the waiters arrived to clear away the plates, she swung into action. She took several plastic freezer bags from her handbag and started to discreetly drop pieces of turkey, sausages, bacon and anything else that Beans might fancy, into the bags.

For the first time in days, we laughed as she carefully removed the best leftovers from everyone's plates into the 'doggie bags.'

'I think you should have brought a bin bag for that lot, never mind a freezer bag,' I said, as another sausage joined its companions in the bag.

I looked around the restaurant to see if anyone was watching us, but nobody was. Thankfully, they were all too engrossed with their own meals. Who knows, perhaps they were even shovelling their own leftovers into little bags.

Some people would be too embarrassed to sneak food off plates, but not Rita. After all, the meal was paid for. They were our leftovers. I just wondered whether Beans' appetite would recover enough to eat the splendid Christmas Dinner that had been prepared for her.

Something of a miracle happened when we got home later on. Jan took the bag of leftovers and tipped it all into Beans' bowl. She called Beans into the kitchen, quite expecting her to do nothing more than sniff the food and then listlessly walk away.

To our amazement, she polished most of it off, leaving only a few scraps in her bowl. Considering she'd hardly eaten anything for days, it was totally unexpected, but nevertheless a delight to see.

What had made her want to suddenly eat, we could only guess. Perhaps it was because this was something different – a treat – and not what you'd call 'proper' dog food that had rekindled the desire for food. It was so good to see her enjoy eating again, but sadly our joy was to be short-lived.

Over the next few days, the cough that had never really got any better began to worsen and she started to lose interest in food again. We couldn't even get her to go for a short walk, other than up the road to the grass for a bit of a sniff. We'd let her out in the garden, she'd do what she needed to do and then come back in. The rest of the time she stayed in her bed, curled up asleep.

We tried taking her in the car up to the start of the path, to see if she fancied a walk to the stables, but she only managed a few yards before wanting to come back. It was a horrible, grey, cold day, so I couldn't blame her. We didn't really want to be out either.

Between the two of us, we had plenty of leave booked that week before the New Year. Beans needed us more than work did. On one of the days I *did* have to work, Jan phoned me in the afternoon. She was almost in tears down the phone.

'I think we'll have to put Beans to sleep,' she said, her voice faltering. 'Mum's been on and she thinks we should take her to the vet.'

'What's happened?' I asked. I felt sick with worry.

'She won't go out, she won't eat, she's just lying here and her cough is worse. I don't know what to do.'

To hell with work, I thought; I had to be with them both. I left early and drove home. My mind wasn't on tedious office politics or boring admin work. It could go and take a running jump. They could even sack me – I didn't care.

When I arrived home, Jan was upstairs on the computer, with Beans lying at her side, curled up on her bed. Unlike me, Jan could work at home. It had been a godsend that week.

Beans looked up at me and wagged a little as I bent down to stroke her.

'I phoned the vets before I left,' I said to Jan.

'What did they say?'

'That we'd know when it was time. They said we could bring her in tonight if we were worried.'

We were now in that dreaded, horrible position where it was obvious our dog was suffering, but to what degree? How we wished she could tell us. How do you decide when an animal has had enough? In my heart, I think I knew that Beans had already made that decision by stopping eating. She couldn't walk far and had lost control of her bodily functions. Her dignity and quality of life was gone. The only way an animal can tell you is by not eating and losing interest in all those things they used to enjoy. We were at that point.

'I'll phone the vets again,' I said, 'we'll take her tonight.' How many times had I dreaded having to make *that* call?

At that moment, as I carefully got Beans into the back of the car, I hated the winter. It wouldn't have made things any easier, but at least Beans could have spent her last days lying in the sunshine. She loved the summer, and I so desperately wanted her to make it to the next one.

We didn't want to distress Beans any more than she was by lifting her on to the examination table, so Richard bent down to examine her where she was. He greeted her and stroked her, before carefully listening to her chest. His face gave away what he was about to say.

'Her heart's all over the place,' he said, 'there's quite a murmur and all that fluid on her lungs is making things worse.'

He mentioned other things that were going wrong, but they didn't register. We both knew what was coming and we were about to face that heart-breaking decision that all pet lovers must eventually face. I needed to know how bad it was for Beans.

'Is she suffering?' I asked Richard.

'She's suffering,' he replied.

He then went on to tell us that we could leave things as they were, but that there was no chance of recovery. Beans was only going to suffer more and more as the days went by. To let that happen would be cruel. There was only one choice we could make.

'Would you like me to leave you alone for a few minutes?' Richard asked. I looked up at him from stroking Beans. He was almost in tears.

'Can you come to our house to do it?' I asked him. My mouth was quivering as I fought back the tears. Jan was quietly sobbing.

'Yes, of course,' he said.

We arranged a time for the next morning – New Year's Eve – and left the surgery. Beans would be happier in her own bed, in her own home, surrounded by all the familiar things. We needed one more night with her.

That evening, wrapped up against the bitter cold, we took Beans up the road to the grass for one last time. She sniffed and peed, but then wanted to go back. It had taken all her strength to walk even that short distance, but now all she wanted was her bed and to be out of the cold. As we slowly walked back I wondered whether we were doing the right thing, but seeing Beans trying to go just that short way helped to dispel any doubts I might have had. Even so, sleep – if it came at all – would be a long time coming that night.

Later that night, Beans made her way up to the little room next to ours and curled up on her bed. It was such an effort for her, but that was where she wanted to be. We made her as comfortable as possible, covering her to keep her warm.

After lying in bed for ages, unable to sleep, I got up and went to check on Beans. As I knelt down beside her, she opened her eyes. I couldn't go back to bed. Instead, I lay down beside her and held her paw. Then, I found myself talking to her. I told her that everything would be okay, that we loved her and that I was sorry for those times when I'd been cross with her. As I held her foreleg I felt her paw squeeze my hand slightly. I think she understood.

After a while, I said goodnight to her, stroked those soft ears, and went back to bed.

Morning soon arrived; as cold and grey as it had been for several days. My stomach lurched, as it does when you awake to the sudden realisation of something that sleep had erased for a few hours. Not that either of us had slept very well.

Richard was due about eleven, after his morning appointments. Before he arrived, all we could do was spend our last few hours with Beans and for her sake, try to act as normally as possible. It wasn't easy, but dogs can sense emotion. We didn't want to unsettle or upset her. She'd been out in the garden, but it had been a slow process getting her there. Now she was back in the warmth of her bed.

Time seemed to stand still in those few hours before Richard arrived. We didn't want to alarm Beans and smother her with cuddles, but every now and then I'd bend down to stroke her. Jan sat with her the whole time, just stroking her. It sounded morbid, but I'd read

283

somewhere about someone cutting a few locks of their pet's fur as a permanent reminder of the animal. I wanted to do the same, but Jan wasn't so sure. We were keeping her favourite red collar, her identity disc and the little collar bell, but I needed something of *her*. In the end, Jan agreed, so we carefully took a little bit of the white fur from Beans' chest and some of the lovely fawn-coloured fur that had given her such a distinctive fox-like appearance.

As we placed the locks in a small plastic bag, how I wished, at that moment, that she'd suddenly make a dramatic improvement – even a small one – and we could phone the vets and tell them to cancel the visit.

Then Richard arrived. We let him in and Beans looked up at him as she recognised him.

'Hello Beans,' he said, trying his very best to sound normal and upbeat, 'and how are you today?' She wagged her tail a little.

He got his stethoscope out. 'Let's have a look at you,' he said.

As he carefully listened to Beans' chest I silently prayed that he'd tell us there had been some improvement overnight.

'She's still the same,' Richard said, dashing our hopes, 'her heart's still bad.' There was nothing more that could be done.

'We'd like to leave her in her bed,' Jan said.

'No problem,' Richard replied, 'just move her a little this way.' He already had a syringe prepared, filled with a blue liquid. Jan and I desperately tried to compose ourselves; it was vital not to upset Beans.

We moved the bed a little way from the radiator; Jan cradled Beans' head in her lap, while I stroked her back. Richard carefully shaved a little fur away from her leg. I looked at him. He was trying to be as professional as possible, but he'd known Beans for a long time. I could tell he was fighting the tears back himself.

'She might cough or judder slightly,' he warned us, 'but try not to be too alarmed.'

As the needle went in, Beans' lips curled up. She still had that tiny spark of fight in her, but there was no strength left in her for any more action.

Jan stroked her head and talked quietly to her. She was being so strong for Beans' sake. Richard withdrew the syringe.

'You go and play with all the funny birds,' I said to Beans, gently stroking her back. I watched as her eyes started to shut and her head relax. 'You go and play with all the funny birds,' I said again. It was all I could think of to say.

Beans' head had now slumped completely in Jan's arms. Richard waited a few minutes and then gently rolled her eyelids back.

'She's gone,' he said.

There had been no suffering, no upsetting noises. With dignity, Beans had slipped quietly and peacefully away.

There was to be no burial in the back garden. We'd already decided where we wanted to put Beans' ashes. The Cloud, where she'd spent so many happy days, would be her final resting place.

After thanking Richard, he took Beans back to the surgery and left us to our thoughts. They'd phone us in a few days to come and collect Beans' ashes. As I shut the front door, all the emotions of the last few days and hours came out, and Jan and I collapsed in each other's arms. We both cried like we'd never cried before. Beans was gone and the house was suddenly so empty. I had never known such grief. I felt bad, because I couldn't remember being this like this when my beloved grandparents had passed away, but Beans had been almost like a child to us. We'd been there for nearly all her life, from the first few weeks until her final days.

As we held each other, I looked up at the beautiful watercolour painting Jan had done of Beans, hanging on the wall opposite. For some reason, a thought came in to my mind that seemed almost inappropriate in the circumstances.

'I'm going to write a book about her,' I said to Jan. She was crying too much to respond.

Sometime later, still in a daze of grief and numbness, I was standing at the front window, just staring into the distance, my eyes blurred with tears. As I looked down, I noticed the deep scratches etched into the white paint of the windowsill by Beans' claws. Then I remembered the window cleaner.

Beans always greeted the arrival of the window cleaner outside our house with much enthusiasm and a great deal of frantic barking and running around the house. As far as she was concerned, he was an intruder trying to enter the house, and had to be seen off. The zeal with which she carried out this mission had to be seen to be believed.

Starting with the downstairs windows, she'd jump up at the windowsills, barking madly at the smiling man as he cleaned the windows. Then he'd move to the back and she'd follow him. Wherever he went, she was there, making sure he didn't try to get in. Most of the time, this performance took place while we were at work, but when we were off, we'd see exactly what she got up to. It was bedlam.

The best part of the entire show was when he cleaned the glass at the bottom of the kitchen door. As his chamois leather circled the glass, she'd follow its every movement; round and round, up and down, left to right, barking the entire time. It was hilarious – a wonder to behold – and must have made the window cleaner's day.

'She likes to let you know she's there, doesn't she?' he said to us one day.

As this happy memory flooded back, I knew that I had to tell Beans' story.

Goodbye Beans

The days immediately after Beans' death were a struggle. There were more tears than either of us had ever known, and an empty, numb feeling that wasn't helped by the gloomy winter weather. The house had always been more cosy and complete with Beans around; now it just felt empty and lonely. Its heart had been ripped out.

Reluctantly, we went to my parents on New Years Day, but we were in no mood for any celebrations, which everyone understood. We tried to take an interest in my sister's children's Christmas presents, we even tried to be cheerful, but it was only an act. It was too early and it felt wrong. Worst of all, going out meant that we had to go back – to an empty house. There would be no enthusiastic, wagging greeting, perhaps with a squeaky toy offering. How we wished to see Beans' face, with her squeaky dumbbell or rugby ball between her teeth.

Without our morning and evening walks with Beans, we were lost. I went out for walks by myself, but it didn't feel right. Having a dog at your side for so long becomes a part of who you are. I took the route we always did with Beans; up to the stables, across the golf course and through the woods, alone with my thoughts.

I made the next days' sandwiches every night, in the kitchen, imagining I could still see Beans, sitting by the door, eagerly waiting for a few scraps to 'accidentally' fall into her mouth. I even started thinking I could hear her, walking across the living room.

One night, after I'd gone to bed, I woke up hours later and was sure I could sense Beans, sitting quietly by the side of the bed, waiting for me to let her out in the garden. As I lay there, I became aware of a familiar 'doggie' odour. There was no fear; Beans had come to let me know she was alright. For many weeks after, I would keep waking up in the small hours, but I never noticed the odour again.

We thought we'd cried all the tears we had; in those private moments when we were alone or when a memory suddenly came back, but there was always some reminder to bring them back. Dog hairs around the house, walks we'd always done with Beans became almost unbearable, photographs, and even that Famous Grouse advert all brought back the memories.

Some weeks after losing Beans the time came to also say goodbye to our faithful little diesel car. It had been the most reliable we'd ever had, but now the mounting costs of essential repairs and maintenance were starting to make it unworthwhile keeping it going any longer. We'd had many journeys in that car and it had served us well. Beans had left her stamp on it and despite cleaning it ready for sale, some of those hairs remained, in the places where the vacuum cleaner couldn't get. As we left it for the last time, driving away in our new car, Jan started to cry.

'Beans isn't going to recognise the new one,' she sobbed, remembering her ability to pick out our car in the car park.

'She will, because she'll know it's us in the car,' I replied. My response seemed inadequate, silly perhaps, but we felt strongly that Beans was still with us, sitting on the back seat of the car, going off on some adventure, or trotting along beside us, when we walked those familiar routes in the Peak District.

Jan went over to her Mum's every Friday, so sooner or later I had to face the prospect of coming home on my own to an empty house. I was dreading it. Opening the front door that dark evening when I got home was almost unbearable. I entered the living room to almost total darkness and switched on the light. Then an overwhelming sadness overcame me and I sat down in tears.

Some days after Beans' death we got a phone call from the vets.

'Hello Mr Johnson, we've got Beans' ashes here if you'd like to come and collect them,' the receptionist said. It was the call we'd been dreading, but it would give closure and allow us to do the one remaining thing for Beans that we'd always promised her.

Later that morning we walked into the surgery. There was no-one else there, just Mandy the receptionist and Jane, the kind vet who'd last seen Beans back in October. Mandy went to a room at the back and returned a few seconds later carrying a little box, inside of which was a small pot, decorated with flowers. At that moment, Jane, who'd looked really upset, said how sorry she was and then disappeared into the back of the surgery.

We left the vets and took Beans back home with us.

We didn't lay her to rest straight away. While that little pot was still there on the mantelpiece, it was as if she was still with us. It was that one final act that we had to face and there always seemed to be a reason why we didn't make that last walk up the Cloud with her. We wanted a nice sunny weekend, but the winter weather just wouldn't go away. In the end, we couldn't put it off any longer. The day we chose was chilly, but at least it wasn't raining.

We made for a little rocky outcrop, away from the main path, where we planned to lay Beans to rest.

We'd gone there a few times before and it had always been one of those few places on the Cloud where we could be alone while Beans watched the trains passing over the viaduct below.

Sitting down amongst the heather, we took out the little pot and removed the lid. Inside was a plastic bag containing Beans' ashes. Jan cleared away a spot just below the rock, opened the bag and gently poured the ashes onto the ground. Then she smoothed them over and covered them with grass and heather. We held each other tightly, the tears falling again.

'I need to say something to her before we go,' I said to Jan. I already knew what I wanted to say.

'Bye bye Beans. You go and run in the heather and watch the trains. We'll see you later.'

And then, our arms around each other, and with a last look back at Beans' resting place, we left her in peace.

EPILOGUE

August 7th 2004

The heather is in bloom on The Cloud now; a beautiful purple blanket that sadly only lasts a few short weeks throughout August and early September, filling the air with its intoxicating fragrance.

On a hot Saturday August morning we made one of our regular pilgrimages to visit Beans' resting place. On a day like this everything seemed even more poignant. Beans loved it up here in the summer, prancing through the heather and then suddenly stopping to roll madly in it, allowing the heady aroma to permeate her fur, an activity she seemed to relish, right back to her early days playing in the heather on Lindow Common. After tiring herself out, she would then just lie there soaking up the sunshine, a picture of true contentment.

No hike up The Cloud would be complete without a visit to her favourite rock viewpoint to watch the trains passing over the viaduct far below. If there was a breeze she loved it even more, just standing into the wind sniffing the air. We both love that invigorating, on-top-of-the-world feeling you get standing on summits and there was no doubt that Beans did too.

So now, seven months after her death, the memories came flooding back, but there were no tears this time; it was too nice a day for that. As we sat by Beans' resting-place, alone with our thoughts, meadow pipits flitted to and fro and swallows wheeled overhead, gathering insects by the beakful. We realised there was no better place for Beans to be. The Cloud seemed like the centre of our – and Beans' – world, and everything that Beans had loved was there: the heather, the trains to watch and the woods, where she became the 'wild wolf of the woods,' getting lost among the trees as she pursued one fascinating smell or another.

We can see our favourite hill from home and from the summit a whole 360° panorama of all our other special places presents itself: Alderley Edge, Gun Moor, Shutlingsloe, Rudyard Lake and The Roaches – places where Beans had enjoyed so many adventures in her life.

'This is the best place for Beans,' Jan said, as we headed down from the summit, echoing my own thoughts exactly.

'Yes and it gives us another reason to come up here regularly to visit her,' I replied.

It seemed right. We could see Beans' resting place every day and it would be as if she was there, watching over us. It somehow felt comforting.

As we walked down through the heather towards the woods, I felt that Beans was with us in spirit, enjoying this warm summer day and bouncing through the heather, restored to her youthful vigour. She will always be with us: both in our hearts and in all those places that hold so many happy memories.

Goodbye Beans. We love you and we will never forget you.

POSTSCRIPT

31st December 2004

Back in October, a new dog came in to our lives: a feisty, but delightful little Skye terrier, who we named Dougal, after his famous namesake character from the *Magic Roundabout* children's show. Beans could never be replaced, but it had become a very empty house without a dog around.

Like Beans before him, Dougal was a rescue dog, and just as Beans had done, all those years before, he chose us. With his delightful comical appearance and feathered ears typical of his breed, he made sure he was the one we'd be taking home.

Today, a year after Beans left us; we took Dougal up to the old shooting cabin on Middle Moor, where Beans enjoyed her first ever 'proper' hike. As this became one of her favourite grouse watching places, it seemed the perfect place to be to mark the year since her passing.

As we sat on the step outside the cabin having our lunch, Dougal started to take a very keen interest in the grouse that were flying around, making their familiar 'go back, go back' calls.

I think we are going to have many more years of fun with our new companion. Perhaps one day he'll have his own story to tell.

In life the firmest friend, the first to welcome, foremost to defend.

'Of a Dog.'

Lord Byron

Acknowledgements

First of all I'd like to thank my wife Jan, for putting up with me during the years it took me to put this book together. It's not easy living with someone trying to be a writer. I also want to thank Jan for designing the wonderful cover for the book.

To Aleta Donaldson, at the Famous Grouse Whisky, for helping me get my dates correct and reminding me of those wonderful television adverts that Beans loved so much. I now have a little Skye terrier who seems to have followed in Beans' footsteps, where Red Grouse are concerned.

I'd like to thank fellow author Simon Whaley for all his help and advice with my numerous queries. Also, Hilary Johnson, of the Hilary Johnson Authors' Advisory Service, for an extremely helpful report on the manuscript, which showed me that – at least where my writing was concerned – I was on the right track.

To protect their privacy, I have changed the names of several people mentioned in the book.

Finally, to Beans, for giving us sixteen years of love and companionship, and a wealth of wonderful memories for this book.

Further reading and useful addresses

The following books are well worth reading:

Goodbye, Dear Friend – Coming to Terms with the Death of a Pet - By Virginia Ironside, Robson Books. A lovely, comforting book from a popular author.

Goodbye, Friend – Healing Wisdom for Anyone Who Has Ever Lost a Pet - By Gary Kowalski, Stillpoint Publishing. A wonderful book from the US, available on Amazon.co.uk.

Absent Friend – By Laura and Martyn Lee, Henston Publishers.

Living With a Rescued Dog – By Julia Barnes. (Dogs Trust). Ringpress Books Ltd.

Useful addresses

ROYAL SOCIETY FOR THE PREVENTION OF CRUELTY TO ANIMALS (RSPCA)
Wilberforce Way, Southwater, Horsham,
West Sussex, RH13 9RS
www.rspca.org.uk
0300 1234 999 (cruelty) 0300 1234 555 (advice)

BLUE CROSS Shilton Road, Burford, Oxon., OX18 4PF
www.bluecross.org.uk
0300 790 9903

DOGS TRUST 17 Wakley Street, London, EC1V 7RQ
www.dogstrust.org.uk
020 7837 0006

INTERNATIONAL FUND FOR ANIMAL WELFARE (IFAW) 87-90 Albert Embankment, London, SE1 7UD
www.ifaw.org.uk
020 7587 6700

HUMANE SOCIETY INTERNATIONAL
5 Underwood Street, London, N1 7LY
www.hsi.org/world/united_kingdom
0808 126 1880

PEOPLE'S DISPENSARY FOR SICK ANIMALS (PDSA) Whitechapel Way, Priorslee, Telford, Shropshire, TF2 9PQ
www.pdsa.org.uk
0800 917 2509

WORLD ANIMAL PROTECTION (formerly the WSPA)
5th Floor, 222 Grays Inn Road, London, WC1X 8HB
www.worldanimalprotection.org.uk
0800 316 9966

GREYHOUNDS IN NEED
33 High Street, Wraysbury, Middlesex, TW19 5DA
www.greyhoundsinneed.com
01784 483206

PEOPLE FOR THE ETHICAL TREATMENT OF ANIMALS (PETA)
PETA Europe Ltd., PO Box 70315, London, N1P 2RG
www.peta.org.uk
020 7837 6327

BATTERSEA DOGS & CATS HOME
4 Battersea Park Road, London, SW8 4AA
www.battersea.org.uk
0843 509 4444

MANCHESTER & CHESHIRE DOGS HOME

(Two sites in Manchester and Cheshire)
www.dogshome.net
0844 504 1212

THE MAYHEW ANIMAL HOME

Trenmar Gardens, Kensal Green, London, NW10 6BJ
www.mayhew.org.uk
020 8962 8009

THE CINNAMON TRUST

10 Market Square, Hayle, Cornwall, TR27 4HE
www.cinnamon.org.uk
01736 757900

A wonderful organisation who look after the pets of elderly or terminally ill people, or those who are moving to residential care and cannot take their animals with them.

INTERNATIONAL ANIMAL RESCUE

Lime House, Regency Close, Uckfield, East Sussex, TN22 1DS
www.internationalanimalrescue.org.uk
01825 767688

Pet Bereavement

The Blue Cross, in association with the Society for Companion Animal Studies, runs a wonderful Pet Bereavement Support Service. The Support Line telephone number is: 0800 096 6606 - daily 8.30am - 8.30pm. For further information contact the Blue Cross at the above address.

Finally

Please support as many of the above organisations as you can. They are all working hard to stop the abuse and cruelty of animals at home and abroad. On a more local level, why not support one of your local animal rescue groups; they are often desperately in need of funds and, who knows, the dog (or cat) of your dreams could be waiting there for you.

14584107R00180

Printed in Poland
by Amazon Fulfillment
Poland Sp. z o.o., Wrocław